NEOLIBERAL RELIGION

NEOLIBERAL RELIGION

FAITH AND POWER IN THE TWENTY-FIRST CENTURY

Mathew Guest

BLOOMSBURY ACADEMIC
LONDON • NEW YORK • OXFORD • NEW DELHI • SYDNEY

BLOOMSBURY ACADEMIC
Bloomsbury Publishing Plc
50 Bedford Square, London, WC1B 3DP, UK
1385 Broadway, New York, NY 10018, USA
29 Earlsfort Terrace, Dublin 2, Ireland

BLOOMSBURY, BLOOMSBURY ACADEMIC and the Diana logo are trademarks
of Bloomsbury Publishing Plc

First published in Great Britain 2022

Cover design by Rebecca Heselton
Jesus image: Graffiti artwork by Loretto, 2018, London © Christina Hemsley / Alamy Stock Photo

A catalogue record for this book is available from the British Library.

Library of Congress Control Number: 2022932163

ISBN: HB: 978-1-3501-1639-9
PB: 978-1-3501-1638-2
ePDF: 978-1-3501-1640-5
eBook: 978-1-3501-1641-2

Typeset by Deanta Global Publishing Services, Chennai, India
Printed and bound in Great Britain

To find out more about our authors and books visit www.bloomsbury.com and
sign up for our newsletters

For Kate

CONTENTS

ILLUSTRATIONS

ACKNOWLEDGEMENTS

I wrote this book almost entirely at my desk in our house in South Yorkshire. The process of getting there, however, took me much further afield.

I have learnt a great deal from many transatlantic trips to the United States and Canada over the past fifteen years, including a valuable period as visiting research fellow at the Centre for Studies in Religion and Society at the University of Victoria, British Columbia. I'm grateful to those who graciously offered wisdom, friendship and hospitality along the way, especially James Bielo; Paul Bramadat, Karen Palmer and Max Bramadat; Rebecca Catto; David and Hannah Davies; Art Farnsley; Amber Fischer; Joe and Heather McLendon, and Richard Topping.

I owe an immense debt to the postgraduate students whose work has inspired many conversations and from whom I have learnt a huge amount. Special thanks go to Danielle Baker, Chris Chok, John Coggin, Tim Dixon, John Dyer, Alex Fry, Rob Haynes, Jamie Howard, Warren Linton, Noreen Mansuri, Jo McKenzie, Flo O'Taylor, Glenn Packiam, Michael Simants and Nick Toseland.

Some of the ideas behind Chapters 1, 6 and 7 were developed with the benefit of discussion at an excellent seminar organized via the Ruhr-University Bochum in November 2020. Many thanks to the organizers – Maren Freudenberg, Sebastian Schüler and Martin Radermacher – and the other seminar participants for sharing their scholarship and critical conversation.

Chapter 5 is informed by my collaborative research on the 'Representing Islam on Campus' project between 2014 and 2020. For support, conversation and shrewd insight during the course of this venture, I am grateful to Tarek Al Baghal, Sariya Cheruvallil-Contractor, Kareem Darwish, Yenn Lee, Shuruq Naguib, Aisha Phoenix and Alison Scott-Baumann.

Various chapters have benefitted from constructive, helpful comments from friends and colleagues, who kindly agreed to read earlier drafts. Many thanks to Paul Bramadat, Rebecca Catto, Dan DeHanas, Katie Edwards, Richard Flory, Gordon Lynch, Therese O'Toole and Sam Reimer. Linda Woodhead read an entire manuscript; her characteristically astute feedback helped identify aspects that needed more thought, and I'm grateful to her for that.

It is difficult to convey the true value of working in a collegial university department without sounding glib and somewhat less than convincing. However, Durham's Department of Theology and Religion has been my academic home for twenty years now and I wouldn't have had it any other way. My sincere thanks to the colleagues who have lent their support, friendship and sound advice over many years. My own work has benefitted immeasurably from their conversation, judgement and learning; any remaining errors, gaffes or disasters in the text are my responsibility alone.

Finally, none of this would be worthwhile without the love and support of Kate, who has brought me so much happiness. This book is dedicated to her.

INTRODUCTION

This is a book that started out as one thing and ended up being another. It started out as a book about evangelical Protestantism – specifically, how this branch of Christianity has been persistently caught within the logic of Western capitalism and how this relationship has produced some novel expressions of religion over recent decades. These expressions caught my attention because of their dependence on forms of thinking commonly associated with commerce, economic markets and consumerism. This in itself is nothing new, of course – Max Weber observed something similar over 100 years ago – but these distinctive forms of religious expression seemed to be extending their reliance on capitalistic or consumeristic patterns of thought and behaviour. They were doing so in ways that were becoming embedded, normative, everyday, and I thought this deserved further scrutiny.

As I explored this relationship in greater depth and became familiar with a larger range of examples, I began to realize that the patterns I was observing extended well beyond the remit of evangelical Christianity. It was true that some of the most remarkable, and most blatant, cases were to be found within this tradition, but it became increasingly clear that if this tendency to merge religious with capitalistic thinking had become important within evangelicalism, it had also broken out of this movement and become commonplace elsewhere.

This book has two main aims: one more general, the other more specific. Its general aim is to explore themes for the sociology of religion that reflect the circumstances of the twenty-first century. Its more specific aim is to address how debates about neoliberal culture illuminate the distinct manifestations of religion we encounter at this time.

Within the pages of this book, the 'norms and values' we are most interested in may be captured in the term 'neoliberalism'. But what does this mean? Without repeating a much more extensive account featured in the first chapter, I am using the term 'neoliberal' to refer to a set of cultural conditions indebted to the principles of neoliberal economics. These conditions may be summarized as a heightened individualism that prioritizes the freedom of the consumer over shared identities, a taken for granted assumption that market competition is the best measure of value and a tendency to treat cultural objects as commodities. These are all expressed in complex and diverse ways. One example, though, might serve to illustrate both how neoliberal assumptions become manifest and how pervasive they are.

The new normal

In recent years, the social circumstances of the world have undergone a dramatic set of changes. At the time of writing, the coronavirus pandemic has claimed the lives of almost five and a half million people across the globe. The level of disruption has exceeded so many wars, natural disasters and outbreaks of disease that, in the past, had seemed so extreme. In order to quell the spread of this virus, the nations of the world have put into practice a number of social conditions that have transformed the way we live our lives. They may continue to do so for some years to come.

As a book rooted in the *sociology* of religion, it would be impossible to ignore this dramatic change of circumstances, especially as it has had such profound consequences for the way social life takes place. As we embrace 'social distancing' as a necessity, this inevitably changes the way we relate to one another as social beings. In the UK, as theatres, cinemas, restaurants and cafes closed as a means of checking the spread of coronavirus, so did churches and other places of worship, and so we find ourselves seeking out new ways of being sociable and new ways of expressing our religious identities.

But at the same time, our apparently unprecedented circumstances have not eradicated the cultural trends that prevailed in pre-covid times. The contours of social life, while perhaps distorted, disrupted or frustrated by the pandemic, still reflect the norms and values that have distinguished cultures across the globe throughout their journey into the twenty-first century. In fact, the pandemic has, in many ways, illuminated their enduring power and significance. One of the most striking examples has to do with the relationship between the rights and responsibilities of individuals. As the threat of a further spike in Covid-19 cases looms ever on the horizon, the UK government has found itself calling upon the population to be mindful of its social responsibilities, as the health of the nation depends on the behaviour of each of us. And yet many appear highly reluctant to relinquish their consumer choices – especially those associated with the night-time economy – in order to observe social distancing and limit the spread of infection. This is not simply feckless selfishness; it is the expression of a set of values consistently reinforced over recent decades and characterized by the elevation of the sovereign individual, the pre-eminence of consumer choice for those who can afford it and a corresponding relegation of collective identities and loyalties as of secondary importance at best. Covid-19 is difficult to control in the UK in part because we have become a neoliberal nation.

The coronavirus pandemic has provoked a variety of reactions among citizens across the world. Government-sanctioned restrictions on human contact have called upon us to find new ways of being social and have tested the extent to which we are willing to give up – albeit temporarily – some of the everyday freedoms we have come to take for granted. Social distancing has severely limited the patterns of human interaction that ordinarily characterize our lives as employees, family members and citizens of local, national and global communities. It has also entailed restrictions on the economy, as businesses have been obliged to close, employees furloughed and travel restricted in order to prevent further spread of the virus. These circumstances have made painfully clear the social inequalities sustained by neoliberal economics. One example constitutes a tragic case of the 'gig' economy and the heightened risks to which Uber drivers are exposed. In April 2020, a news story appeared about Rajesh Jayaseelan, an Indian cab driver working in London. Jayaseelan, working in the UK while his wife and two sons waited back home in Bangalore, had been locked out by his landlord on the grounds that he was 'high risk', as an Uber driver coming into contact with customers. Unfortunately, Jayaseelan had already developed symptoms of Covid, and while he found somewhere else to live, he was frightened of seeking medical care in case he might lose his accommodation again. After he got worse, he drove himself to hospital but developed pneumonia and died soon afterwards.

From a sociological point of view, one of the most interesting aspects of this strange set of circumstances has been how different groups of people have responded to demands that their behaviour change and their normal habits of consumption be curtailed. With society-wide restrictions covering entire populations, compliance has not realistically been enforceable by the authorities and so has depended in large part on voluntary behaviour change. As such, the coronavirus situation is a potentially insightful measure of the cultural embeddedness of neoliberal social norms. How do populations respond when told they cannot gather, socialize in bars, clubs and restaurants or go to the cinema? What happens when normal patterns of consumer behaviour are labelled irresponsible and a threat to public health? What do acts of public defiance indicate about people's priorities or values, or their opinion of scientific professionals whose advice they are openly ignoring?

The Covid-19 pandemic has exposed the embeddedness of neoliberal assumptions in certain societies over others. This has become manifest in both the responses of governments and the reactions of the general public. Those countries that appear to have been most successful in controlling the spread of the virus – Vietnam, South Korea, perhaps China – have put in place systems of track and trace that, some libertarians might argue, amount to mass surveillance of the population. Rules about social distancing and hand-washing are inevitably more likely to command widespread compliance in more authoritarian states, where following government-issued guidelines is normative. But what we find in the United Kingdom and the United States especially is a reluctance to put public health before freedom of movement and freedom of commerce to a degree that far exceeds other liberal democratic nations. Covid-19 tests the neoliberal society because it calls for a level of restraint at the individual level and it calls on governments to endorse that restraint. In the UK, we have arguably never witnessed in such stark terms how neoliberal our society really is.

At the same time, we find ourselves at a good point in time to assess the consequences of the neoliberal age, which some suggest has reached its conclusion. The coronavirus has triggered economic and social upheaval on a global scale. Governments across the world have struggled to manage the fallout, and the inevitable soul-searching has prompted much reflection on whether new ways of thinking and living need to replace those that were previously dominant. Have global markets exacerbated or enabled international attempts to contain the virus? Has the consequent closure of borders thrown into question the globalization in which neoliberal economics thrives? How has our presumed entitlement to act freely and without constraint compromised the social distancing necessary to limit the spread of infection? When governments have prioritized commercial over civic recovery – opening shops before public libraries, for example – how does this expose the limitations of neoliberal thinking as a programme for positive social change? In many ways, the pandemic has thrown into crisis the neoliberalism that has maintained pre-eminent global influence for decades. How nations respond will tell us a lot about our collective ability to challenge the status quo and about the resilience of neoliberal perspectives.

The book

My argument in this book is that such changes demand a rethink of how the sociology of religion is conceived, including a fresh nomenclature, a more concerted engagement with other disciplines and a jettisoning of strict notions of ethical neutrality. The discussion spanning the following nine chapters takes for granted the observation that 'religion' (in its widest sense) has shown itself capable – albeit with varying degrees of success – of adapting to the cultural conditions of late modern societies. It is its strategies of adaptation and their consequences that are the principal conceptual focus of this book.

The following analysis is distinct in several ways. First, it is conceptually led rather than tradition led. There is much more discussion of Christianity and Islam in the United Kingdom and the United States, for example, than about Buddhism in Sri Lanka or Aboriginal religion among indigenous Australian people, precisely because the former are more shaped by the cultural forces of neoliberalism than the latter, although we need to be careful in how we draw boundaries here. This is a reason to do with external influence; there is also a reason that has to do with priorities that are internal to particular religious traditions. Given their conversionist tendency, it is not surprising that Christianity and Islam would furnish us with some of the most striking examples of neoliberal religion, for they are the traditions that typically engage most concertedly in conversations with neoliberal cultural environments. However, they do not have a monopoly on this, and there are plenty of examples of religion outside of these traditions that illustrate the geographically widespread realities of neoliberal influence.

Second, it is driven by a desire to write an accessible book about the sociology of religion that is not a survey of the field nor an introduction or 'how to' guide. Rather, I wanted to write an account of religion in the contemporary world through a specific conceptual lens, one that, I am convinced, has radically changed the way religious identities are negotiated, as well as the way religion is viewed across the globe.

Third, while rooted in the sociology of religion, it attempts to draw illumination from other disciplines and sub-disciplines. This is in part an echo of Max Weber's own influence – which stretches into economics, history and across many fields within sociology – but also is intended to challenge contributions to the sociology of religion that have paid insufficient attention to thinkers beyond a fairly traditional canon. I have found it highly illuminating to engage with ideas and research from the disciplines of human geography, international development, political science, as well as history and anthropology. They have often converged on the same cluster of concepts and sometimes the same secondary sources. So it has felt like tapping into a network of conversations.

Finally, the book has an ethical dimension. At least, there is a final chapter that addresses ethical responsibility in the sociology of religion. I believe the changes in wider neoliberal society make ethical questions unavoidable and so call for a debate about how we might exercise ethical responsibility within this sub-discipline. This is meant to be an opening contribution and is therefore partial and provisional, but it is intended to provoke as well, in order to get the discussion going.

After delineating some of the distinguishing features of this book, it may be helpful also to explain what this book is not. While it is deliberately written so as to be accessible to a broad scholarly readership – both across disciplines and across levels of understanding – it is not a comprehensive account of the sociology of religion. As my interest is in aspects of religious development that relate most closely to neoliberalism, certain traditions, as well as certain topics and questions, feature more prominently than others. There are a number of debates within the social scientific study of religion that, while undoubtedly important, are not addressed here. The ongoing dynamics of secularization are only engaged tangentially, as there is a more than adequate literature already available that covers this topic. Religious organizations, myths and rituals are only addressed insofar as they shed light on the cultural relationship between religion and the forces of neoliberalism. Where I omit extended discussions, I hope the cross-references to other scholarship prove helpful to those wishing to read further. For those wishing to delve deeper into the themes explored in these pages, a selection of recommended further reading appears at the end of each chapter.

CHAPTER 1
RELIGION IN A NEOLIBERAL AGE

Introduction

It is one of the grounding assumptions of this book that social change has overtaken the sociology of religion as conventionally practised. Put another way, things have changed to a point where the tools of the sub-discipline need to be reconsidered. What follows is a discussion of a particular, connected set of cultural-religious relationships. This book is not about all forms of religion nor all forms of society. It is about how we make sense of those religious phenomena that emerge from and embody an engagement with neoliberal social conditions. This is why this book is entitled *Neoliberal Religion* and not *Religion and Neoliberalism* or *Religion in Neoliberal Times*. It centres not on general social changes nor philosophical narratives, asking how religious movements have responded to them. Instead, it focuses on the instances of religio-cultural engagement that stand out as especially interesting and especially significant when viewed through a neoliberal lens.

Placing neoliberalism at the heart of how we understand contemporary religion enables a degree of critical distance from theoretical models that have dominated the sociology of religion in the past. The theory of secularization in particular has arguably functioned as a kind of 'theoretical blinder' (Cadge and Konieczny 2014: 558), exerting such a profound influence over sociological thinking about religion that it's prevented us from recognizing a range of interesting developments. As Gorski and Altinordu put it, secularization 'has often led scholars of religion to focus narrowly on a scientifically unanswerable question [i.e. what is the fate of religion in modern times?] and ignore other, more tractable ones, some of which are, arguably, just as urgent' (2008: 75). Not all scholars of religion take this view, and some have retained secularization theory within a more complex account of global change (e.g. Pollack and Rosta 2017). However, when religion is *predominantly* bound up in questions of society-wide decline and the task of measuring that decline, a momentum builds that leads the sub-discipline to repeatedly undermine the validity of its purpose. Religion becomes conceived in terms of decay or vitality, cases of the latter viewed as residual exceptions that prove the rule, leapt on uncritically by some as counterexamples rather than as interesting in their own right. This is not to suggest the secularization debate has not produced significant insight. We continue to learn from the accounts of social and religious change formulated by Bryan Wilson and David Martin in the 1960s and 1970s, for example, as well as the later, revisionist analyses by scholars like José Casanova (Casanova 1994; Martin 1978; Wilson 1966). But the dominance of secularization, alongside its ossification into simplistic, generalist accounts at the more popular level, has stymied the sociology of religion for too long. The deferral to a master narrative of secularization has obscured our vision and limited our capacity to formulate new ways of theorizing, researching and imagining religion as a social phenomenon.

In this opening chapter, I set out the main ideas associated with neoliberalism in three stages: neoliberal economics, neoliberalism as cultural change and neoliberalism as a lens through which to examine religious phenomena. I then clarify the approach of this book, before offering an account of the chapters to come.

The rise of neoliberal economic conditions

The economics of neoliberalism is usually traced to the thought of Austrian-British economist Friedrich von Hayek. In 1947, Hayek founded the Mount Pelerin Society, attracting like-minded intellectuals committed to what they viewed as a 'free society', drawing on the principles and practices of free market economics. A cluster of ideas and debates, rather than a coherent school of thought, neoliberalism nevertheless developed momentum as a major alternative to the Keynesian branch of economics that was dominant at the time. Keynesianism took its inspiration from John Maynard Keynes, the British economist who advocated a 'managed capitalism' (Moberg 2017: 42), with the policies and interventions of state actors key to the long-term stability of capitalist economies. Heeding the lessons of the Great Depression of the 1930s and chastened by the instabilities triggered by the twentieth century's two world wars, Keynesianism favoured centralized regulation as a means of securing durable economic prosperity. The market was key to this, but it was also a force whose positive capacity could not be taken for granted or left to chance. The state remained important as an active manager of capitalism. The heyday of Keynesianism coincided with the establishment of a range of ambitious innovations that drew on state power working in cooperation with capitalist economies. At the national level, there was Britain's welfare state, founded after the end of the Second World War; at the international, interstate level, there was the International Monetary Fund, the World Bank and the Organisation for Economic Co-Operation and Development. All assumed that economic activity needed to be managed if it was effectively to enrich the public good, and all assumed that states and representative cross-national bodies were the right agents for this job.

The neoliberalism of Hayek offered a very different vision for economic and social order. Rather than view markets and nation states as best organized into a collaborative relationship, Hayek was an advocate of markets remaining free from state intervention. His neoliberal perspective arose as a response to the perceived failure of the classical liberalism of the nineteenth century, which was viewed as placing too much faith in the state and in the moral-philosophical reasoning often used to justify state authority. It was also a critical response to a rising 'collectivism', which Hayek saw in communism and socialism, but also in more moderate forms of state-centred governance. Hayek and other neoliberal thinkers argued for the replacement of political or philosophical discourse with economic measurement. Liberal politics was viewed as vulnerable to ambiguity and the unreliable idiosyncrasies of passing ideologies and changing governments. Collectivism was vulnerable to state despotism. Societies would, according to neoliberals, be better organized according to the principles of the free market, with value conceived and measured in terms of explicit, quantitative, economic indicators. Economics was conceived as a source untainted by the vagaries of politics or ideological bias. Insofar as this approach transcended the interests and inherited privileges of particular actors or institutions, and instead presumed an equal playing field governed only by the rules of free competition, it was perceived as a more effective guarantor of both efficiency and fairness (Hayek 1944). In fact, in anticipation of the later, more expansive influence of neoliberal ideas, Hayek understood economic liberty to be essential to all aspects of a social order that is open and free.

While its intellectual roots lie in the early twentieth century, neoliberal economics achieved international influence only in later decades. Instrumental to this rise was US economist Milton Friedman, the leading figure in the Chicago School of Economics, who was influenced by Hayek's ideas. Friedman argued that a serious limitation of the 'big government' model inspired by Keynes was its propensity to cause high levels of inflation through price controls. Friedman instead advocated monetarism, which favoured the free market as the only effective regulator of supply and demand. Friedman was awarded the 1976 Nobel Prize for Economics, and it was during this decade that neoliberalism achieved pre-eminence as an economic model among 'Western' nations. During the 1980s, a neoliberal approach – distinguished by economic deregulation, privatization of state assets and liberalization of trade – was adopted and legitimized in political terms by the Thatcher government in the United Kingdom and the Reagan administration in the United States. By the 1990s, the same economic model was not only integrated into such nations' foreign policy; it also shaped conditions attached to financial aid issued to poorer nations in the global south. Instrumental in enforcing this globalization of neoliberalism were the international institutions previously established under the Keynesian model: the IMF and the World Bank.

A variety of economic characteristics are associated with neoliberalism as a philosophical rationale for free market capitalism. These are chiefly structured around deregulation, marketization and privatization. The pre-eminence of global financial markets is endorsed along with the assumption that their free operation is more important than the political agendas of particular states. In the economic sphere, the liquidity of capital is viewed as more important than the stability of employment. Binding the two is the belief that social contracts are less effective than the logic of the market (Marti 2020: 194). The pre-eminence of markets is also accompanied by a conviction that it is deregulation of these markets that enables the full realization of their potential (Harvey 2007). This fosters ease of borrowing and an increase in consumer debt, disempowerment of the state and heightened risk, but these consequences are assumed to be worth the benefit of the economic rewards. To be sure, the state has a role within the neoliberal vision, but it is a minimal one, and its principal purpose is to ensure the 'maintenance and facilitation of laissez-faire capitalism' (Moberg and Martikainen 2018: 420).

The growth in influence of neoliberal economics has paralleled and informed successive changes in the industrial and commercial life of powerful capitalist nations. The mass production of the early twentieth century – often dubbed Fordism after the assembly line methods of Henry Ford's motor car factories – gave way to a 'post-Fordist' economy characterized by flexible, service-oriented industries. Since the 1980s, there has been additional importance attached to the 'knowledge economy', reflecting the acceleration of information production and dissemination enabled by the birth of the internet. This was buoyed by the exponential growth in dot.com corporations and subsequent dominance of digital giants like Microsoft, Facebook and Google. Increased economic precarity, coupled with limited regulation of employment practices, has triggered the rise in short-term or zero-hours contract work. This 'gig economy' has been lauded by some for the freedom and flexibility it affords to mobile workers, while being condemned by others for the lack of job security, especially among those with families to support. Such developments have lent weight to suggestions of an acceleration of neoliberalization, as economic conditions signal a heightened deregulation for a wider range of workers.

It is fair to say that neoliberal economics has achieved the status of global hegemony. As David Harvey puts it, there has been, across the world, 'an emphatic turn towards neoliberalism in political-economic practices and thinking since the 1970s' (2007: 2). Its embeddedness as economic orthodoxy was made painfully clear in the aftermath of the global economic crash of 2007–8. Triggered by a deregulation of financial and real estate markets in the United States, and higher rates of risky borrowing and investment, the interconnectedness of global markets ensured the crash had a ripple effect around the world. It was also clearly attributable to neoliberal economic policies that had become normative in the preceding decades, something acknowledged by world leaders and economists. As British prime minister Gordon Brown commented, 'The old world of the Washington Consensus is over' (quoted in Steger and Roy 2010: 133). Except it wasn't over. Ironically, the most significant state response to the crash was the decision by the governments of most industrialized nations to issue multibillion-dollar bailout packages to support ailing financial markets. This return to state-aided capitalism was accompanied by a joint communiqué issued by the G20 group of nations advocating for reform of the global banking system, including tighter regulations and an integrated, international support package devised to sustain economic stability for richer and poorer countries. And yet these measures appear to have lost teeth under pressure from vested interests over time, so that the neoliberal economic momentum, while perhaps not quite so gung-ho as it once was, has resumed and assumed the status of political common sense. This persistence has understandably attracted critical comment, with neoliberalism condemned as a system here to stay so long as those in power stand to benefit from its continuance, even if the majority suffer in the long term (Harvey 2011: 12; Marti 2020: 187).

The aftermath of the financial crash also reveals an important dimension of neoliberal economics as it is practised. Rather than reflect a market free from state interference, neoliberal interests often depend on the state for legitimation and support.

While rooted in economic thought and practice that has its axis in Western Europe and North America, neoliberalism has also gained traction as a global export. This process has proceeded along two parallel lines: via the commercial activities of transnational corporations and financial markets as they extend their reach across the world, and via the influence of transnational organizations like the IMF and World Bank, whose promotion of economic development reflects a neoliberal approach. These have both been augmented by radical developments in the digital world, with the global circulation of ideas, images and services accelerated by a gradual narrowing of the digital information gap, developments in smart technology and an explosion in social media engagement. The interconnectedness of global economic markets has been illustrated in the way a crisis in the domestic US mortgage industry precipitated the global economic crash of 2007–8. The circulation of goods, services and ideas on a global level has, in one sense, reduced the size of the 'global village', in line with arguments about globalization that emerged in the 1990s. We are reminded of George Ritzer's concept of the 'McDonaldization' of society, which traced how norms of standardization, calculability, predictability and control migrated from fast-food restaurants into a variety of social spheres across a range of global contexts (Ritzer 2004). Ritzer's emphasis on the standardization of commercial products may need some updating in light of subsequent developments in social media and social enterprise, but his observation that standard templates tend to come from particular corners of the globe remains valid. Indeed, these same processes highlight major imbalances of power, as when particular commercial giants define norms of engagement across the world. Furthermore, the capacity of Amazon, Facebook, E-bay and Google to shape our everyday buying habits has implications well beyond the economic; they have come to have a major influence over our cultural lives.

Neoliberalism and cultural change

One of the reasons why neoliberalism has endured so robustly beyond the market crash of 2008 has to do with its embeddedness in spheres of life well beyond the economic. Indeed, William Davies suggests neoliberalism, following the crash, entered into a 'contingent' state, 'in which various failures of economic rationality are dealt with through incorporating an ever broader range of cultural and political resources' (2017: xxi–xxii). Part of the emergence of neoliberalism as a dominant paradigm has to do with the pre-eminence of economics over other forms of thinking. In other words, neoliberalism represents a set of assumptions that has its originating context in economics but which exerts an influence over a much wider range of cultural spheres (Delanty 2019: 11). This is what political scientist Wendy Brown calls the 'economization' of all realms of human life (Brown 2015). In this sense, according to Brown, neoliberalism is best viewed not as an economic policy, or even an ideology, but 'a normative order of reason developed over three decades into a widely and deeply disseminated governing rationality' (Brown 2015: 9).

It is in this respect that neoliberalism does not merely advocate a limited role for the state in economic affairs. It also has an expansive mission, characterized by the widespread assumption that all spheres of social life – in order to achieve maximal efficiency and potential – should be subjected to market conditions. In other words, all segments of society, whether falling within the realms of education, politics, health care, welfare, employment or leisure, would be better off if they functioned more like economic markets. It is in this way that the term 'marketization' becomes useful, pointing to the increasing adoption of market idioms into non-economic spheres of life (Moberg and Martikainen 2018: 430).

To be sure, this is not an indiscriminate, wholesale adoption of economic norms. Indeed, analyses that equate the 'neoliberal' with just about everything within the social realm risk proposing a theory that is too all-encompassing to be useful (Flew 2015). Moreover, *neoliberalization* proceeds in degrees, varies hugely by cultural context and prioritizes certain neoliberal ideas over others. Nevertheless, there are three strands of influence that are especially significant, both because they appear so culturally prevalent and so indicate important ways in which neoliberalism reshapes social life, and because they appear especially portable and hence embody significant potential for cross-cultural dissemination. These three strands are interrelated and may be summarized as choice, competition and commodification. First, neoliberalism conveys and reinforces the notion that consumer freedom and choice are universal goods. In this way, it contributes to 'the definitive establishment of consumerism as the dominant cultural ethos of late-modernity' (Moberg 2017: 45). This in turn heightens an existing tendency towards individualism as personal needs and preferences are viewed as the most legitimate gauges of value and meaning. A heightened individualism tends to present the empowered consumer as the driver of social change, over and against collective action or shared identities. Indeed, this is a focus of much critique of the expansion of neoliberalism, which is associated with a diminished civic sphere and, according to some, a weakened democracy (Brown 2015).

Second, there is the valorization of competition as a supremely reliable measure of efficiency. This means 'market logic' – the idea that the best is elicited from a given social field by pitching social actors against one another to compete for finite resources – takes precedence over cooperation, which becomes associated with inefficiency and a lack of dynamism. In this sense competition is treated as not just the best way to allocate resources but also the most effective means of fostering creativity and fresh ideas. It is ironic, then, that the same emphasis on competition drives a tendency to elevate standardized forms of measurement as a means of managing information and adjudicating the merits of competing claims. This is most visible in the migration of quantifiable measurements of value across various areas of social life, especially in the pre-eminence of statistics, but also in the importance of league tables, scoring systems and consumer ratings across cultural spheres, from school exam results to Amazon reviews (Beer 2016).

Third, as more and more activities are treated like markets, so the constituent 'goods' at stake within a given situation are more likely to be treated as commodities.

In some cases, this style of thinking proceeds in a partial or metaphorical sense, as when university courses are 'sold' to prospective applicants as options within a higher education market. Degree programmes might be treated as commodities insofar as they are promoted and marketed using methods universities have adopted from private business, but the conditions of exchange are quite different from those that pertain when we purchase a commodity like an item of clothing, a laptop or a meal in a restaurant. Students do not receive a degree simply because they have paid their tuition fees; they also have to attend lectures, learn the curriculum and pass the required assessment to a given threshold. In other cases, the similarity to a conventional 'commodity' is more subtle and its implications more profound. For example, in her book *Consumer Culture*, Celia Lury discusses the ways in which women have been objectified in art and in consumer commodities, defined by the male gaze as an object of sexual interest. While all individuals emerge in this context as potential consumers, their experience is highly gendered, so that the active agency of men may be contrasted with the more subordinate status of women, whose role is subject to the expectation that they will carry out the work of femininity. Markets for beauty products, for example, thereby construct women not as active consumers but as 'bearers of a culture that they do not own' (Lury 2011: 127). In the act of consumption, women are both consumers and images being consumed. Using other language associated with neoliberalism, women become the entrepreneurs of their own images (Genz 2006); whether this constitutes a mode of gender empowerment or disempowerment is a live debate within contemporary feminism. Either way, women become commodities available for consumption. As we will see later in this book, this process of personal commodification has become a notable feature within particular religious movements.

The cultural expressions of neoliberalism include elements that, from one point of view, represent universals of human life. Anthropologists have long noted how the exchange and consumption of goods are not simply a matter of survival but a key social act, structuring social relations and defining hierarchies of status and responsibility (Godelier 1999; Parry and Bloch 1989). 'Goods', as Gauthier, Woodhead and Martikainen put it, 'are the visible part of culture, and it is through their exchange that social life is made to exist' (2013a: 11). This is the case whether one is in rural India or urban Indianapolis. What occurs in cultures shaped by neoliberal assumptions is something quite distinctive, however. Specifically, there is a heightening of the importance of consumer goods as symbolic markers that individuals may harness in the service of self-expression, together with a valorization of market logic as a mode of thinking that makes this possible.

The predominance of neoliberal assumptions within the economic life of powerful nations has not gone without opposition and ethical critique. Many point to heightened levels of wealth inequality, leading to deprivation and various social problems as consumer aspirations outpace the means to achieve them. Others focus on the exploitation of the global south, which pays for its financial aid from richer nations not only in massive debt, but also in relinquishing state resources via neoliberal deregulation. The consequent importation of neoliberal assumptions into the cultural realm brings its own problems.

The privileging of individual choice – encouraging citizens to put their own preferences before any shared concerns – makes it more difficult to mobilize political resistance against the status quo. In this sense, consumerism can be a profoundly conservative social force, keeping individuals focused on their own desires and hence distracted from the injustices that the system inflicts. Neoliberalism's expansive reach has also provoked ethical debate. The reduction of issues of education and health to matters of resource governed by a cost-benefit analysis; the distorting effects of an assessment-led school system, in which teachers are incentivized to teach to the test, while pupils learn enough to get through; the way online rating systems put small businesses at the mercy of customer feedback, no matter how simplistic, fair or valid. All highlight the ethically dubious consequences of living in social conditions heavily coloured by neoliberal assumptions about what counts as value and how best to measure it. Seeking to challenge this, academic studies have highlighted the complicity of neoliberalism in maintaining a range of social problems, including violence against women (Bradley 2017), mental ill-health among university students (Lawrence 2021) and the stigmatization of the poor and homeless (Tylor 2020).

Perhaps the most insidious quality of neoliberalism is the way it sustains and depends on the myth that markets are governed only by objective economic efficiency, and so exist beyond the interests of individuals. A related assumption is that markets function as mechanisms and therefore do not embody values (Sandel 2012: 113). Both assumptions lend weight to claims that the effectiveness of neoliberal markets is beyond question and that to ask moral questions about their consequences is somehow improper or irrelevant. This presumption of non-accountability evokes Block and Somers's analogy between religion and neoliberalism: both are dependent on 'a claim to truth independent of the kind of empirical verification that is expected in the social sciences' (2014: 3). Such qualities protect neoliberalism from direct challenge. Its capacity to endure crises that promise its undoing – the 2008 financial crisis led some to predict a post-neoliberal age that never emerged – underlines this resilience (Mavelli 2020). The recognition that neoliberal conditions generate systems that appear to carry their own justification, as if they do not require justification beyond their capacity to reproduce themselves, is also applied within non-economic spheres. For example, Stefan Collini's critical essays on the state of the contemporary university point to the internalization of market logic within the bureaucracy of higher education. Emergent processes are rationalized not in terms of an external goal to which they are oriented but simply because market-driven systems are viewed as intrinsically more desirable and more efficient (Collini 2012). This idea was at the heart of Hayek's vision, and yet subsequent research into the social consequences of neoliberal economics paints a very different picture (e.g. Allen 2014; Brown 2015). Markets are rarely, if ever, 'neutral' in the sense that opportunity arises from a level playing field. Pre-existing inequalities play a huge part in dictating who is enabled to harness economic resources. Markets, while complex, are still products of society and history. To view them as value neutral is to sidestep important sociological and ethical questions concerning accountability, fairness and power.

Religion through the neoliberal lens

Many studies that attend to the relationship between economics and religion are ultimately indebted to Max Weber's work *The Protestant Ethic and the Spirit of Capitalism* (originally published in 1904–5), which has generated a vast literature that stretches to the present day, reflecting the richness of Weber's analysis. Unlike Karl Marx, Weber was not convinced by the argument that the key drivers of social and religious change could be associated with inequalities of wealth and economic status. Rather, Weber was more interested in the influence of economic *ideas* insofar as they impinge upon the cultural realm. Just as Weber was charting an apparent correspondence between a particular form of religion in the seventeenth century – Calvinist Protestantism – and rational capitalism, so the conditions of neoliberalism invite us to consider whether cultural resonances have made their way from the economic sphere into more recent expressions of religious identity. But Weber only takes us so far in answering this question. The neoliberal affinity between religion and economic spheres is the direct opposite of what Weber predicted for the future of modernity. Weber argued that the modern age would evolve further into disenchantment, involving the separation of religion and morality from the economic realm (Mavelli 2020: 61). What we find in the twenty-first century, as we will see through subsequent chapters, is not a separation but a complex convergence. As Jean Comeroff puts it, religion has become 'reciprocally entailed with economic forces' (2009: 32).

One expression of this relationship might be described in terms of an *affinity*; in Weber's case, this was a particular affinity between certain forms of Protestantism and rational capitalism. Read as an argument about historical causation, Weber's *Protestant Ethic and the Spirit of Capitalism* develops the case that elements of Protestantism gave rise to capitalism by incentivizing a disciplined orientation to work while discouraging indulgence in the fruits of one's earned wealth. Put another way, Protestantism encouraged particular ways of viewing the world and engaging with it, and these were especially compatible with capitalistic enterprise, characterized by hard work, a desire for this-worldly success and an imperative to reinvest profit. Some sociologists are sceptical of the causative elements of Weber's argument – the historical evidence appears much more complex – but nevertheless retain the affinity argument as an enduringly useful means of making sense of religious change. Peter Berger points to the twenty-first-century reality of the Protestant Ethic, especially in Pentecostal movements in the developing world, where it appears to empower poor communities to achieve social and economic mobility (Berger 2010). In other words, Protestantism still motivates capitalist engagement, with material consequences for those on the margins of society.

An extension of this affinity argument relates to forms of religion that legitimize or affirm identifiably capitalistic values. The most striking example can be found within those forms of charismatic Christianity that fall within the 'prosperity' or 'faith' movement. According to advocates of the 'prosperity gospel', material wealth is a sign of divine favour and the persistent acquisition of wealth a divinely endorsed ambition (Bowler 2013; Coleman 2000). More than this, the prosperity gospel transforms Christian identity into a source of power. As Birgit Meyer puts it, writing about the movement in Ghana, for prosperity believing Pentecostals, 'Faith, circumscribed as spiritual eye and spiritual hand, is a device, rather than an inner attitude, which promises the Born Again believer to be assured of God's blessings' (Meyer 2007: 15). The kind of Pentecostalism Meyer is writing about exemplifies an embrace of a distinctively neoliberal strand of capitalism. Its preoccupation – unlike the Calvinists of Weber's analysis – is not earnest productivity but material consumption, the wealthy pastor with the expensive clothes and Mercedes car a symbol of how true faith in God can lead to real-world transformation. Importantly, this turn towards material gain exists *alongside* faith in the power of the Spirit, material and non-material spheres of life interacting within the Pentecostal quest to harness the powers that will change the world.

More subtle correlations emerge in cases where religious movements attempt to adapt to conditions generated by neoliberalism. A decline in popularity can lead to a greater dependence on wider economic norms, as religious groups develop ways of coping with fewer resources and attempt to attract new members. For example, Jens Schlamelcher explores how these challenges have triggered a change of orientation within the German Evangelical Church (GEC). Previously able to take for granted a steady income generated via the state implemented 'Church tax', since the 1990s the GEC has faced financial decline as its membership grows older (and retired people do not pay church taxes) and as more opt out of this payment as they abandon church membership. Two consequences follow. The Church is forced to economize as it downsizes its activities and learns to work with a more limited budget. And it becomes more 'customer oriented', putting on services and activities designed to appeal to a broad audience via churches based in more heavily populated cities. These activities include dance classes, healing and power sessions, meditation and religious lectures. They require no moral obligation on the part of the participant and some charge a small fee to take part. As Schlamelcher finds, the mode of engagement comes to reflect the neoliberal economic circumstances with which the Church is attempting to contend. Specifically, 'One can come, consume and go, without being subjected to any further demands. There is no request for any personal commitment' (Schlamelcher 2013: 65).

The same argument about a 'turn to the self' may be used to explain the emergence of what have sometimes been called 'self' religions, those forms of 'alternative' religion (sometimes called 'spirituality') oriented around practices understood as meeting the needs of the individual. The emergence of contemporary forms of Paganism, Wicca, occultism, holistic healing and the plethora of practices associated with the term 'New Age' fall into this category (Heelas 1996). If the shift towards individualism undermines some traditional forms of religion, it lends an enhanced cultural resonance to alternative spiritualities, which share the value it attaches to individual choice and subjective experience (Heelas and Woodhead 2005).

The neoliberal age finds alternative spiritualities increasingly commercialized, as products and services are marketed and sold to interested customers. Indeed, the proliferation of such phenomena has only been possible due to market forces and the opportunities for promotion and engagement possible via digital media (Gauthier,

Martikainen and Woodhead 2013: 270). The counter-cultural movements of the 1960s and 1970s have been replaced by a market much more closely aligned with the norms governing mainstream culture. In this sense alternative spiritualities may signal momentum away from an *expressive* individualism – treating identity as defined by personal experience – towards *acquisitive* individualism, where identity is defined by our consumer purchases (Lyon 2000: 32–3). Of course, it may not be helpful to draw a clear distinction between the two, especially given the pervasiveness of consumerism within neoliberal society. As this book will try to demonstrate, a wide range of religions are profoundly shaped by the neoliberal assumptions that influence wider society, including those we might describe as traditional, collectivist or even sectarian. Those who portray alternative spiritualities as superficial and narcissistic often overlook the ways in which values associated with individualism, choice, marketability, competition, self-empowerment, branding and image management make their way into the thinking and behaviour of 'traditional' religious movements (Moberg 2017).

This momentum also runs in the other direction, with corporate business taking on motifs and ideas derived from religious or spiritual contexts, for example in advertising (Marmor-Lavie, Stout and Lee 2009). This correspondence has been remarked upon in a polemical study by Jeremy Carrette and Richard King, who argue that forms of 'alternative spirituality' have been co-opted into the marketing of big business, which uses 'religious' language in building product brands in order to reinforce the sense that they are selling not just a product but an experience, with its own values and philosophy (Carrette and King 2005: 159–60). In this way, phenomena within the 'spiritual milieu' become vehicles for the dissemination and maintenance of neoliberal values. Carrette and King's study is instructive in highlighting the ethical issues that arise from the neoliberalization of religion but in focusing on Western contexts, it overlooks some important variations. For example, there are distinctive ways in which neoliberal assumptions enter into expressions of Islam in Turkey via the Islamic fashion industry, Christian nationalism in the United States, secularism within contemporary France and even global networks of alternative spirituality, which do not easily fit into their analysis.

That religious groups should become caught up in neoliberal ideas and values is not surprising insofar as they are, like all human phenomena, shaped by the cultural contexts in which they are situated. Religious groups are also subject to changes in law or government, and emerging legislation or policies can embody neoliberal assumptions. This has been exemplified in various nations through changes in models of welfare provision. Neoliberal governance typically includes a more limited role for the state in providing centralized welfare services, and religious organizations and charities have been viewed as well-established alternative providers. A reduced state and the deregulation of welfare provision open up new roles – and often funding – for religious organizations. This was the thinking behind the 'Big Society' initiative launched under Prime Minister David Cameron's Conservative government in the UK, as well as the White House Office of Faith-based and Community Initiatives, established under President George W. Bush in 2001. Religion can be subject to neoliberal assumptions when those assumptions make their way into the thinking of those in power, influencing policy and law (Beaman 2013).

These patterns all reflect what James Beckford has called the 'deregulation of religion' (1989: 172). Religion has, within the late modern age, achieved a level of unpredictability and flexibility that exceeds earlier times. It is less bound by traditional structures and meanings, and is freed up to forge novel relationships and connections with a range of non-religious social phenomena. It is for this reason that Beckford argued that religion is best conceived as a cultural resource; it has been put to use by a variety of interest groups, whether to legitimate political ambitions or lend meaning to commercial endeavours. We need to recognize this deregulation within approaches to the sociology of religion, as only then will they be able to account for the complexities of the twenty-first century. As David Lyon puts it, 'Without its crippling conceptual tether to local community or to social institution, religion may be rethought in fresh ways' (2000: 9).

This observation has exerted a major influence on the sociology of religion over recent decades, but all too often deregulation has been read as an unstructured and unfettered religious 'free for all'. The 'turn to the self' has been understood as arising from a fragmentation of tradition that leaves individuals to pick up the pieces and put them back together, constrained only by the choices they make. Indeed, this is the idea behind the unhelpful caricature of 'pick and mix religion'. As this idea has gained traction in both academic and more popular circles, the sovereignty of the self has been overstated, and as a consequence, some important patterns in the *social* expression of religion have been overlooked. As the subsequent chapters will show, neoliberal assumptions often have a structuring influence over religious phenomena. Even while celebrating individual freedom and choice, their consequences are social, not least in their capacity to reconfigure patterns of identification, empowerment and recognition that occur within the contexts of human relationships (Gauthier, Martikainen and Woodhead 2013: 272).

A critical cultural approach

The cultural approach pursued in this book can be described in terms of a critical engagement with the work of Max Weber mentioned earlier. This in turn can be understood as a critical response to Marxist sociology and its assumption of the primacy of economic factors. A critical approach to neoliberalization benefits from this angle because, as Terry Flew observes, much of the scholarship has tended to oversimplify issues of power, treating neoliberalism as a vehicle for the imposition of class interests (Flew 2015: 319). Re-engaging with Weber can be a useful way of guarding against this because, while acknowledging the close relationship between religion and economic forces, for Weber, this relationship was complex, variable and only one factor among several in any account of how and why religious phenomena develop as they do. Indeed, Weber's influence may in part be indebted to his appropriation – especially by US academics – as a more acceptable foil to the more subversive Marxist tradition (Barbalet

2020: 907). Weber was arguing against economic determinism, instead offering an account of how *ideas* can become 'effective forces in history' (Giddens 1992: xix). This is one of the reasons why his work still repays consideration among sociologists of religion. At a time when economic forces appear to shape cultural life with particular power, it is tempting to analyse religious phenomena in deterministic terms, either as a direct consequence of economics or as a counter-response to economics and consequent social inequalities. Just as Weber sought to guard against the myopia of a Marxist perspective, so we may learn from his work as we guard against deterministic thinking in the present day.

At the same time, while Weber advocates for a complex perspective that takes seriously historical and social contingency, he also takes economic forces seriously. While we must guard against economic determinism, we cannot at the same time capitulate to the assumptions of a cultural sociology of religion that pays no attention to economic factors. Indeed, the latter is possibly a greater danger, given how the sub-discipline has developed over recent decades. It is the contention of the present book that the sociology of religion needs to take economic forces seriously while situating them within cultural frames of reference, if it is to take proper account of the manifestations of religion distinctive to the twenty-first century. Put another way, I hope to provide an account of contemporary religion that takes seriously the permeation of economic forms of thinking and practice but which conceives of their influence on religion in cultural terms: variable, not always predictable and subject to creative negotiation as well as more direct mirroring.

Existing studies of the interface between neoliberalism and religion have tended to treat the former as a general account of social conditions to which religious movements are responding. One approach would be to borrow the language that Roy Wallis used in his volume *The Elementary Forms of the New Religious Life*, in which he differentiated between new religious movements that were world-affirming, world-accommodating and world-rejecting (Wallis 1984). If we follow Wallis's framework as a template, we might differentiate between religious responses to neoliberalism in terms of affirmation, accommodation and rejection. In substantive terms, there are those religious movements that explicitly embrace market logic as a universal regime of 'success', strategically deployed to further their key goals; those which internalize neoliberal norms as culturally commonplace; and those which openly oppose neoliberalism as complicit in social injustice.

This is a potentially useful approach; however, the emerging analysis would not tell us much about *how* such movements *engage* with neoliberal forces. It would assume a simple orientation (affirmation, accommodation, rejection) while not leaving room for *active* negotiation. James Beckford offers a similar critique of analyses that relate religious innovations to generalized accounts of 'late modernity'. While placing phenomena like the New Age movement and alternative spiritualities within a given cultural milieu – which may or may not reveal important affinities – it does little to attend to the specific ways in which such practices *relate* to this milieu or aid the complexities of empirical investigation to inform a more intricate picture (Beckford

2003: 5–6). As the examples in the following chapters will show, the relationship between religious movements and neoliberal norms is not simple, static or straightforward. It moves in different directions, includes counter-movements and manifests in social configurations that are often unexpected. To borrow the words of François Gauthier, it represents 'a new kind of rapport between religion and economics in which they are profoundly intertwined' (2018: 388). It is subject to changing circumstances and differential levels of power and influence. And yet it is not random. It follows patterns – clearly identifiable patterns that, while moving in a direction that is not predetermined, are nevertheless distinct enough for us to learn something by taking them seriously. It is in this sense that the approach taken in this book may be summarized as *probing the cultural space within which economics and religious forces come together to achieve meaning and social expression*. Religion acquires new significance in this cultural realm, but it is one often structured in relation to social norms tied to neoliberal economic conditions.

The emerging discussion is *not* a universal model or theory, or a call for all religion to be viewed as somehow neoliberal. For some strict forms of religion, free choice is anathema, associated with Western decadence, immorality or the worship of false gods. Clearly not all contemporary religious movements can be collapsed into neoliberal themes, although increasingly few – I would argue – remain able to sustain an existence while ignoring neoliberal forces entirely. Furthermore, what I propose is *not* a causal argument but an argument about the expansion of cultural affinities between certain kinds of thinking and social organization and certain forms of religion. This expansion is not linear nor inevitable but has gained enough momentum by the end of the second decade of the twenty-first century for a set of distinct patterns to be identified.

The structure of the book

This book considers the major elements of neoliberal cultural circumstances and explores how they change how religious identities are expressed. The analysis breaks down into five themes, each highlighting how religious phenomena emerge in novel forms out of a dialogue with neoliberal conditions. Each theme is considered in a separate chapter via examples drawn from a range of cultural contexts, chiefly the United States, the United Kingdom, Australia and continental Europe. These chapters explore five cultural forces that are especially important as sites of neoliberal influence. These forces are marketization, populist politics, the destabilization of knowledge associated with the 'post-truth' era, securitization and an entrepreneurial orientation to selfhood.

Following this, broader themes are addressed in chapters on power and religious difference, and on non-religion and secularism, which addresses how neoliberal appropriations of religion also re-frame affirmations of non-religion and arguments for a secular society. A final chapter considers the ethical responsibilities incumbent upon those undertaking the social scientific study of religion within a neoliberal age, arguing for a fresh debate about the values underpinning and driving this endeavour.

It is necessary to make a note here on the selection of examples featured in this volume, many of which are drawn from developed nations in the global north. This bias is partly due to the boundaries of the author's own experience and expertise, which has been framed by a career studying and working as an academic in the United Kingdom, supplemented by a brief period living in Canada and multiple research trips to various locations in the United States. My research has also focused predominantly on religious movements in Anglophone 'Western' nations, especially the United Kingdom and the United States, and, while my teaching in the sociology of religion has sought to stretch this scope, I am inevitably confined by what can be covered well within the limitations of space available. My reading continues to be stretched by colleagues, whose perspective and experience are broader than my own, and I hope those elements of the current book that venture beyond my comfort zone do so responsibly and with an emphasis on questions being explored, rather than conclusions drawn. There is also a more conceptual reason for retaining this bias and that has to do with the global forces that have been the most significant carriers of neoliberal conditions. Consumer society is not ubiquitous and exists in more or less developed forms in different parts of the world; however, these developments often take as their templates initiatives that emerge from particular centres of power (Stolz and Usunier 2018: 2). To understand the contours of the cultural conversations that generate 'neoliberal religion', we need to understand how neoliberal conditions emerge as dominant or at least influential, and this demands attention to the impact of dominant world powers on the global south (Wuthnow 2009). While I cannot claim to have explored this process in full here, I hope to have said enough about the direction of travel to trigger discussion among others better qualified to continue the journey. In the meantime, I am more than happy to keep my own 'first world' assumptions under the critical microscope and disrupt the authority they might often assume.

CHAPTER 2
RELIGION AND THE MARKET: RELIGIOUS DIVERSITY IN NEOLIBERAL CONTEXTS

Introduction

The sociology of religion has, in recent years, made increasing use of the market as a category of analysis. It has been used to capture how religions operate, how they recruit new members and how they relate to broader social contexts. Applications of market language have stretched across the globe, including prosperous and developing nations (Moberg and Martikainen 2018). As Stievermann et al. comment, 'Religious adaptation of market techniques and technologies is everywhere', adding that it has become, in the United States, 'just standard practice' (Stievermann, Goff and Junker 2015: 1–2). To speak of the religious or spiritual in the same sentence as the market resonates with our neoliberal context, and this is reflected in the abundance of academic publications that adopt this language. What this reflects, I would argue, is not just changing theoretical fashions in the discipline. It points to a growing recognition of market-like themes within the life of religious movements.

The question of markets runs in parallel to the question of neoliberalism, for neoliberal economics has spread throughout the world via market forces. This is not to collapse neoliberalism into markets alone; there is much more associated with the neoliberal as a cultural phenomenon, as the following chapters will demonstrate. However, markets, marketization and market thinking are axiomatic to it, serving as both *vehicles* and *enablers* of neoliberal initiatives. It is the impact of these initiatives on religion that serves as the focus of the present chapter. We start by revisiting the market as a metaphor and examining critically its usefulness in conceptual terms.

Markets and rational choices

While an economic theory of religion that includes elements of market thinking can be found in Max Weber's work (Bourdieu 1987; Stolz 2006), the explicit use of the market as a metaphor for understanding religion sociologically emerges much later. In *The Sacred Canopy*, Peter Berger describes pluralistic situations, in which religious monopolies have broken down, as 'dominated by the logic of market economics'. According to Berger, when religious traditions are multiple and depend on voluntary allegiance, they become 'marketing agencies and the religious traditions become consumer commodities' (Berger 1969: 138). The use of this analogy among social scientists has grown in tandem with the expansion of neoliberal markets themselves (Moberg 2017: 3). It was studies emerging in the 1980s that inspired R. Stephen Warner's formulation of a 'new paradigm' in the sociology of religion, framed by economic metaphors – for example, 'competition in the religious marketplace' – rather than by religion conceived in terms of society-wide 'sacred canopies' (Warner 1993: 1051). In this influential group of studies, market competition, rather than an accelerator of secularization, is presented as a stimulator of religious vitality (Finke and Stark 1992). Just as free competition stimulates a market economy, so a free market of religions stimulates the religious landscape. Finke and Stark's *The Churching of America*, for example, argues that the deregulation of religion in the fledgling United States established the conditions of a free market, in which different religious groups competed for followers. The maintenance of this arrangement has engendered a relatively high overall level of religious engagement, at least compared to other economically prosperous 'Western' nations. The causal link here has to do with a free market's capacity to accommodate the needs and preferences of a diverse population (in contrast to societies in which a single religious tradition retains dominance), as well as the in-built incentive for religious movements to be enterprising in their attempts to recruit and retain participants, rather than lose them to the competition. It is the established presence of a free market for religion, so Finke and Stark argue, that explains why the societies of Western Europe are characterized by religious decline while the United States at the same time experienced religious vitality (Finke and Stark 1992).

Finke and Stark's explanation is admittedly neat and at first sight might seem compelling. It echoes Warner's discussion of the 'new paradigm' and, indeed, might be said to exemplify it within a fresh and novel theory. It draws attention to the limitations of using a framework suited to the European context within the very different United States. It also has the virtue of being testable against available evidence. It should, in theory, be possible to compare different societies (and more localized subcultures) in order to demonstrate whether 'free market' conditions do foster religious vitality, while religious monopolies lead to religious stagnation. Others have applied the same logic to societies beyond the United States, arguing for a more wide-ranging significance of market competition as a stimulus to religious growth (e.g. Iannaccone 1991). However, their analysis has also been subjected to serious criticisms among both historians and sociologists of religion (Goldstein 2006). Some point to nations characterized by virtual religious monopolies – such as Ireland and Poland – where there is evidence of relative religious vitality, compared with others where there is religious deregulation and decline (Casanova 2007). Others have charted changes over time, to see whether deregulation stimulates religious vitality, as with Jörg Stolz's study of the disestablishment of the Protestant Reformed Church in Switzerland. Again, the evidence is against the market model, with a weakening of the relationship between church and state and a heightened programme of religious marketing having no discernible effect on a pre-existing pattern of secularization (Stolz 2018). The empirical evidence does not appear to support Finke and Stark's model as a universal theory.

Many critics have focused on their dependence on a 'rational choice theory' (RCT) of religious identity. Religious actors are treated as freely choosing their religious engagement from among a range of available options, subject to a cost-benefit calculation. Religious affiliation and practice are motivated by self-interest. In other words, people choose the religions that accrue most benefits and incur the lowest costs. Costs here are not – at least not predominantly – imagined in financial terms but mainly in terms of time, energy and opportunity costs, while benefits are understood in terms of community support, sense of identity and answers to existential questions. According to RCT, the religious human has their eye permanently on the internal balance sheet.

The assumptions of rational choice theory, as Kathryn Lofton argues, both embody and uphold the logic of neoliberalism (Lofton 2017). In a remarkable mirroring of Freidrich von Hayek's own thinking, it is the *market* that enables the optimal outcome. 'Market' thinking can appear deceptively simple and logical, rational and internally consistent. It constitutes a form of knowledge that is communicable across cultural contexts and carries the appeal of appearing universally accessible. And yet because it assumes human decision-making is governed by rules that supercede cultural differences, rational choice theory overlooks the cultural construction of rationality and the ways in which differential access to power shapes the different opportunities available to different people (Edgell 2012: 249). Rational choice theory also tends to assume stability of religious preferences over time, as if the motives people have for aligning themselves with one religious group over another do not change (Hefner 2009: 163). There are also problems with how RCT imagines the religious market itself. As Pollack and Rosta argue, this approach underestimates the influence that distinct cultural frameworks have on patterns of religious vitality and decline (2017: 432). Applied in the United States, RCT has been criticized for overlooking the challenges faced by many immigrants and non-Christian groups in adapting to a context that privileges a distinctively Protestant model of religious organization, i.e. the congregation (Edgell 2012: 252). Religious choice is not entirely 'free and unregulated' but is framed by pre-existing privileges and an unequal distribution of power (Berger, Davie and Fokas 2008: 20–1). Differences of national history and culture matter. Some fascinating case studies emerge from Eastern Europe, for example, in which the absence of religious regulation is accompanied by high levels of disinterest and disaffiliation. To take one case, following the collapse of the Soviet Union, the Estonian government introduced a more neoliberal approach to religion, characterized by freedom of practice, limited state intervention and a free market of religions. But a deregulation and diversification of the religious landscape was not, as rational choice theorists might expect, accompanied by an increase in religious vitality and growth, something Ringvee attributes to the historically weak relationship between religion and Estonian national identity (Ringvee 2013). The 'market' is not a singular, stable phenomenon.

Markets as fields of opportunity and risk

The arguments associated with rational choice theory may be contentious, but they raise an important and enduringly relevant question: to what extent do the social fields within which religious behaviour occurs function like an economic market? Returning to the key cultural facets of neoliberalism discussed in the previous chapter, is there evidence of consumerism, competition and commodification? And if so, with what kinds of consequences for the social status of religious phenomena? It may be problematic to make sense of the religious fate of an entire culture using a market model, as if it were simply replacing the society-wide ambitions of secularization theory. But given the influence of neoliberalism on twenty-first-century cultural life, is it wise to jettison 'the market' completely? If market thinking and market forces have an impact on religious phenomena, how should we understand this relationship, while avoiding the pitfalls of rational choice theory?

One observation is undeniable: there are indeed examples of religious behaviour that mirror those associated with economic markets. Indeed, in some contexts, the mirroring is blatant, and religious practices assume a form remarkably similar to the consumption of commercially marketed goods. Benjamin Soares finds this pattern in the West African state of Mali. Here, a 'religious economy' has developed populated by Islamic saints, preachers and practitioners of esoteric sciences or magic, offering their services for a fee for those seeking health, wealth or success. This 'religious economy' has, over time, come to resemble the broader neoliberal economy, and these religious entrepreneurs have adjusted their practice accordingly. Economic uncertainty has been met with flexibility and adaptability, production of religious commodities and the use of online media to market individual personalities (Soares 2017). Comparable developments have been noted in Kerala in southern India, where anthropologists Osella and Osella find the circulation of wealth and workers has generated a 'commoditization' of Hindu ritual practices (Osella and Osella 2003: 134). In a study of *kuthiyottam*, a blood sacrifice to the goddess Bhadrakali, the authors describe how this ritual is expensive to facilitate and functions in part as a 'public sanctioning of wealth and status' (2003: 110). However, the high caste elite who have traditionally dominated this ritual tradition have had their status disrupted in recent years by families and communities traditionally excluded from it. People of low caste status but newly earned wealth derived by migrant work in the Persian Gulf have used this wealth to sponsor *kuthiyottam*, in turn translating economic opportunities into affirmations of prestige and status. Migrant labour is not only significant in funding conspicuous consumption among lower caste communities, though; it also feeds a pattern of neoliberalized religious innovation through the association of migration with power and opportunity. Osella and Osella describe the associated changes in wider Keralan society:

> Kerala temple committees have been quick to react to this migration-led 'consumer' demand by introducing, for example, long-distance bookings – by fax or email – for *nercha* (temple offerings), or by organising the performance of obscure Vedic rituals (for example, a 1994 *yagna* organised at a local Shiva temple which on the last day attracted more than 25,000 people); local Brahmins have become willing to perform hitherto relatively uncommon *homams* (fire sacrifices, especially to Ganapathi) in the house of whoever is able to afford the costs, regardless of caste

status; and some Brahmins have opened up their family temples to the public, cashing in on the ritual reputation they hold. Astrologers, sorcerers (*mandravadi*), Ammas, Tantris and ritual specialists in general have all been able to exploit this burgeoning religious market. (2003: 117)

The studies by Soares and by Osella and Osella both illustrate how the influence of neoliberal economics in developing societies extends to modes of engagement among religious practitioners. One dimension has to do with market resemblances. Religious activity takes on some of the features of economic markets insofar as there are goods that are sold and opportunities seized to promote religious – and economic – interests further. Another dimension relates to the secondary consequences of the movement of labour and capital that are brought about by neoliberal economic change. Just as a deregulation of market forces can disrupt traditional distributions of wealth and status, so it can disrupt traditions of religious practice that uphold those arrangements. The link between the two highlights the complex relationship between religion and power.

Competition between religious 'providers' is easier to imagine within contexts characterized by high levels of religious pluralism and unstable economies. But how might this become manifest within more prosperous, 'Western' societies? One approach that offers a useful perspective on this issue, and which combines insights from rational choice theory *and* secularization theory, is offered by Jörg Stolz and Jean-Claude Usunier. Stolz and Usunier (2018) associate modernization with a breakdown in traditions and a consequent increase in the importance attached to individual choice. Religious identities cease to be traditions one inherits from one's parents or which are ascribed by virtue of birth into a particular culture. Instead, they emerge as voluntary organizations, functioning in a comparable way to sports clubs and charities. Participation in religions becomes a matter of personal choice. These changes take place at a different pace within different locations, and Stolz and Usunier remark on differential patterns in the United States and Europe, but the overall trajectory remains the same. It is distinguished by a shift from religion as something prescribed to religion as something chosen. This means religious groups have to compete for the attention and commitment of potential members, but it also places them in a situation of what Stolz and Usunier call 'generalized religious-secular competition', as 'religious suppliers compete with secular suppliers concerning specific human needs' (2018: 5). Religious organizations might offer support for those with mental health problems via pastoral care, but individuals could also seek the services of a healthcare professional for medication or counselling, or perhaps psychotherapy. Religious groups might offer clear and compelling answers to some of life's most difficult questions, but individuals could instead go to educational institutions, literature or science. A sense of community might be a benefit of belonging to a religious congregation, but individuals might get this via a sports club, campaigning organization or friendship network. Whereas, at one time, all of these functions might have been exclusively provided through religious organizations, there is now a range of outlets from which to choose. Moreover, faced with this choice, many individuals in Western cultures are choosing non-religious options. This is why Stolz and Usunier 'observe a simultaneous process of marketization, individualization, and secularization' rather than understanding these as mutually exclusive (2018: 5).

Stolz and Usunier's approach is helpful in incorporating non-religious providers of meaning and belonging; their integration into a market model allows for an approach that takes marketization *and* secularization seriously as concurrent social processes. It also moves away from the common assumption among rational choice theorists that while the 'supply side' of the equation varies, providing different religious options for interested individuals, demand for religion tends to remain constant, an especially difficult assumption to justify in sociological terms. Stolz and Usunier recognize the importance of market-style thinking while also acknowledging the reality of a market choice to *reject* religion as an option. In calling attention to how religions in the twenty-first century need to compete for the attention of individual citizens, Stolz and Usunier identify an element of market thinking that is difficult to deny, even in societies with minimal religious diversity. Even if only competing with non-religious providers, religious groups may need to develop strategies of self-promotion in order to stave off the possibility of dying out in the longer term. And yet patterns of declining religious engagement across a variety of prosperous capitalist nations – some of which exhibit profound levels of neoliberalization – suggest marketization by no means guarantees religious growth (Stolz and Usunier 2018: 15).

The analysis advanced by Stolz and Usunier highlights the importance of local conditions in framing experiences of religious – and non-religious – diversity. It also draws attention to the issue of perception. The reality of religious diversity within a given context and the perception of that diversity by religious actors within it may be markedly different. Indeed, the beliefs of a particular religious group may predispose it to view the world in binary terms – black and white, truth and falsity, good and evil – and so struggle to formulate a positive view on the religious variety in their midst. It is in these contexts that complex patterns of religious difference are collapsed into simple, often pejorative categories: pluralism, the faithless, heathen or lost. For many conservative or sectarian religious groups, there is no religious diversity; there is only the faithful and everybody else. There is also the issue of visibility. How do we read the social landscape around us and do we have the knowledge to be able to notice and interpret signals of religious identity or diversity? To have an orientation to religious diversity we need to recognize that it's there. This is of course germane to the experience of the solitary observer, the person walking the street or driving through a city centre. But it also has to do with the experience of religious groups and the motivations they might have to be seen and if so, by whom. How visible is religious symbolism within a given environment? And what range of meanings are attached to its communication of difference? (Watson 2005) We will explore these questions in relation to the social forces that drive religious intolerance and prejudice in later chapters.

In this way market thinking can sensitize us to the ways in which religious behaviour is framed by what we might call fields of opportunity. We use the term 'field' here in a similar sense to French sociologist Pierre Bourdieu, who wrote about a social field as a structured system of positions, defined by the distribution of particular resources, or forms of capital. In other words, social fields are contexts defined by the goods that are at stake within them. In one of the few articles Bourdieu devotes to religion, he even speaks of 'goods of salvation', the transaction of religious power between religious officials and laypeople, and 'competition for lay followers' (1987: 129, 133), indicating the compatibility of his thinking with market models. However, Bourdieu's perspective differs from rational choice theory in several important respects. Importantly, he does not imagine humans to function according to consciously rational calculative logic, but as a result of more complex combinations of factors, including learnt practical sense and what he calls *habitus*, an embodied disposition that informs the orientation of the individual agent. In this way, Bourdieu takes the distribution of power and status seriously but without collapsing a religious field into a rationally governed marketplace. We cannot treat religious individuals as 'pre-social', calculative rational actors capable of acting independently of their social identities (Gauthier 2018: 383). Rather, if we treat religion as functioning within social fields in Bourdieu's sense, we are forced to attend to the ways in which opportunity as well as risk emerge differentially according to the status of different people.

Bourdieu recognizes that the social field is never a level playing field, with status and success determined primarily by individual effort and skill. Rather, it is structured by inherited distributions of power and status, and is also influenced by its relationships with other social fields (Bourdieu 1984). This latter observation is especially useful in assessing the significance of online fields of religious engagement, encompassing what scholars have called 'digital religion' (Campbell 2013). Online accessibility represents a potentially massive expansion of the religious market available to any one individual. Indeed, early research into religion online raised the possibility that the internet might constitute an arena of religious possibility capable of bypassing the limitations of the offline social world, perhaps generating a mass abandonment of traditional, 'offline' religious practice (e.g. Brasher 2001). Subsequent experience has encouraged a more cautious perspective; however, two observations might be made, which are apposite for an understanding of how online engagement relates to fields of religious opportunity.

First, online engagement has become domesticated and normalized over the past two decades. Contrary to early warnings about the capacity of the internet to revolutionize social reality, our everyday lives are now so entangled with online communication that it hardly seems meaningful to draw a clear distinction between the two. This is perhaps especially the case for younger generations, like the 'GenZers' born after 1995, who have only known a world in which the digital is integral to everyday interaction (Katz et al. 2021). Moreover, online engagement does not operate independently of the offline world but in complex relationship to it. What were once called 'new media' now feature in the way we do our supermarket shopping, organize a night out with friends or share family photos. The ease with which so many religious communities transferred their communal acts of worship onto video conferencing platforms during the coronavirus pandemic reflects how what was once the stuff of radical novelty has become the mundane everyday. That being said, what is a blurred line for many nevertheless represents a precious source of safety and opportunity for others. Writing of online churches, Tim Hutchings notes that while the boundary between online and offline is insignificant for some, 'for others that boundary is the foundation and guarantee of any value the online church can offer them' (2017: 232). The option to assume multiple identities also affords opportunities to express doubt and heterodox ideas inconceivable in one's everyday offline life (Fader 2020). Online spaces – whether interactive gaming, anonymous online forums or social media platforms like Twitter, TikTok or WhatsApp – can enable expressions of vulnerability and subversion that would be difficult to imagine in offline contexts (Freitas 2017).

The second point is that in the twenty-first century, online environments are often heavily structured by neoliberal economic forces. A large portion of online engagement occurs through social media platforms and so is framed both by a particular kind of technology and by the commercial interests of the corporations which maintain these platforms. Search engines filter our online engagement via algorithms that tailor our experience according to prior patterns in our consumer preferences (Mavelli 2020: 69). These in turn get synchronized with the apps on our smartphones, our email address lists, our wish lists and 'likes' as stored on various websites, TV subscriptions and social media accounts. Through our online activity, our exposure to and engagement with the world is comprehensively filtered through an interconnected network of commercial interests. A similar observation is made in Possamai and Lee's (2011) research on 'hyper-real' religions, which mix elements of traditional religion with elements of popular culture. Neo-pagans who draw inspiration from J.R.R. Tolkein's *Lord of the Rings* novels, or those citing their religion as 'Jedi' on recent census returns are just two examples. The web is a key site for inspiring such innovations, and yet the most prominent examples derive from commercially successful movie franchises, such as Harry Potter, Star Wars and The Matrix. Once we trace the ways these connections relate to, enable or collude with offline activities – whether through education complemented by online learning environments, collecting retail credit via store card points or using video conferencing software for work meetings – we might find ourselves agreeing with Kathryn Lofton's comment that 'the distinction between what is the market and what is not seems wholly impossible to determine' (Lofton 2017: 7). The important point here is that online engagement opens up new possibilities for religious expression and experimentation, but these possibilities are not unfettered or limitless and are often structured around commercial interests.

Marketization: The internalization of market norms

Having attempted to develop a nuanced understanding of how the market metaphor might help us understand the broader context of religious engagement, we turn to a slightly different perspective. This I am describing as marketization and refers to the internalization by religious movements of methods and ideas commonly associated with commercial business.

It was Alexis de Tocqueville, the nineteenth-century French aristocrat whose travels in the United States informed his influential two-volume work *Democracy in America*, who observed the constructive role religion played in American democratic society, in contrast to the antagonistic relationship in his native France. He famously attributed this to the separation of religion from the state, but he also noted the significance of commerce in energizing American democracy. The craft of the businessman is upheld as signifying vigour and ambition, so much so that even those in religious ministry aped his methods and standards as a route to success (Hofstadter 1964: 50). In his book *Selling God*, R. Lawrence Moore traces how religious leaders in nineteenth-century America entered the 'marketplace of culture' in order to confront what they saw as the damaging influence of the emerging leisure and entertainment industries, not least popular theatre. Their initial attempts to ban or discourage, however, soon gave way to a determination to offer more spiritually wholesome products of their own, adopting the methods of the market for religious purposes (Moore 1994).

In the twenty-first century, the ubiquity of market norms within American religion – if not their universal dominance – is undeniable (Lofton 2017). In her book *Brands of Faith*, Mara Einstein traces how a variety of religious movements have adopted the norms of the marketing world. They have done this, Einstein argues, in order to remain relevant within the context of a commercial culture characterized by a 'multitude of competing messages' (Einstein 2008: 13). In other words, the absorption of market norms is symptomatic of the effort among religious groups to adapt successfully to the cultural circumstances of the twenty-first century. While by no means discrete, it is possible to disentangle two main strands through which this absorption of business norms has occurred. The first relates to the expansionist tendency in free market capitalism; the second relates to the methods modelled as a successful means of achieving this.

Einstein's book covers a range of examples, although a good number of them derive from the world of evangelical Christianity. This is not surprising, as evangelicalism is the form of religion most readily associated with the logic of capitalist economics. Both evangelicalism and free market capitalism share what historian Grant Wacker calls an 'expansionist impulse' (Wacker 2015: 79). Alongside biblical authority and an emphasis on conversion (being 'born again'), evangelicalism has traditionally prioritized mission and outreach as a means of bringing non-Christians to faith. This invites an obvious parallel with commercial bodies marketing their goods and seeking out new customers. Evangelical churches – and I count Pentecostal churches within this category – have recognized this parallel and have been among the most enthusiastic adopters of methods and strategies drawn from the world of private business. But the adoption of marketing techniques among evangelicals is a complex and multifaceted process. On one level, it has emerged organically, as part of an almost intuitive emulation of business strategies that is arguably as old as evangelicalism itself. Here, Weber's 'Protestant Ethic' combines with an anti-institutionalism deeply entwined in the legacy of the Protestant Reformation. The emerging individualism is characterized by a privileging of personal faith and an instinctive wariness towards established institutions. The persona of the enterprising evangelical – resourceful and determined – becomes an important and empowering motif. The emphasis on conversion also encouraged evangelicals to view life as something that could be turned around, that radical change was possible here and now, dependent only on will and faith. When viewed in this way, we are reminded of how religion needs to be considered not simply as a response to social circumstances but also – potentially – as an active agent in bringing about social change. It matters that evangelicals have viewed the world as something that can be transformed, because this changes what is imagined to be possible.

This expansive impulse leads to an extension of evangelical initiatives into spheres of life previously unassociated with religion. One aspect of this has been the establishment of museums or theme parks designed to promote creationist ideas, and examples can be found across the world. Often viewed as an expression of Christian tourism, these attractions are typically framed around '6-day' or 'young earth' creationism, hence taking issue with evolutionary science as incompatible with what is taken to be a faithful reading of the Bible. The museums are understood by those who run them as vehicles for evangelism and as opportunities for believers to engage with – and be entertained by – an experience that reflects their own religious convictions. Museums like these borrow from the forms and media of the natural history museum, as they similarly seek to convey knowledge to the public and demonstrate its plausibility. Those behind creationist museums in this sense believe themselves to be in the same game as mainstream scientists, trading in evidence, explanations and arguments. They also try to strengthen their claims by anticipating the doubts of sceptics, with exhibits featuring explanatory signs that attempt to 'close gaps' typically cited by sceptical observers (Bielo 2019: 46). The Ark Encounter (founded in 2016) is a massive reconstruction of Noah's ark apparently built according to the exact proportions stated in the book of Genesis and populated with models of all of the species claimed to have been on board (Bielo 2018). Both the Creation Museum (in Petersburg, Kentucky) and the Ark Encounter (located just up the road) are attractions built by the organization Answers in Genesis (AiG), which anthropologist James Bielo describes as an 'empire of cultural production'. According to Bielo, both attractions integrate 'religious tourism, pedagogy, fun, and devotional piety' (Bielo 2019: 43). In their materialization of the Bible, they also illustrate how a shift into new markets extends both the reach and symbolic expression of pro-creationist Christianity (Figure 1).

This expansion into news realms of social experience pushes against the social differentiation commonly associated with secularization theory. Rather than reflect the retreat of religion into the private realm, it suggests an occupation of an expanding range of spheres, thereby extending the possibilities of its cultural expression. We can find further striking examples in publishing and movie entertainment (Strombeck 2006). Another arena of innovation is the business world. To take a non-Christian example, Rudnyckyj (2009) examines the ways in which neoliberal values and Islam are converged within a training programme for employees at an Indonesian steel factory. These programmes, which combine Islamic ethics with management knowledge, are run by 'spiritual reformers', 'to enhance Indonesia's transnational competitiveness' (Rudnyckyj 2009: 105). Spirituality is reconfigured as a site in which management may intervene, and work is conceived as a spiritual endeavour, effectively reforming Islam into a set of practices for the formation of a self compatible with neoliberal conditions.

Figure 1 The Ark Encounter, Williamstown, Kentucky. *Source*: Anthony via Flickr.

A different strand of marketization has seen the adoption and adaptation of practical strategies learnt from commercial contexts. When Billy Graham, Carl Henry and others launched what became known as neo-evangelicalism in the 1940s, their point of distinction from earlier, more socially withdrawn fundamentalists was their contrasting enthusiasm for *engaging* with culture as a means of reaching the unsaved. Their chosen bridging strategies were indebted most of all to templates derived from the business world. Vineyard Church founder John Wimber had been a successful businessman within the entertainment industry; during the early 1960s he was managing and playing keyboards for the Paramours, the pop group that became the Righteous Brothers. Bill Hybels, founding pastor of the Willow Creek megachurch ministry, based in Chicago, is the son of an entrepreneur who was inspired by his father's work ethic. Hybels, alongside fellow megachurch pastor Rick Warren, cites as a major influence famous management consultant Peter Drucker, Warren consulting him for twenty years about the 'purpose driven' approach he pioneered at Saddleback Church in southern California (Maddox 2012: 154). At each step, the most influential evangelicals have to some extent modelled their ministry after methods, skills and virtues associated with business.

The US megachurches also make for an illuminating example in their highly innovative approach to church organization, based around meeting the needs of a market niche (Ellingson 2013). Rick Warren's Saddleback Church, which boasts a regular attendance of over 20,000 individuals, is a striking example, but the same client-oriented approach can be found across the evangelical and Pentecostal world. Also significant are the range of evangelistic courses established over the past few decades. *The Purpose Driven Life*, based on Warren's multi-million selling book of the same name, is forty days of spiritual exercises tailored to the imagined needs of the individual 'seeker'. *Alpha*, originating in

Holy Trinity Church, Brompton in London, is a ten-week introduction to Christianity structured around the key elements of charismatic evangelicalism. Each week is devoted to a particular topic, with interested parties attending a meeting based around a meal, a talk and small group discussion. *Christianity Explored* offers a conservative evangelical variant, also structured around weekly meetings but with content focused around a week-by-week Bible study of the Gospel of Mark. All three have accompanying merchandise and serve as brand identities for the large evangelical churches where they originated. All three also function as franchises, with materials available for any church, school, prison or other social gathering to use as they put on their own course. Importantly, an effort to retain control over the product is reflected in carefully maintained brand identities and legal measures – such as citing copyright protection of course materials – against the risk that deviant variants might emerge.

This packaging of evangelical outreach takes advantage of the processes of commodification common in commercial settings. The founding organizations are managing a global product, and the courses are subject to careful marketing, packaging, advertising and promotion. But feeding into this is a more bespoke adaptation of marketing as a technique for developing evangelical church life, one that can be traced to the church growth movement, which emerged during the 1970s. Church growth theory was the brainchild of Donald McGavran, an experienced overseas missionary keen to develop new methods of reaching the unsaved. His experiences in India, observing mass conversions in some regions but negligible numbers in others, inspired him to figure out what made mission successful. It was in his influential book *Understanding Church Growth*, published in 1970, that McGavran devised the concept of the 'homogenous unit principle', defined as a 'section of society in which all the members have some characteristic in common' (McGavran 1970: 85). McGavran uses this idea elastically to designate common language, tribe or caste, denomination, political or geographical units. In terms used within academic social science, he was referring to the benefits of cross-tabulating data by a range of different variables, this way identifying whether pockets of church growth within a given area might be attributed to some common factor. McGavran's book teaches that successful evangelism rests on understanding one's mission field in social scientific terms and identifying which segments of that field are most receptive to Christian mission. His 'homogenous unit principle' has been developed among subsequent generations of church growth writers and church founders, but remains well summarized in the lesson that growing a church depends on knowing your target audience and meeting their distinctive needs. McGavran's work established a genre of 'church growth' literature, typified by books issuing their own distinctive step-by-step recipes for growth, targeted at ambitious church leaders keen to unlock the hidden potential for revival within their local areas. Rather than present evangelism as merely a matter of personal will or charismatic rhetoric, the church growth movement conceives evangelism in terms of research, method and the application of evidence-based strategies.

Protestant evangelicalism undoubtedly provides the most visible and long developed examples, but the embrace of marketing initiatives among religious movements extends well beyond the Christian world. Building on Patrick Haenni's research on the Middle East, François Gauthier remarks on the emergence of a 'Market Islam'. Recent religious revivals in this region are not, he argues, best understood as a conservative retrieval of traditional Islam nor a resurgent political Islam but as developments that draw inspiration from Western consumer capitalism. What emerges are religious movements preoccupied with the values of 'self-realisation, health and economic as well as relational success' (Gauthier 2018: 404). He takes the example of the business-trained spiritual guru Amr Khaled, a popular speaker whose message emphasizes the needs of the subjective self, emotional health and happiness: 'More of a "coach" or a "big brother" than a charismatic leader in the classical sense, sporting a business suit without a tie nor a beard, the Egyptian-born Khaled insists that the Prophet Muhammad was a rich and successful merchant in preaches that are relayed worldwide via a media empire that includes satellite television and Internet' (Gauthier 2018: 405).

Khaled's conspicuous consumption is echoed in a prosperity-focused message. The fact that 'Market Islam' casts personal success and affluence as signs of *baraka* (grace) is reminiscent of the prosperity gospel message within Pentecostal Christianity. The willingness to adapt in order to compete in a public marketplace of ideas is even evident among conservative Muslim scholars. Robert Hefner describes how the availability of mass secular education within Muslim countries during the late modern period led some to believe that the authority of religious legislators would be eroded. However, 'the '*ulama* have adapted to the competitive religious market with impressive skill, and have reasserted their religious influence' (Hefner 2009: 158). He refers to their composition of popular tracts and use of television and online platforms to promote their judgements on Islamic law.

Mira Niculescu grapples with examples within Judaism, especially counter-intuitive as a traditionally non-proselytizing religion. Drawing on research in North America, Niculescu notes the concern among Jewish religious leaders that younger generations are falling away from traditional religious practice and marrying out of the Jewish community, threatening its future survival. An overlapping development has seen large numbers of Jews embracing what are considered to be the more culturally meaningful practices of Buddhism, or appropriating New Age ideas, a pattern Kaplan and Werczberger (2017) find among middle-class Jewish communities in Israel. A perception emerges that it is necessary for Judaism to develop 'competitive strategies and cultural adaptations' in order to retain appeal among younger generations and win back the support of those who have already drifted away (Niculescu 2013: 100). A variety of innovations can be identified, including the blending of Eastern spiritualities into Judaism and rebranding Judaism using the media of popular entertainment. All reflect an attempt to retrieve a sense of relevance and appeal among emerging generations.

Intersectionality, markets and religious difference

While the market analogy can shed light on religious fields and on methods of social engagement, neither proceed in a way that is divorced from deeper layers of identity and experience. Religious orientations to social reality, including market realities, are subject to what I am calling a *framing identity*. This framing identity is not intended to mean simply a given person's context. Rather, it is meant to capture the particular significance that religious orientation plays vis-à-vis other aspects of identity. This is the issue of what is called *intersectionality*, the various ways in which different markers of identity interact to generate different opportunities and patterns of exclusion (Crenshaw 1989; Hancock 2016). We will come back to this term in later chapters, particularly with respect to issues of race, gender and religion. Within the context of the present chapter, I am incorporating intersectionality into our discussion of markets in order to highlight how different constellations of identity frame orientations to a given religious landscape. A couple of examples will make this clearer.

Take the case of converts to Salafi Islam, the ultra-conservative tradition researched by Anabel Inge in her book *The Making of a Salafi Muslim Woman*. Inge studies the lives of women who have converted to Salafism within the UK context, exploring their motivations and 'paths' to conversion. Salafism makes high demands on its followers, advocating a return to the traditions of the 'ancestors' (*salaf*), the first three generations after the Prophet Muhammad, who are thought to have practised a pure form of Islam. The Salafi Muslims Inge encountered in her research tended to practise full-face veiling (wearing the *niqab*), strict obedience to their husbands and seclusion from other men. And while this commitment is a radical one, signalling adherence to a conservative, literalist reading of the Qur'an, Inge finds that the process of conversion for these women was still preceded by an experimental period characterized by careful deliberation and evaluation of religious alternatives within Islam. In other words, the commitment to Salafism was the end point in a process compatible with the logic of the religious marketplace that aligns closely with the religious pluralism of twenty-first-century London. As Inge explains:

> The pattern that has emerged here suggests another form of conversion, specific to liberal, religiously diverse societies in which a religious seeker is free to 'shop' in a religion 'market'. I term this pattern '*delayed conversion*'. Here, an individual resists affiliation with a group after initially encountering it, due to something off-putting. Involvement occurs only after exploration of and/or experimentation with other groups has proven disappointing, prompting a reinvestigation of the original group, which subsequently emerges as more attractive. (Inge 2016: 98)

The example of Salafi converts highlights how the *framing identity* includes intra-religious orientations. In other words, we are not simply discussing what happens when individuals confront multiple religious traditions but also multiple strands within the same tradition. Various recent studies of churchgoing in Anglo-American societies have found a tendency for individuals and their families to try out a number of different churches before settling on the one that works best for them (e.g. Guest et al. 2013; Reimer, forthcoming). The appeal of church depends upon its ability to serve one's needs as an individual or the needs of one's family (childcare and welcome of children are undoubtedly important in many cases). With the possible exception of Roman Catholicism, the denomination of one's upbringing seems to have only a tenuous influence over one's choice of church in adulthood. Personal choice is central, but it is framed by boundaries defined by one's pre-existing tradition.

Another example encapsulates what are often called 'alternative spiritualities', usually referring to nature religions such as Wicca, complementary forms of health care, the appropriation of 'Eastern' traditions like meditation and yoga, human potential movements that root fulfilment in the exploration and affirmation of personal experience, and the various traditions, movements and practices associated with the New Age. These have often been grouped together as expressions of what Robert Bellah et al. (1985) refer to as 'expressive individualism', marked by a tendency to locate truth and meaning not in the process of conforming to the external traditions of the past but in embracing the subjective experiences of the self. Variously interpreted as a continuation of the 1960s counterculture, a religious form of 'Western' individualism and a celebration of neoliberal selfhood that merges consumerism, 'spirituality' and the 'well-being' industry, this constellation of developments has often been linked to the idea of the 'spiritual marketplace' because of its shared emphasis on individual empowerment and eclecticism (e.g. Carrette and King 2005; Heelas 1996; Heelas and Woodhead 2005; Roof 1999). Véronique Altglas's book *From Yoga to Kabbalah*, published in 2014, addresses patterns of engagement among those interested in what might be called 'alternative spiritualities' but arrives at a more complex analysis compared to those advanced in previous studies.

Altglas conducts her research across a broad range of cultural and religious contexts. Researching case studies at centres of Siddha Yoga, Sivananda and Kabbalah, her empirical investigation spans France, Britain, Brazil and Israel. She frames her book as a study in religious exoticism – in particular, the fascination with 'foreign' religions among people within advanced industrial societies. Why do so many 'Westerners' exhibit such strong enthusiasm for practices like meditation, yoga and mystical traditions like Kabbalah, while they have such a limited interest in the world religions from which these traditions emerge? How should their engagement with these 'Eastern' traditions be characterized? Altglas takes as her conceptual focus the notion of *bricolage*, famously theorized by French anthropologist Claude Lévi-Strauss in his studies of myth. Roughly translating within everyday French as 'DIY', bricolage is used by Lévi-Strauss to describe the process whereby meaning is secured by the maker of myths – or *bricoleur* – who inherits narrative traditions and fills in any gaps by drawing on resources at their disposal. Altglas is interested in the way in which this term represents a tendency among sociologists of religion to characterize religion in modernity as the escalation of a radical individualism. Bricolage is associated with the formation of eclectic, personal religiosities made up of whatever resources happen to be available and are constrained by little aside from the agency of the individual. It is this version of bricolage that has found its way into popular parlance within expressions like 'do it yourself religion', 'pick 'n' mix religion' and 'spiritual shopping'. According to this perspective, religion – or, more often, 'spirituality' – is entirely at the mercy of personal choice: unconstrained by tradition or convention, capricious, changeable and largely uninterested in any body of teaching or knowledge that might have given birth to the various ideas or practices associated with its repertoire. Adoption of a market-based approach arguably pushes this argument even further, so that the 'religious consumer' is presented as empowered not just by free choice but by a market of religious possibilities at their disposal.

Altglas takes issue with this understanding, arguing on the basis of her findings that important social dimensions to religious exoticism have been overlooked. Foregrounding individual liberation from the constraints of tradition, personal choice has been extracted from the social contexts that define and delimit it. This is not to deny the close relationship between these phenomena and neoliberal markets, and Altglas describes how the practices of bricolage among agents who set themselves up as spiritual 'experts' or alternative therapists 'need to be understood as the continuous re-skilling of freelancers involved in competitive and unregulated markets of specific symbolic goods' (Altglas 2014: 18). However, the reflexive identity construction that some commentators have placed at the heart of their orientations to religion is never as free, as unhindered or as self-directed as is often claimed. As Altglas puts it, 'inflating the eclectic and personal nature of practices of bricolage has led to a neglect of their social and cultural logics' (2014: 6). Rejecting notions of bricolage that assume a relatively unfettered process of reflexive identity construction, Altglas argues that social class is an especially powerful shaping influence (2014: 282). Her interviewees consciously distance themselves from professional ambitions and material comforts as unfulfilling, instead affirming the values of 'self-realization, happiness, finding one's true self, and the "spiritual"' (2014: 288–9). However, Altglas finds that 'the emphasis on different values (ethics and spirituality versus ambitions and greed), used to differentiate oneself from "others", denotes a discourse about social positioning' (2014: 287). In this way, the choices of spiritual traditions pursued and the meanings attached to them by participants mirror the politics of identity construction distinctive to the urban, educated middle classes. Put another way, and echoing the work of Bourdieu discussed earlier, bricolage is shaped and informed by pre-existing social conditions. Recognizing this, we need to study not just the fact or degree of religious eclecticism within a given environment but also variant patterns of bricolage, the processes that make different spiritual resources available or unavailable and the strategies people use to engage with those resources.

Conclusion

In the world of commercial marketing, the selling of products is often presented as a simple response to consumer demand, and yet the 'feedback loop' between consumers and producers is imperfect and imbalanced. Put another way, the 'producers' have a much greater say in how products are designed and packaged than those 'consumers' who purchase them. (This is one reason why the common claim that 'the market just supplies what the public demands' is so problematic.) The illusion of a 'level playing field' can be seen in both this context and marketized contexts of religious expression.

In the commercial world, the power of the big corporations can easily crowd out smaller businesses that do not have the same resources nor access to the economies of scale that allow prices to be kept low. In the religious world, those movements or organizations with relatively high levels of wealth, scale and visibility can often attract greater interest than smaller religious movements with more limited resources. In crude terms, the size of your building, the professionalism of your website, the number of regular participants (and donors) – all matter when it comes to securing an enduring social presence. In this sense, the market metaphor works insofar as it illuminates how religious groups present themselves in ways they consider to be compelling. They borrow from neoliberal norms in presenting themselves as 'successful' and 'accessible'. The market metaphor is also helpful in a different sense, one that demands a more critical perspective on the dynamics of 'free markets' than that often affirmed by neoliberalism's apologists. Specifically, it alerts us to how the distribution of resources that enable this kind of presentation has as much to do with pre-established power and privilege as it does with a group's capabilities in working the 'market' to its advantage. This is one important reason why it is helpful to consider religion within a neoliberal framework: not simply because religion might be viewed as functioning like products in a neoliberal marketplace – although that might be part of the picture – but because the critical discussion about neoliberal economics illuminates how religious concerns are caught up in a wider distribution of power and opportunity.

One of the principal weaknesses of market-based approaches has to do with their tendency to assume that markets somehow sit beyond the constraints imposed by social conditions. This is a common conceit that is reinforced by neoliberal assumptions, particularly the assumption that social complexity can be collapsed into mathematical logic. It is misleading for two related reasons. First, no set of social conditions – including economic factors – can ever be entirely collapsed into measurable equations or figures without doing violence to the social phenomena being studied. Insofar as religion is treatable as an aspect of social conditions, then it is subject to this rule in the same way as phenomena to do with education, employment, leisure or health care. An unqualified use of the market metaphor risks papering over this complexity and so misrepresenting religious movements. Second, to apply the market metaphor as a singular template across all forms of religion is to overlook the differential ways in which market logic *is actually operative* within different religious movements. Market-type thinking is undoubtedly important, but not everywhere and not in the same way wherever we look. This is where we depart from some thinkers who dismiss rational choice theory and in so doing abandon all talk of markets when addressing religion, as if religious phenomena are somehow beyond such crass theorizing. I would argue they risk throwing the baby out with the bathwater. Market-type thinking remains important but selectively, unevenly and as an aspect of the cultural spaces in which religion operates. One way of getting at this more cultural expression of neoliberal religion is by examining recent ways in which religion has been mobilized in relation to political identities. Specifically, we find neoliberal religion at the interface of religion and populism, and it is this topic that we turn to in the next chapter.

Further reading

The rational choice theory approach has now been discussed and critiqued in a wide range of impressive studies (e.g. Stolz 2006), including those which conceive it as a vehicle for neoliberal assumptions (Goldstein 2006). It has also been reconceived and applied in ways that reflect the distinctive cultural circumstances of the twenty-first century (e.g. Stolz et al. 2016). Other discussions of religion and marketization adopt a cultural approach more in keeping with the present book. Especially insightful are Gauthier (2018) and Moberg and Martikainen (2018).

CHAPTER 3
RELIGION AND POPULISM

Introduction

If global markets are an economic driver of neoliberalism, they are not without counter-responses at the cultural level. On the left, antiglobalization movements (e.g. Occupy) have focused on the injustices and inequalities associated with global capitalism, protests often targeting multinational corporations and the international organizations accused of advancing private profit over public good. While commanding support from many left-leaning religious citizens, these agendas are usually formulated in purely secular moral terms. The appeal is to a common humanity and to principles of equality, honesty and justice couched in humanistic language. A rather different phenomenon has become increasingly visible in recent years: the politics of populism. While sharing with groups like Occupy a suspicion towards supranational agendas and powers, populist movements react against globalization at the cultural level, often reaffirming nationalist and nativist identities. As such, they are often – although not exclusively – of the political right. Moreover, with nationalist advocates in countries as diverse as Greece, Austria, Hungary, Brazil, the Philippines and the United States, the current surge of populism is an international phenomenon.

Populist movements share with some religious ones an interesting set of ideological and organizational features, and sociologists, theologians and political scientists are noting the ways in which religious and populist agendas are intertwined within different regions of the world (DeHanas and Shterin 2018; Marzouki et al. 2016). Within Donald Trump's America, a populist narrative became caught up in the values and aspirations of white evangelical Christians, a constituency to which the president largely owed his election victory in 2016. Meanwhile, populist movements on the European continent have sought political capital in the demonization of Muslims, illustrating how religion serves as both a force for validating populism and a resource in the redrawing of nationalist boundaries of identity. Largely established within liberal democracies, and dependent on electoral support, populist parties are nevertheless characterized by authoritarian rule. Their charismatic figureheads are often willing to bypass the normal systems of political accountability in the interests of bringing the 'will of the people' into being. In this they share qualities with some religious movements, appealing to a truth that transcends the conventional structures of human life.

The interface between religion and populism is a useful case study for challenging the common misperception among social scientists that religious movements are for the most part marginal and deviant phenomena (Beckford 2003: 9). The populist political movements of recent years have exhibited a willingness to draw heavily on religious symbolism and religiously inflected forms of ethno-nationalism in attempts to win the support of a grassroots base. In such cases, religion is not simply epiphenomenal window dressing. It appears instrumental in commanding popular support and plays an important role in shaping emerging new identities within the public realm.

What is populism?

Scholarly definitions of populism tend to be organized around three related notions, all featured in the rhetoric of populist leaders, writers and political activists. First, a presentation of society in terms of a clear-cut dichotomy between 'the people' and corrupt elites. These elites might be identified in the political establishment, the church, the mainstream media, the intelligentsia, the landed wealthy, big business, civil servants or other segments of society popularly associated with privilege or status. Their importance is in their symbolic differentiation from 'ordinary' citizens, whose experience of injustice, marginalization or hardship can be blamed on the elites who exploit them. Second, there is a tendency to present 'the people' as sovereign, unified and relatively homogenous. Populism has no truck with diversity, conceiving 'the people' as all sharing the same values and interests. Consequently, it has tended to alienate or demonize minority groups who do not fit into its conception of 'the people'. Its rhetorical preference for simple oppositions is mirrored in its exclusivist perspective on who is 'one of us' and who is not. As Jan-Werner Müller puts it, 'The core claim of populism is thus a moralized form of antipluralism' (Müller 2017: 20). Third, populist leaders claim to be the sole faithful representative of 'the people' and their interests. Only they can grasp what 'the people' want and need, and in this they claim moral high ground over the corrupt elites motivated by their own interests, rather than the people's. Once in power, the populist leader will also typically disparage any democratic procedures already in place that might frustrate their agenda, an agenda that is claimed to have special legitimacy by virtue of representing the will of the people.

Populism tends to be characterized by a sense of nostalgia. Populist politicians invoke a memory of past times now lost, an imagined past that highlights all that is wrong about the present. They join 'the people' in lamenting its loss and promise to build it again. Donald Trump promised to 'make America great *again*'; Boris Johnson and others campaigning for the UK to leave the European Union urged Referendum voters to 'Take *Back* Control'. Such slogans share an assumption that in supporting the right candidate, citizens can retrieve a social order they thought was lost. But as Ruth Braunstein (2017) argues in her analysis of faith and politics in the United States, nostalgia also has an appeal that's connected with a loss of status, so that a desire for an imagined past signals a yearning for greater status in the present. Hence the appeal of populist politics among those who perceive themselves to be marginalized.

This emphasis on the *perception* of marginality is important. Populism doesn't always emerge among those we might conventionally define as socially marginal.

Media coverage of some of the more extreme or alarming incidents associated with a populist resurgence – the storming of the Capitol in Washington, DC following the 2020 presidential election, for example – tends to highlight the involvement of poor white people, responding to their alienation from establishment politics with anger and aggression. However, research into the demographics of Trump supporters paints a more complex picture, as we will discuss later.

At this point it is important to note that while its most well-known advocates have been on the political right, populism is not an exclusively right-wing phenomenon. Its key distinguishing feature is a call to unite the people under a common, anti-pluralist banner, but this banner can be rooted in ideologies that are progressive, socialist, nationalist or even neoliberal (Ádám and Bozóki 2016: 101). The fact that politicians as ideologically diverse as Venezuela's Hugo Chavez, Nazi Germany's Adolf Hitler and Argentina's Juan Perón are all described as populists is testament to this. Progressive populists also remain influential within the European context, for example Spain's Podemos Party, Greece's Syriza and Italy's Five Star Movement, although their lack of interest in religion makes them less relevant to our purposes here. It is also possible to conceive of populism as a 'political style' (DeHanas and Shterin 2018), a useful corrective as it allows for the use of populist strategies among politicians who might not usually be described as populist in their approach.

In its more substantive forms, populism is often – and especially in its authoritarian right-wing expressions – a form of nationalism, structured around an understanding of a given domain that has clear boundaries. It presumes a clarity about who belongs and who does not. Christophe Jaffrelot argues that the phenomenon of nationalism was born in Western Europe as part of the broader Enlightenment project. Early conceptions in the sixteenth and seventeenth centuries were part of an effort to establish a more egalitarian sociopolitical order and displace the power of an aristocratic elite. Self-determination – at an individual and national level – was a key value. Emergent nationalist projects – for example in France – were justified in terms of the rights of man, leaving little room for God or religious loyalties that might compete with nationhood as the basis of identity (Jaffrelot 2009). For these reasons, the history of nationalism is often associated with anti-religious sentiment (in the case of France, this is retained as an entrenched ideology in the twenty-first century – see Chapter 8). However, other forms of nationalism have evolved through a more collaborative relationship to religious identities. For example, in some cases nationalism and religion merge in a shared project of 'cultural defence', coalescing into a common identity in reaction to a significant imminent 'other' (Bruce 2002: 31). One striking example would be Northern Ireland, where Roman Catholic nationalism (in the sense of support for the reunification of Ireland) and Protestant loyalism (retaining loyalty to the British state) have formed a pair of mutually reinforcing religio-political identities since the early twentieth century. Such enduring mutual opposition has had divisive and violent consequences, as evident in the 'troubles' that afflicted the province from the late 1960s until 1998.

The populism of recent years signals a departure from earlier alliances between religion and politics or between religion and nationalism. From one perspective, religion for the populist is a political resource, valuable because of its power to bestow legitimacy and reinforce a common sense of identity. Religious allusions can also confer credibility on criticisms levelled at one's opponents or dissenters. However, this is only the case insofar as a given religious identity can be convincingly called upon to coincide with 'the people' at large (or at least, 'the people' as conceived by the populist party's support base). This is summarized by Yabanci and Taleski as the 'religionization of politics', signifying the mobilization of religious identities for tactical reasons among political actors (2018: 286). Religious identities are here invoked as a means of reinforcing the dichotomies favoured by populists – us versus them, the people versus the elite, the true patriots versus the unwelcome newcomers. This can be an especially resonant mix within contexts characterized by a state or majority religion, as myths of national identity can be associated with nationalist politics and religious tradition. Religion can be a powerful unifying identity, cutting across ethnic, class-based and sectarian boundaries to convey an illusory sense of a united, homogeneous population.

In this chapter, we consider three contrasting examples that illustrate how religious identities have been invoked within populist politics in recent years. This is followed by a more extended discussion of the United States and the relationship between populism, religion and racial hierarchies. A final section considers the religious dimensions of populism as a facet of neoliberal cultural conditions.

Turkey's Islamic populism

Turkey sits on the edge of Europe, both geographically and politically. Its population is also religiously atypical in being approximately 90 per cent Sunni Muslim. Its Islamic status is an important reference point for many far-right groups hoping to preserve a pan-European white Christian identity from what they see as unwelcome Islamization. Indeed, fear of Turkish incorporation into the European Union was exploited by the pro-Brexit campaign in the UK in 2016 (Ker-Lindsay 2018). Getting out was a means of keeping Islam out. While outsiders often associate Turkey with its Muslim population, it is also distinguished by a state that has been determinedly secular since the establishment of the Turkish Republic in 1923. Some have described Turkey as a uniquely successful merger of secularism and religious conservatism, referred to as the 'Turkish paradox' (de Medeiros 2018: 148). However, it has experienced significant instability in recent years, including an attempted military coup in 2016 and the rise of a powerful, authoritarian rule by a populist political party with strong connections to Islam.

The Justice and Development Party – a translation of Adalet ve Kalkınma Partisi, summarized in the acronym AKP – was established in 2001 and has been in power almost continuously between 2003 and 2021. It is led by Recep Tayyip Erdoğan, who has continually served as either president or prime minister during this period. At its foundation, the AKP affirmed an 'allegiance to the free market (in line with the interests of their own increasingly bourgeois support base), parliamentary democracy, and the EU process' (Tuğal 2012: 34). At the same time, while not identifying itself as a religious party, it has effectively united the Muslim voice over against secular parties within the Turkish public sphere. This needs to be understood against a background of long-term state-directed religious oppression in Turkey, in accordance with the secularizing agenda initiated by the Republic's first president, Kemal Atatürk, in the 1920s. Under Atatürk, the sultanate was abolished, the last holders of this religious title exiled, Islamic courts were dissolved and religious education was abolished, replaced by a national secular system (Gökariksel and Mitchell 2005: 151–2). For much of its life, the Turkish Republic has been defined by the state in terms of its secularity, with public affirmations of Islam viewed as impediments to the country's path to modernity.

In its early days, the AKP did not appeal explicitly to Islamic teaching to justify its policy proposals, preferring instead the language of equal rights and freedoms, and citing the traditional values of Turkish society. This generic claim to represent the circumstances of 'the people' was markedly narrowed in 2008, in the context of the divisive debate about wearing headscarves in public institutions. Erdoğan claimed banning the headscarf would be a "violation of freedoms" within a nation in which such an overwhelming majority are Muslim. During their second and third terms in power, Erdoğan and the AKP consolidated this move to conflate 'the people' with the Sunni Muslim majority. This discursive strategy has reinforced an 'us versus them' dualism that is deployed by the AKP to its advantage, portraying itself as loyal to the Islamic values of the people, while condemning its dissenters as 'enemies of the national will' (Yabanci and Taleski 2018: 300). Significantly, this hostility has extended beyond the secularist establishment – for example the military, secularist political parties – to include religious and ethnic minorities (e.g. the Alevi and Kurdish communities). Islam has been incorporated into a public discourse that legitimizes the AKP and its government and demonizes those who dare to oppose it. With religious and political identities bound together, dissenters from the AKP are not only condemned for their betrayal of 'the people' but also excluded from the category of the 'devout'. To oppose the government is to place oneself outside of the Muslim community.

The AKP has also consolidated its grassroots religious support through institutional means. The *Diyanet* (Directorate of Religious Affairs) is an official state institution that has, since the beginnings of the Turkish Republic, been responsible for training imams, overseeing the administration of the life of mosques across the country and educating children in the Qur'an. As well as administering Turkey's 85,000 mosques, it also oversees 2,000 mosques overseas. Under the AKP government, the power of the Diyanet has increased dramatically. By 2019 its budget exceeded most other government departments, in 2012 it launched its own 24-hour news channel and the *fatwas* (rulings) it has issued with increasing frequency in recent years serve as a powerful means of clarifying norms of proper conduct among the Turkish population. Many now view the Diyanet as a mouthpiece for the government. With such an extensive and abundantly resourced network of mosques, imams and media, it is in a powerful position to influence public opinion and has done in a partisan direction during recent elections and referenda.

The career of the AKP is not something that can be explained simply as a cynical 'religionization of politics', making use of religious symbols and rhetoric to build support

Figure 2 Recep Tayyip Erdoğan, president of Turkey, during an official visit to Russia in 2015. *Source*: Press service of the President of the Russian Federation/Wikimedia.

among a majority Muslim population. This is certainly part of the picture, but the AKP has also aligned itself closely with the neoliberalization of Turkish society. As Tuğal writes in 2012:

> A bourgeois-Islamic civil society slowly came into being in the atmosphere the AKP created, and the existing Islamic civil society molecularly changed in a market-oriented direction. Cultural centres, networks of friends, mosques and Islamic schools manufactured a pragmatic and business-oriented spirituality. For example, whereas the Welfare Party and Virtue Party leaders encouraged their members and contacts to pray whenever called upon, the AKP leaders and members chose to emphasize how hard work itself is a part of religion. (Tuğal 2012: 39–40)

The neoliberalization of Turkey's economy and society has followed an uneven course since its inception in the early 1980s. Turkey joined the EU's Customs Union in 1995, a transition that aided the rise of a 'new entrepreneurial class of conservative businessmen with roots outside of the country's urban, secular elite' (Gökariksel and Secor 2010: 315). This shift in economic power was reinforced by the AKP, which sought to combine its support for neoliberal programmes of economic reform with an alignment with the religious sympathies of the Muslim population. For example, a shrinkage in state welfare programmes has paralleled a greater emphasis on third sector provision for the poor, including charities financially supported by Muslim entrepreneurs (Moudouros 2014). Since 2015, the AKP's maintenance of power has been characterized by an effort to undermine its political opponents – opposition is labelled as anti-democratic –

which has emboldened its neoliberal agenda further. As Bozkurt-Güngen argues, this strategy enabled the AKP government to undermine collectivist efforts to represent workers' interests, instead engaging with members of the labour force as 'consumers, credit users and social assistance recipients' (2018: 233). Within this political context, religion is invoked as a means of legitimation *and* a populist tool of power, incorporated into a larger agenda that includes a heightened neoliberalization of Turkish society. Its global standing has been aided by a perception among some Western observers that this market-friendly, democratic Islam constitutes a preferable alternative to 'radical Islam', a powerful binary within a post-9/11 context.

Far-right opposition to Islam in Europe

Far-right populism organized around opposition to Islam is rather different to many other forms of populism that invoke religious identities. Rather than be rooted exclusively in a nativist rhetoric about nationhood as such, it invokes a broader understanding of identity that founds its ethno-nationalism on racial and cultural difference. In this sense, far-right groups in Europe – while committed to defending what they see as true British, French or Austrian identity, for example – find common cause among groups in other countries who share an allegiance to a white nationalist agenda, defended against a racialized 'other', often associated with immigrant communities. Such groups often resemble movements of colour racism which had their heyday in the 1970s and 1980s, although in recent years their opposition has been more focused on Islam. Indeed, populist political parties defending a vision of national identity based on an othering of Islam have recently emerged in Austria, Bulgaria, the Czech Republic, Denmark, Finland, France, Germany, Greece, Hungary, Italy, the Netherlands, Poland, Portugal, Slovakia, Spain, Switzerland and the UK.

The invocation of Islam as a significant 'outgroup' within the European context has a long history. Talal Asad points to documents in the Middle Ages, which suggest a persistent historical strand whereby Turkey (the 'Turks') are understood as a threat to Europe. This he connects not to national boundaries but to religious and cultural ones. Europe is treated as coterminous with Christendom, with the Turks an alien force outside of the ambit of the Western Christian family (Asad 2003: 162–3). This binary between Islam and pan-European identity remains important in the twenty-first century, overlaid with racialized notions of who belongs and who does not. The invocation of Christianity as integral to this identity is also persistent within political discourse. At the same time, ethno-nationalisms have emerged within a variety of European nations, many of which maintain Islam as a principal 'other' (Yabanci and Taleski 2018: 284). Patterns of migration from Africa and Asia into Europe, including among refugees, have fed into this nativist counter-reaction, Muslims viewed not simply as unwelcome outsiders liable to be a drain on the state but also as cultural aliens, whose religion signals their incompatibility with 'Western' values. The post-9/11 context also marks them as a security threat (Mudde 2016: 296), a perception reinforced by counter-terrorism measures introduced by European states that validate fear of the 'enemy within' (see Chapter 5).

One of the most striking cases is France, where secularism – or *laïcité* – implies the removal of religion from French identity. Religion is believed to be compatible with French society, so long as it is preserved for the private sphere, with minimal visibility in public life. This understanding has engendered a series of tense stand-offs involving the country's Muslim population, who are especially visible for reasons of religious clothing, and because of skin colour, most Muslims in France tracing their heritage to North Africa or the Middle East. The mainstream of French culture has a difficulty with Islam, many believing Muslims seek religious protections incompatible with French traditions of free speech. The populist far right in France – not least the Front National (now called the National Rally) led by Marine Le Pen (figure 3) – presents Islam in even more hostile terms. For Le Pen's political party, Islam is a social problem in France that illustrates how multiculturalism has failed. It has led a corrupt political elite to neglect hard-working French citizens, the 'forgotten' (*oubliés*), underlining the party's embrace of all those feeling left behind by mainstream French politicians (Ivaldi, Lanzone and Woods 2017: 361). They campaign for what they refer to as the de-Islamization of France, Islam conceived as both a security threat and an alien cultural force. This is reflected in its tendency to fuse security and immigration concerns, its call for a tightening of France's borders combined with a valorization of a French identity that is secular, white and native-born.

The Netherlands presents a contrasting example. The narrative of Dutch identity promoted by populist parties rests partially on a progressive understanding of 'Western'

Figure 3 Marine Le Pen at a meeting of the Front National, 2012. *Source*: Blandine Le Cain via Flickr.

values. Dutch national identity is commonly associated with women's rights, gay rights, freedom and tolerance. Contrasted with a depiction of Muslims as backward and intolerant, the message of cultural incompatibility is used to justify hard-line policies on immigration and counterterrorism. Here, the political rhetoric is focused on what Brubaker (2017) calls 'civilizationism', which presents Islam as a threat to the Dutch way of life. Significantly, it was the murder of two outspoken critics of Islam – the politician Pim Fortuyn in 2002 and the film director Theo Van Gogh in 2004 – that triggered a heightening of this rhetoric. Geert Wilders, who has led the populist right-wing Party for Freedom since he founded it in 2006, has campaigned against the 'Islamization of Europe' and has drawn comparisons between the Qur'an and Adolph Hitler's book *Mein Kampf* (Modood 2019: 171).

The rise of populist politics has also had a profound effect on the British context, most strikingly in recent debates surrounding the UK's membership of, and then departure from, the European Union (abbreviated as 'Brexit'). The UK had joined the then European Economic Community (EEC) in 1973 under the Conservative government of Edward Heath, ratified two years later via a referendum called by his successor, Labour's Harold Wilson, who had committed to re-negotiating terms of membership. The public voted 67 per cent in favour of continued membership, with a voter turnout of 64 per cent. Forty-three years later, in 2016, another referendum was held, called by Conservative prime minister David Cameron. This time the public voted 52 per cent in favour of leaving the EU, with a voter turnout of 72 per cent. The political contexts of the two referenda were very different. In the mid-1970s, there was significant cross-party consensus about the desirability of EEC membership (aside from some divisions in the Labour Party), as well as strong support from the electorate. Brexit was much more divisive. And while instigated by Cameron to appease the Euro-sceptic wing of his party, at a campaign level it was bound up in issues concerning immigration and national sovereignty.

Recent debates about British identity have inevitably been framed in relation to the European question. While Brexit campaigning featured relatively few explicit references to religion, religious differences were mobilized as symbolic markers of ethno-cultural difference, especially among smaller parties and movements backing a nativist vision for Britain. Even though such groups have achieved no or very minimal success at the ballot box, they were arguably instrumental in shaping the political climate that led to Brexit in the first place. Islam was often cited as a marker of cultural difference, either in the context of Turkey's potential membership of the EU or in expressions of British identity that draw on Christian symbolism. The far-right group Britain First has expressed its anti-Islam stance by engaging in 'Christian patrols' of areas heavily populated by Muslims, marching with large crosses and distributing Bibles in mosques. Three years before the Brexit vote, former leader of the UK Independence Party (UKIP) Nigel Farage was calling for 'a much more muscular defence of our Judaeo-Christian heritage' (Odone 2013). During the Brexit campaign, Farage promoted a billboard poster featuring a long queue of individuals of visibly Middle Eastern appearance with the caption 'Breaking Point', calling for the UK to retake control of its borders. Quite aside from its implicit Islamophobia, the poster was criticized for its close resemblance to anti-Semitic images used in Nazi propaganda in Germany during the interwar period. (Interestingly, Hungarian populist leader Viktor Orbán used the exact same image in his 2018 campaign for re-election.) By 2017, UKIP had included a ban on the burqa as one of its policy commitments (Modood 2019: 167).

While the relationship between Christianity and Islam is arguably marginal to European affairs (although admittedly not to the case of Turkey's campaign for membership), it has been mobilized by far-right groups as a symbolic boundary in their fight against immigration. In emerging disputes in the UK, Christianity comes to be associated with white British identity while Islam symbolizes the cultural 'other'. This association is especially powerful because of pre-existing cultural alignments between Christianity and British identity. In the heavily secularized British context, very few are regular church attenders (perhaps 5 per cent of the population attend weekly), but a much larger proportion self-apply the 'Christian' label, which carries a complex cultural, rather than religious, meaning (Guest, Olson and Wolffe 2012). This is what Abby Day has described as 'ethnic nominalism', where those who are not actively religious in any conventional way may nevertheless claim a Christian label as a 'marker of ethnic identity' (Day 2013: 183). Simply put, Christianity becomes conflated with national identity, and while this remains relatively benign among many, the association has allowed others to mobilize Christian symbolism in the service of far-right agendas (Busher 2016). A related pattern can be seen in the correlation between identification with the Anglican Church of England – the established national church – and support for independence from the European Union. Greg Smith and Linda Woodhead analysed national survey data to reveal a strong correlation between the two. Almost 66 per cent of Church of England members polled said they voted to leave the EU, compared to the national figure of 52 per cent, 55 per cent of Roman Catholics, 49 per cent among those of non-Christian faiths and 47 per cent among those of no religion (Smith and Woodhead 2018: 207). While the Christian–British association clearly varies in its political expressions, from quietly conservative and nationalist to openly far right, the association remains a powerful identity resource for populists.

The case of Hungary offers another distinct variation. The fall of communism in 1989 was followed in Hungary by two decades of economic instability as the country attempted to establish itself as a liberal democracy. Widespread disillusionment with communism and its apparent capitalist alternative led to the rise of Viktor Orbán's nationalist Hungarian Civic Alliance (or *Fidesz*) Party, which won an absolute majority in the Hungarian parliament in 2010. The party with the third largest share of the vote was the Movement for a Better Hungary (*Jobbik*), which won 17 per cent of the popular vote. Jobbik was also right-wing populist, but at that point more extreme than Fidesz, maintaining an anti-EU message alongside hostility towards Jewish and Romany minorities. With left-wing and centrist parties securing less than 20 per cent of parliamentary seats in the 2010 national election, Hungary's politics moved decidedly to the right, with no effective opposition to a right-wing populist hegemony.

Its post-communist legacy has left Hungary largely secularized, and so its right-wing populist parties do not position themselves as directly representing the Christian churches. At the same time, with leftist parties historically tending towards secularism, the space for more traditionalist moral and religious sentiments falls on the right of the political spectrum. While populists invoke a 'Christian' identity, 'Christianity in this context rather signifies a degree of social conservatism and traditional nationalism than expressing any substantive religious reference' (Ádám and Bozóki 2016: 108). A similar argument is made by Olivier Roy about the Front National in France, which invokes Christianity as symbolic of a mythic national past and as a marker for 'non-Islam' (Roy 2016). In Hungary, for the Jobbik party, according to Ádám and Bozóki, the language of 'Christian' is used to designate non-Jewishness, reflecting the party's anti-Semitism. Indeed, its more moralistic/nationalistic use of the term 'Christian' is reflected in orientations to religion among its supporters. Among all of Hungary's political parties, it is Jobbik that has the highest proportion of atheists and of non-religious people (Ádám and Bozóki 2016: 109–11). For Fidesz and Jobbik, Christianity is deployed as part of a repertoire of symbolic resources suited to the defence and legitimation of nationalist claims.

Their orientation to Islam has, however, been more complex. Fidesz has maintained a strong campaign against Muslim migrants, conceived as a security threat, and has exploited the fears of the electorate and reinforced a sense of symbolic nationhood that treats Islam as its principal 'other' (Thorleifsson 2017). Jobbik, on the other hand, has maintained a unique stance among right-wing nationalist parties in Europe in adopting a pro-Muslim stance. This is partly rooted in its promotion of a contested alternative history of the Hungarian people, which traces their ancestry to Turkey and the Islamic East. According to this narrative, Hungarians and Muslims are kin, embodying a common identity and professing shared values. Expressions of Hungarian nationalism emerging from this tradition place Muslims on the patriotic side of the divide, as distinguished from the Jewish and Romany communities. Islam has also served as a symbolic focus of Jobbik's opposition to globalizing free market capitalism. Jobbik leader Gábor Vona has presented traditional Islam as 'a ray of hope (reménysugár) in the fight against Western globalisation and neoliberalism' (Pap and Glied 2018: 1043). Islamic nations have been looked upon as admirable examples of resistance to US-led commercialism which, effectively spread across the globe, has further extended the wealth of Western elites at the expense of ordinary people. The foreign policy of Jobbik was built around criticism of Israel and support for an independent Palestinian state, alongside the building of relationships with China, Russia and the Islamic East as a means of challenging the power of the European Union and United States. Its pro-Muslim stance was integral to its anti-neoliberal stance. Following its poor performance in the 2014 election, Jobbik moderated its position on anti-Semitism in order to enhance its credibility as an electable alternative to Fidesz (Svitych 2021: 52). However, this backfired following the 2015 migrant crisis, which heightened public opposition to immigration and, by association, to Muslims. Fidesz capitalized on this anti-immigrant feeling and fiercely opposed the EU quota proposal, which would have obliged EU member states to accept a set number of forced migrants. As a moderate conservative political force, Jobbik had weakened its electoral power. So it reversed its position on Muslims in order to win back some of the public support then enjoyed by the ruling Fidesz party. Its more recent anti-immigrant message has predictably undermined its connections with the Muslim electorate in Hungary and created a dissonance between its historical message and its current policies. Anti-Muslim rhetoric – often conflated with anti-immigration rhetoric – remains a potent force among Europe's populist parties.

Christian nationalism in the United States

In November 2016, Donald J. Trump, the real estate magnate and former reality TV star, was elected the 45th president of the United States. His victory was unusual in several respects. It was a close run, and while Trump secured 304 electoral college votes to his opponent Hilary Clinton's 227, he received almost three million fewer votes overall, only the fifth candidate in US history to win the presidency while losing the popular vote. Trump's victory was also a surprise, with mainstream media and political pundits expecting Clinton to win. This expectation was reinforced by Trump's background and campaign performance. While he quickly became the Republican front runner during the primaries, he had no political experience, frequently affirmed contradictory views and made alarmist, sometimes false, claims. Consequently, he was not often taken seriously by political stalwarts on either side. Ironically, Trump's dismissal by those in the political establishment ultimately worked to his advantage, confirming his populist claim to speak for the American people rather than the political elite. Furthermore, his status as a billionaire businessman did not appear to undermine his populist credentials; being in business rather than a career politician was viewed by his supporters as an advantage. Trump was not corrupted by being part of a political class that had lost touch with the American people and his business background lent credence to claims of his having 'real world' experience, a proven leader in the corporate world. As Gerardo Marti comments, Donald Trump's candidacy makes special sense within the context of Christian Libertarianism, for which the 'ultimate exemplars of virtue are successful entrepreneurs' (Marti 2020: 114).

During his four tumultuous years in office, Trump both delighted his supporters and horrified his critics in a series of unprecedented, often controversial, initiatives. Many, including the border wall with Mexico and the ban on incoming travellers from several majority Muslim countries, were subject to contestation in the US courts. The president's avid, frequent and apparently unfiltered use of Twitter to promote his initiatives ensured they received immediate and global media coverage. His hostile attacks on his political enemies and detractors reinforced the impression of a leader untroubled by the usual conventions and procedures traditionally followed by holders of his office. This lack of constraint even extended to live, and highly critical, commentary during legal hearings concerning his policies or political appointments. Trump's invocation of dubious or unfounded claims on social media attracted widespread criticism and eventually led to his tweets frequently being accompanied by fact-checking warnings. He was eventually banned from Facebook, Twitter and Instagram. Trump's use of misinformation as a political tool is something we will consider in the following chapter; for the present purposes, it is important as an indicator of his populist profile. Donald Trump epitomized an American expression of twenty-first-century populism: grandiose in his proclamations; hostile and merciless to his critics; openly dismissive of mainstream media, political elites and (when in his interests) the courts; blatantly uninterested in political traditions or process; allergic to compromise, apologies or collaboration; and unflinching in his claim to represent the hitherto neglected lives of grassroots, hard-working US citizens.

And yet there are reasons to view Trump's populist message as a very particular form of ethno-nationalism, one that, more than any of the other cases discussed in this chapter, has religion at its centre. The strong alignment between conservative Protestantism and US politics has been well-established since the founding of the nation, arguably heightened with the emergence of the so-called New Christian Right during the 1970s. That a Republican president should invoke God repeatedly in his speeches, develop strong relationships with evangelical lobby groups and promote a set of moral values closely in line with evangelical teachings is no surprise. This is part of maintaining the party's support base and was especially evident during the previous administrations of Ronald Reagan and George W. Bush (Kruse 2015). What distinguishes Trump's presidency is the extension of this pattern into a distinctively libertarian, Christian nationalist direction (Figure 4).

In the years following Trump's election, a number of academic studies emerged which attempted to make sense of his rise to power and the cultural forces that underpinned his electoral victory (e.g. Du Mez 2020; Fea 2018; Marti 2020). One of the

Figure 4 Donald Trump in front of St John's Episcopal Church, Washington, DC, June 2020. *Source*: Trump Whitehouse Archive via Flickr.

most impressive is *Taking America Back for God: Christian Nationalism in the United States* by Andrew Whitehead and Samuel Perry. It is based on national attitudinal survey data, supplemented by fifty in-depth interviews with a cross-section of US citizens who affirm a range of perspectives on the privileging of Christianity within the civic life of the United States. Their overall focus is on the emergence of Christian nationalism as a movement distinguished by the use of Christian language and symbolism to reinforce and promote a particular nationalist agenda. Whitehead and Perry conceive of Christian nationalism as a 'cultural framework – a collection of myths, traditions, symbols, narratives, and value systems – that idealizes and advocates a fusion of Christianity with American civic life' (2020a: 10). The authors find that those who subscribe to this outlook are also more likely to support authoritarian kinds of leadership, 'traditional' (heteronormative) models of the family and an understanding of American identity that privileges those who are Christian, white and native-born. Based on national survey data, Whitehead and Perry generate a typology of US individuals organized around a spectrum of support for Christian nationalism. *Rejectors* are those who are most sceptical. For *Rejectors*, Christian nationalists undermine a core aspect of the US political tradition – the separation of church and state – illegitimately fusing American identity with a specific religious identity. In sharp contrast, *Ambassadors* are most supportive of Christian nationalism. *Ambassadors* not only believe in and support Christian nationalism; they are also evangelistic in their promotion of it. *Resisters* and *Accommodators* fall in between these two opposites. *Resisters* lean towards opposing Christian nationalism but may be more ambivalent than *Rejectors* about certain aspects of American public life and the place of religion within it. Indeed, this is reflected in the high proportion of religious people within this category. *Accommodators* share the ambivalence or indecision evident among *Resisters* but lean towards accepting Christian nationalism. Their support, however, is focused on the *values* of Christianity, which they believe to be a positive influence on American life. It is also non-exclusivist; they accept these values can be found in other traditions too and so do not claim that Christianity is *uniquely* placed in its capacity to enhance the life of the American nation.

Significantly, these four types do not correspond precisely to traditional political or religious affiliations. For example, 55 per cent of *Ambassadors* are evangelical Protestants; 56 per cent align with the Republican Party – majorities, but not overwhelming ones, pointing to how, in the context of the Trump presidency, the boundaries of politico-religious identity have been redrawn. Even more striking is that 65 per cent of African Americans are either *Accommodators* or *Ambassadors* and so support Christian nationalism, the largest proportion of any racial category. This warns against simplistic analyses that assume a clear correlation between white evangelicals, support for Christian nationalism and support for Donald Trump. The Christian nationalism associated with Trump supporters *does* privilege white Americans, but it is set within a vision of American identity whose appeal stretches well beyond this segment of the population. As Whitehead and Perry comment, 'It is inaccurate to assume, as many have done recently, that "white evangelical" is synonymous with Christian nationalism or that all Democrats want religion banished from the public sphere' (2020a: 44).

Nevertheless, as Whitehead and Perry demonstrate, these four types are highly predictive of the social attitudes held among the US population. In fact, knowing someone's orientation to Christian nationalism – whether they are an *Ambassador* or a *Rejector*, for example – can tell us 'far more about your social and political views than knowing what denomination you affiliate with, how often you attend church, and even whether you identify as Democrat or Republican' (Whitehead and Perry 2020a: 44). Those most supportive of Christian nationalism are also more comfortable restricting the political freedoms and civil liberties of Muslims, most opposed to abortion, most supportive of 'traditional' gender roles and most likely to have supported Donald Trump in 2016. Moreover, and contrary to much popular and scholarly opinion, Whitehead and Perry argue that being an evangelical Christian was *not* in itself an important predictor of voters supporting Trump in 2016; by contrast, supporting Christian nationalism, as they understand it, was (2020a: 20).

Whitehead and Perry's impressive analysis raises a number of important questions, especially about the significance of Trump's distinctive brand of populism for our understanding of the religious landscape of the United States. Trump's numerous outlandish claims are well documented; his rhetoric was undoubtedly populist, inflammatory and divisive. What we have in Whitehead and Perry's study is a complex, comparative account of the social attitudes that distinguish his supporters. What values do they hold? How do they differ from those with different political or religious perspectives? Trump's approach was so unsettling it is fair to say his critics hoped those supporting him were casting a protest vote against a political system they felt had failed them, rather than favouring Trump because their values aligned with his. There is some evidence to support this, but Whitehead and Perry's account also reminds us that underpinning Trump's support base is a coherent politico-religious viewpoint, held passionately among a sizeable minority (approximately 25 per cent) of the electorate (2020a: 46). Their analysis suggests Christian nationalism is a highly significant identity marker in the twenty-first-century United States. Theirs is not the first study to propose that social changes have led to a redrawing of the boundaries of American religiosity (cf. Wuthnow 1988), but it is the most recent and arguably the most radical. It has a number of important implications, some of which are explored in greater depth in the sections that follow.

From civil religion to Christian nationalism

The first has to do with the relationship between religious and national identities. It was back in the 1960s that Robert Bellah first developed his understanding of US 'civil religion'. Bellah was building on Rousseau's idea, first formulated in *The Social Contract* in 1762, which conceived 'civil religion' as a set of religious beliefs imposed by the state on its citizens as a means of maintaining social order (Aldridge 1999: 144). Anticipating Émile Durkheim's thinking at the turn of the twentieth century, Rousseau presents religion as integral to social stability. Bellah adopts this idea but develops it in a new direction, reflecting the distinctive circumstances of the United States. Rather than being imposed from above, Bellah's 'civil religion' emerges more organically as a shared orientation among the American people and which provides 'a religious dimension for the whole fabric of American life' (Bellah 1967: 3). Civil religion plays an important role in legitimating the United States' major institutions and achieves public expression in the great rituals of American life, like Thanksgiving, the Fourth of July and the inauguration of a new president. Bellah illustrates this with excerpts from speeches by former presidents, pointing to perennial themes that highlight the nation's guidance under God, its special status as the new Israel or new Jerusalem and the close relationship between God's plan and the lives of US citizens. The language is always Judaeo-Christian but rarely exclusively Christian; God is always mentioned, Christ far less so. Bellah argues that this tradition of civil religion does not contradict the constitutional separation of church and state. Freedom of religion remains intact, but the private religious convictions of US citizens coexist with a different, civil religion that belongs in the public sphere. Its principal purpose is the unification of the American people via a common set of religious symbols and rituals. According to Bellah's argument, civil religion must therefore adopt broadly inclusive language and symbolism if it is to fulfil its purpose. It is, in one sense, the sanctification of the American nation as a religiously diverse population unified under a single banner.

While Bellah's article has been highly influential in the sociology of religion and was for many years recognized as an astute conceptualization of an important aspect of American life, it is difficult to imagine it would be received so warmly in the twenty-first century. This is partly because Bellah's claims for an inclusive civil religion – while not unqualified – would probably be viewed as grossly overstated. A Judaeo-Christian discourse of common nationhood may have appeal across the majority of the American population who identify as Protestant, Catholic or Jewish, but the US population is much more religiously diverse than it was when Bellah was writing. What about the growing population of American citizens who identify with non-Christian religions (now over 7 per cent of the population, according to the Pew Research Center)? Or the rapidly increasing proportion of the United States who identify as 'non-religious' (now around a quarter of the population)? And what does a 'uniting discourse' structured around Judaeo-Christian imagery mean for First Nations peoples, whose traditions far predate the introduction of Christianity onto American soil? The notion of 'civil religion' begs many questions about the forms of symbolism capable of uniting the American people. In framing sociological analyses of religion using this concept, we need to ask whether we help to perpetuate the cultural-religious hegemonies we ought to be treating with more critical scrutiny.

Additionally, nationalist discourses of any kind are viewed with much more cynicism nowadays. Their legitimation using religious language is only likely to heighten that cynicism. One of the more socially visible consequences of secularization is the de-legitimization of religious authorities (Chaves 1994). Some sociologists connect this to a general scepticism directed towards traditions of the past that have historically commanded authority over the lives of citizens. According to this argument, the decline of religion is part of a much wider trend encompassing the decline of trade unions, declining trust in governments and an erosion of national pride (e.g. Davie 2002). Invocations of 'civil religion' are especially precarious in an age that valorizes subjective individualism, for they depend on sympathy for old loyalties: to faith and to nation. It is important to recognize that Bellah himself was not entirely sanguine about the way civil religion has been invoked in US history. The example of the Vietnam War from his contemporary context highlights how the discourse of US civil religion can be abused by those overlooking moral impropriety in the interests of forging relationships of global power. As Bellah puts it: 'Those nations that are for the moment "on our side" become "the free world"' (1967: 10). If the United States is one nation under God, does it have an exclusive right to claim God's endorsement for its actions?

Finally, civil religion appears an incongruous concept in the twenty-first century because its integrity has been unsettled by the rise of populist Christian nationalism. In one sense, the two phenomena overlap, especially if we accept how civil religion has a powerful capacity to exclude as well as unite. But the Christian nationalism we have described in this chapter is distinct from civil religion in invoking a far narrower understanding of American identity. It makes no pretence of being non-divisive, nor shows much interest in building bridges with its dissenters. It also has its own symbols and rituals, paraded in the public sphere: pro-Trump rallies, 'Make America Great Again' baseball caps, in some contexts the confederate flag (figure 5). Whitehead and Perry offer vivid descriptions of Fourth of July church services that openly celebrate Christian nationalism, featuring an MC in full military uniform, a pledge by an entire congregation to the US flag and a recollection that Jesus 'gave the ultimate sacrifice for our lives *and for our nation*' (Whitehead and Perry 2020a: 2, emphasis in original). Christian nationalism is a matter of symbolic boundaries, of drawing a marker around who belongs and who does not. In maintaining these boundaries, Christian nationalists can be found to designate certain groups – for example atheists or Muslims – as morally or socially incompatible with the American way of life (Dahab and Omori 2019). In this sense, it promotes a sense of shared cause among supporters united by ethno-nationalistic identities, in contrast to Bellah's civil religion, that invoked common belonging by geography and historical legacy. If civil religion conceives US national identity as diverse but united in a common destiny couched in broad but Judaeo-Christian language, Christian nationalism conceives it in ethno-nationalist terms: narrow, exclusive and hierarchical. For civil religion, the religious element emerges in a general discourse about shared destiny; for Christian nationalism, the religious element is conjoined with a nationalistic programme deployed as a tool of cultural-ethnic exclusion. As Whitehead and Perry summarize, 'Christian nationalism uses Christian language and symbols to demarcate and defend group boundaries and privileges' (Whitehead and Perry 2020: 87). In other words, Christianity is mobilized within Christian nationalism as a symbolic resource used to privilege the interests of white, native-born men. Christianity is deployed instrumentally. We might then ask, does this shift imply a decoupling of Christianity as a symbolic resource from Christianity as an indicator of religious observance?

Figure 5 Trump merchandise. *Source*: Kanesue via Flickr.

Christian nationalism and the question of race

The identification of Christian nationalism as a distinct cultural movement has coincided with a revival of concerns in the United States about racism. While previous studies have highlighted the connection between evangelicalism and white privilege, these have tended to conceive the relationship in terms of what Emerson and Smith (2000) call 'anti-structuralism'. Evangelicals are complicit in allowing racism to continue because they refuse to see racism as anything but a problem of individual attitudes. This indirect relationship, based on an underlying individualism that accords no credence to social-structural causes, has been challenged in recent years, as scholars have identified a more direct relationship between white evangelicalism and racial prejudice. Perry, Whitehead and Davis (2019), for example, examining national survey data, find support for Christian nationalism associated with a tendency to believe police treat white and black citizens the same, and to believe black citizens get shot by police more often because they are more violent. So, is Christian nationalism a vehicle for racial prejudice?

Donald Trump arguably aligned himself with a white nativist narrative of American identity during Barack Obama's time as US president. Trump was a prominent advocate of the so-called birther conspiracy, which claimed Barack Obama is not a US citizen (his birth certificate is claimed to be false) and his religious identity is not Christian but Muslim (advocates often citing Obama's middle name, Hussein). While demonstrably false, this strategy to delegitimize the Obama presidency gained remarkable momentum, supported by public figures and backed by the libertarian Tea Party. It also enhanced Trump's public profile in the years running up to his campaign for the presidency, cementing support among certain elements of the conservative grassroots. The 'birther' movement reinforced the impression of Obama, held by his critics, as a leader inclined to betray the 'core values' of America. He was not American, and not Christian, and so 'not one of us'. Its discrediting of Obama by calling into question his American identity *in these terms* echoes strategies used by right-wing racist movements from the past, like the Ku Klux Klan and John Birch Society. According to Gerardo Marti, central tenets of these movements included 'dedication to preserving an America in which the superior role of white, Christian men, already established in the American social hierarchy, would be secured and reflected in government' (Marti 2020: 167).

In office, Trump appealed to those sympathetic to white nativist understandings of American identity. In August 2017, a rally of right-wing (including white supremacist and neo-Nazi) groups took place in Charlottesville, Virginia. 'Unite the Right' sparked violence on the streets of Charlottesville, culminating with Alex Fields Jr, a white supremacist, driving his car into a crowd who were peacefully protesting against the rally. His act killed 32-year-old Heather Heyer and injured several others, and he was subsequently convicted of her first-degree murder. The event also became significant because of President Trump's reaction. Issuing a statement several days later, Trump condemned the event's 'egregious display of hatred, bigotry, and violence' but added – apparently 'offscript' – that this hatred, bigotry and violence had been evident 'on many sides'. At a press conference following the incident, Trump also claimed there had been 'very fine people, on both sides'. His apparent granting of moral equivalency to neo-Nazi groups and those protesting against them drew angry reactions among politicians across the two main parties, who put distance between themselves and Trump by issuing their own statements. By contrast, neo-Nazi groups on social media expressed their approval of Trump's statement and his refusal to condemn them, adding to the impression that his intention had been to validate elements of the far right whose support he wished to retain (Marti 2020: 210–11).

Trump's alignment with the far right and its racist views illustrates the complex ways in which populist politics draws on other ideologies. When populism emerges within the space usually occupied by the political mainstream, fringe or extreme ideologies can be indirectly legitimated. Parallel patterns have been observed in various European nations, as well as in Turkey under President Erdoğan. In an article on the changing fate of the white supremacist Aryan Nations organization, Robert Balch (2006) addresses the social forces that led to its demise. Balch suggests the group was on the verge of collapse many years before the lawsuit in 2000 that finally brought the movement to formal disbandment in 2001. But might the Aryan Nations – both a far right and explicitly Christian movement – have been reinvigorated following political legitimation of its ideas from the White House? Some evidence suggests it would. For example, Clark and Stoddard claim that 'fliers and pamphlets claiming affiliation with the Aryan Nations or groups with similar names have been spotted throughout northern Idaho and eastern Washington with increased regularity since 2016' (Clark and Stoddard 2019: 148). Trump did not need to openly endorse the far right; it was enough, given his position and the expectations connected to it, to criticize its opposers and to refuse to openly condemn far-right extremism.

But the significance of the Trump presidency for issues of race extends beyond the white supremacist far right. It also exposed racial hierarchies embedded in mainstream US society, as well as the complicity of Christianity in sustaining them. Gerardo Marti's (2020) book *American Blindspot* traces the racial tensions laid bare during Trump's administration in a social history of race, class and religion in US society. Marti's argument is that we cannot understand what happened between 2016 and 2020 without understanding what went before, specifically the enduring tendency to privilege the white man's experience within narratives of American identity. Marti builds a rich account of how the structural inequalities of the US present are deeply rooted in its past, from slavery to reconstruction, Jim Crow laws to the civil rights movement, from George Washington to Donald Trump. According to Marti, it is the sense that this white privilege is being eroded and that the world associated with it is passing away that triggered a populist counter-reaction and Trump's election. It was 'fears of immigrants and a disappearing "American" identity [that] were the most salient issues for Trump supporters' (Marti 2020: 172).

A note of caution is needed here, as recent populist movements have often been mischaracterized as driven by disillusioned older citizens from the white underprivileged, poorly educated classes. Such claims were made in the wake of the Brexit referendum in the UK and were repeated the same year after Trump was elected president. In both cases, counter-reactions among the liberal elite expressed class-based prejudice that only served to heighten existing divisions. To propose that Brexit and the Trump presidency materialized out of the ignorance of ill-informed poor people is to misunderstand the broader picture in a grossly unhelpful way. Statistical analyses of Trump supporters paint a more complex picture, highlighting the prominence of young white voters in exurban areas that have increased in demographic diversity in recent years. As Whiton puts it, among these voters, 'It is whiteness itself that has lost salience as a signifier of social status and class, and it is to this status anxiety that Trumpism is addressed' (Whiton 2021). Other studies have highlighted Trump's ability to exploit pre-existing animosity towards Democrat-linked groups and perspectives (Mason, Wronski and Kane 2021), a vote for Trump perhaps motivated less about what he stands for as what he can stop happening. The issue of *perceptions* is crucial here and recalls the influential book *The Spirit Level*, by Richard Wilkinson and Kate Pickett, which found high levels of social deprivation in countries across the world were linked to high levels of inequality. 'Greater inequality', they argue, 'seems to heighten people's social evaluation anxieties by increasing the importance of social status' (Wilkinson and Pickett 2009: 43). Our perception of how things are – where we stand in society, what we're entitled to, who has usurped opportunities that might have been ours to enjoy – can have a profound influence on the values we espouse and the social movements to which we lend our support, even when the evidence marshalled by established sources is pointing in the opposite direction.

Religion and populism in the neoliberal age

Within recent scholarship on the rise of populism across the globe, academics differ about its significance. While acknowledging how populist parties on the radical right are 'experiencing their biggest electoral and political success' within post-war European history, Dutch political scientist Cas Mudde warns against overstating their importance, highlighting limited influence on policy and limited success at the ballot box (2016: 302). Pippa Norris and Ronald Inglehart, on the other hand, paint a more foreboding picture, arguing that 'authoritarian populism has taken root in many European countries' (2019: 9). Their analysis focuses on authoritarianism and populism as social forces, which, they claim, exert significant influence well beyond their performance in elections. The case of the UK Independence Party (UKIP) backs this up. Securing only two seats in the House of Commons across its thirty-year history, its electoral success has been negligible. However, the party's campaign against EU membership was instrumental in changing the political landscape of the country, pushing the Conservatives to the right and keeping Euro-scepticism in the media, so that the Brexit referendum in 2016 was all the more unavoidable.

There is no doubt that the rise of populist politics has generated new possibilities of public engagement for religious institutions. In both the Turkish and Hungarian cases, Islamic and Christian (Catholic and Calvinist) institutions respectively have been co-opted into promoting the government's message while at the same time receiving new funding and powers from the state (Ádám and Bozóki 2016: 113–14; Yabanci and Taleski 2018). Of course, their new status has come at some cost, and neither are short of critics who see them as selling out to an authoritarian regime. The Turkish case illustrates how the 'instrumentalization of religion' has its limits, with the AKP's blatant use of Islamic credentials to reinforce its own position attracting scepticism, including among some of its political allies (Yabanci and Taleski 2018: 301).

But what about the other way around: populism as a vehicle for the politicization of religion? The case of the United States suggests a strand of Christianity possesses a degree of elasticity that makes it especially suited to co-option by populist interests. This elasticity, I'd like to argue, has to do with a close relationship with neoliberalism, and it is a relationship rooted in a long history. Mark Valeri addresses the relationship between the market and the state in his analysis of evangelical merchants in eighteenth-century New England. Referring to the advocates of mercantilism, he states, 'By describing free trade as an instrument of the state and a means to defend liberty, they linked moral virtue, patriotism, and market dynamics' (Valeri 2015: 70). John Corrigan's book *Business of the Heart* (2002) explores how middle class, white Protestants in nineteenth-century Boston approached their religious practice – including their relationship with God – in transactional terms. Caught up in the 'Businessmen's Revival', they distinguished themselves from outsiders by their distinctive emotionality, the emotional displays of Irish, African Americans or abolitionists judged as unfit for the 'business' of relating to God, as well as for business in the commercial sense. Christianity and commerce emerge in complex relationship and converge in the construction of binary identity markers that signal who is among the faithful and who is beyond the pale. Insofar as this connection has been sustained within the United States, we might expect neoliberal economic conditions to be especially hospitable to forms of ethno-nationalism of a religious or moral flavour. Put another way, Christianity, the free market and the state exist in a relationship of mutual complementarity within the US context (Kruse 2015).

In their excellent study of the global populist turn, Norris and Inglehart (2019) propose what they call the 'cultural backlash' theory as a means of accounting for it. They note the increasing influence of authoritarian populism in recent years, stretching across a wide range of relatively secure, high-income nations. They argue a root cause is the 'silent revolution' from materialist to post-materialist values that occurred during the relative prosperity of the period after the Second World War. An experience of unprecedented existential security led the baby boomer generation to be less concerned with physical and financial security and more interested in individual freedoms. The same sense of security also led them to adopt more tolerant social norms than their parents. The associated shift from more traditional to more socially liberal values gained pace with succeeding generations, reinforced by expanded participation in higher education, urbanization as growing populations sought employment in cities and increasing levels of cultural diversity fed by inward migration. As this more socially liberal orientation to life was heightened and became more dominant, so older citizens felt increasingly alienated, discerning a growing gap between the world into which they had been born and the world as they encountered it in the present. As the authors put it, 'For many older people, same-sex marriage, women in leadership roles, multicultural diversity in cities, and, in the US, an African-American President were disorienting departures from the norms they had known since childhood; they felt they had become strangers in their own land' (Norris and Inglehart 2019: 35).

It is this sense of alienation, so Norris and Inglehart argue, that triggers a counter-reaction among social conservatives, one that sometimes finds expression in support for authoritarian populist parties promising to restore the society they have lost. This certainly tallies well with the rise of populism in the US context. Arlie Russell Hochschild's powerful study *Strangers in Their Own Land* charts how members of the white working classes were feeling increasingly marginalized, beleaguered and economically unstable in the period leading to the Trump presidency (Hochschild 2016: 221). And Robert P. Jones's *The End of White Christian America* charts how the erosion of this previously dominant cultural-religious amalgam triggered the backlash of the Trump election (Jones 2017: 243). This 'cultural backlash', while reacting against the changes of the 'silent revolution', nevertheless retains its preoccupation with cultural over economic issues. Populist movements are typically focused on the presence of ethnic minorities, immigration and the status of refugees, changes in social mores concerning gender and sexuality, and national sovereignty (Norris and Inglehart 2019: 50). Given how these issues often intersect with religious concerns – for example the status of religious minorities or same-sex marriage – it is not surprising that debates about populism often invoke issues concerning religious identities. But what is the relationship between the two?

As we remarked earlier, populism is not inherently right wing; however, the coupling of populist with religious causes takes place for the most part at the intersection of small state, pro-market, socially conservative political parties and religious movements sympathetic to their values. This is not to say that these religious movements are populist themselves. Jan-Werner Müller contrasts populists with some conservative religious people, as the latter do not view 'the people' as 'morally pure and unerring in its will. Not everyone who rejects pluralism is a populist' (2016: 25). So we are not talking about a neat, unqualified tessellation of interests or mirroring of values. Not all US evangelicals supported Trump and not all Turkish Muslims support Erdoğan. Indeed, an area worthy of further research would be the mobilization of *anti-populism* on religious grounds. Religious organizations have hardly been absent from public struggles over the consequences of populist rule.

But if this relationship is not one of simple ideological alliance, how best to characterize it? Two common features are worthy of note here, and while not wishing to brush over important differences of cultural context, they both have conceptual significance for the sociology of religion. The first we might call *discursive dualism*. This refers to a particular way of speaking about collective identities, one that romanticizes a sense of shared 'us', while citing hard boundaries between 'us' and 'them'. Müller argues that one of the appeals of populism is it appears 'to solve a problem to which liberal democracy has no real answer – namely, the problem of what should constitute the boundaries of "the people"' (2016: 75). Populists imagine 'the people' as a singular voice and will; they reify the idea of a united, common community. In this sense, populism shares a feature with many forms of religion, especially those inclined towards sectarian expressions of community and those conversionist faiths that aspire to reshape society. Both uphold an idea of a special community, and both assert that this community is best placed to steer the direction of the nation. Of course, in both cases 'the community' or 'the people' is a construction, defined by leaders claiming to be well placed to represent them. And while, as we noted earlier, religious movements often present 'the people' as a flawed community, they also often claim to have special status all the same.

The second feature I am calling a *strategic orientation to authority*, and it extends across the examples we have explored in this chapter. Numerous commentators have reflected with bemusement on the curious alignment between Donald Trump supporters and evangelical Christians, many questioning how those who so passionately preach high moral standards can find common cause with a president who apparently falls short of those standards on a regular basis. There are various ways of explaining this, including the common claim that Trump is supported not as an example but as *a means of empowering the evangelical cause*, much like the Persian king Cyrus in the Old Testament, who enabled the Jews to return to Jerusalem and rebuild the Temple. Trump has often been referred to as the 'Cyrus candidate', and other biblical analogies have been cited to make the same point. Some companies have even manufactured commemorative coins featuring the image of both Donald Trump and King Cyrus to mark the 100th anniversary of the Balfour Declaration, when the British government stated its support for the establishment in Palestine of a home for the Jewish people, hence merging in material form the Trump presidency, its biblical legitimation and the global politics of the American right.

The important point here is that Trump was viewed as a suitable political figurehead because of the power he held, irrespective of his moral or religious values. In other words, his eligibility was justified in instrumentalist terms and the alliance between evangelicals and Trump was a strategic one. This phenomenon builds on a pre-existing legacy that can be traced back to the New Christian Right of the 1970s and 1980s. Michael Lindsay calls this 'elastic orthodoxy' (2007: 216), a willingness to cooperate with groups who hold a similar view on a specific issue (if not on others) that has been crucial to evangelicalism's success in influencing US politics. Evangelical support for Trump took this principle a step further, justifying an alliance with a leader whose behaviour and professed attitudes were profoundly at odds with their own, but who was nevertheless willing to support their causes in order to retain their vote. Gerardo Marti explains this using the terms of Max Weber's typology of forms of authority: 'today's evangelical conservatives have given up on spiritual revival as a means of change. . . . Borrowing Max Weber's conceptual framework, white evangelicals have turned away from the charismatic authority of the Church in favour of the rational-legal authority of the State' (Marti 2020: 220).

Marti highlights an important shift here, but an additional modification is required in order to draw out the distinctive character of 'strategic authority'. According to Weber, legal-rational authority is associated with the state and its branches of government within modern democracies (Weber 1947: 328). What Marti identifies among evangelicals supporting Trump is a particular *orientation to* legal-rational authority. It is an orientation that mirrors some of the ideas and assumptions associated with neoliberalism, most notably what William Davies calls the 'strategic mindset' (Davies 2017: 67). Simply put, this strategic mindset treats the conventions of public politics as negotiable and their transgression acceptable if this is more likely to result in the desired outcome. Mirroring practices in free market economics, to be adversarial, combative and ruthless is justified as it grants a competitive edge.

The use of power in this 'strategic' fashion may have a special appeal among religious agents who perceive their own power to have diminished in recent times. It is evident in evangelical support for Trump, which included a range of leaders and public figures who had endorsed very different values from Trump's in the past. A high-profile case was that of evangelical theologian and seminary professor Wayne Grudem, whose prevarications over Trump's candidacy in 2016 were the subject of much discussion in the Christian press and on social media. During the primaries, Grudem had spoken out against Trump, but after Trump secured the Republican nomination, Grudem backed him, publishing a now notorious article on the conservative website *TownHall* entitled 'Why Voting for Donald Trump Is a Morally Good Choice'. Trump was, so Grudem argued, a flawed candidate but one who would nevertheless do more moral good for the United States as a nation than his Democratic opponent. Following the release of the infamous 2005 video in which Trump is heard making lewd, offensive remarks about women, Grudem retracted his article, condemned Trump's moral character and called on him to withdraw from the election. A mere ten days later, he changed his mind again, reaffirming his earlier position but in more blatantly instrumentalist terms. This time, Grudem claimed, he found both candidates – Trump and Clinton – morally objectionable, but that he agreed with Trump's policies and believed they were consistent with biblical teaching. A Clinton presidency, Grudem argued, would cause serious damage to the US nation and lead it away from what he considered to be a Christian way of life. Moreover, with such a close race between the candidates of the two dominant US political parties, a third-party vote or a choice not to vote would risk helping Clinton get into the White House. Supporting Trump wins out as an effective strategy for ensuring a Republican victory and keeping a Democrat out of the presidency.

Grudem's actions attracted criticism as they suggested a cynical strategy of courting a divided public. Many Christians across the United States expressed discomfort at the readiness with which he set aside issues of moral conduct and endorsed a form of tactical voting. By the time Trump was campaigning for a second term, however, Grudem had escalated his praise of his candidate to include his character as well as his record as president. By 2020, Grudem was attacking Trump's critics and denying a variety of misjudgements that were a matter of public record. Grudem cited his credentials as a theologian who has written an ethics textbook, before claiming that Trump had never intentionally lied, this despite an abundance of evidence that the president repeatedly made misleading or patently false statements about his own achievements, the Democratic Party, coronavirus, China, 'cancel culture' and Joe Biden, his rival for the presidency in 2020. Reinforcing the populist tone of Trump's campaign machine, Grudem also claimed that all those accusing the president of being a divisive force are 'bearing false witness' (Fea 2020). Despite his earlier prevarication, it seems by 2020, Wayne Grudem had fully adopted the tactics of Trump's populism: speak in simple dualisms, denounce your detractors and deny any wrongdoing.

So the embrace of populist politics among religious leaders has a strong strategic, instrumentalist dimension. It is an approach that makes special sense within contexts featuring religious constituencies that seek social power but feel their status is under threat. Grudem was by no means alone in allowing his avid support for Donald Trump to stretch his moral credibility as a Christian leader. Jerry Falwell Jr, Franklin Graham, Robert Jeffress and many other prominent evangelical Trump supporters have come under attack for peddling a message difficult to reconcile with the moralistic judgements they have preached in the past. With such figures leaving an extensive online record of their past pronouncements and published work, it has been easy for opponents to identify and call out inconsistencies. While this strategy may be less surprising among politicians – such as the AKP's attempts to 'co-opt' religion for its political ambitions in Turkey (Yabanci and Taleski 2018) – seeing it among religious movements marks a step change in the norms of religious engagement in the public sphere. The bigger question is what this means for the potential of religion to secure political power in the future.

Further reading

The literature on populism has grown considerably over recent years. Jan-Werner Müller's short, accessible and highly perceptive volume *What Is Populism?* (2017) is an excellent introduction. Pippa Norris and the late Ronald Inglehart produced a characteristically robust, cross-national study that spans Europe and the United States. Their *Cultural Backlash: Trump, Brexit, and Authoritarian Populism* (2019) is packed full of empirical data and astute commentary. On Trump's America, and its links with Christian nationalism, there is now an abundance of sources. Among the best are Gerardo Marti's *American Blindspot: Race, Class, Religion, and the Trump Presidency* (2020), Andrew Whitehead and Samuel Perry's *Taking America Back for God: Christian Nationalism in the United States* (2020) and *Jesus and John Wayne: How White Evangelicals Corrupted a Faith and Fractured a Nation* by Kristin Kobes Du Mez (2020), which links the popularity of Trump with enduring notions of masculinity in American culture.

CHAPTER 4
RELIGION IN THE POST-TRUTH ERA

Introduction

In 2016, the same year Donald Trump was elected president of the United States, the Oxford Dictionaries organization named 'post-truth' its word of the year. In his book on this phenomenon, journalist Matthew D'Ancona introduces the idea via an episode that occurred early in the new president's time in office. Donald Trump claimed that the crowds at his inauguration in 2017 were larger than those in attendance at Barack Obama's eight years earlier. Responses across the print and broadcast media marshalled clear photographic evidence to the contrary. After an uncomfortable, fractious exchange between reporters and Trump's team, Kellyanne Conway, senior aide to the president, tried to settle the dispute by stating this was a matter of perspective. But she went further, stating on National Public Radio, 'It's kind of like looking at ratings or looking at a glass of half-full water. Everybody has a way of interpreting them to be the truth or not true. There's no such thing, unfortunately, anymore as facts' (quoted in D'Ancona 2017: 13).

This intervention heralded a new and peculiar tendency within the Trump administration, so that expressions like 'alternative facts' and 'fake news' became a familiar feature of political discourse over the subsequent four years. The implication was plain: there was no longer any shared verifiable reality, only a battle for dominance defined not by an external measure of truth but by brute force of volume. On many occasions, Trump did not even attempt to shout down his detractors; he merely dismissed their claims without explanation, as if their tendentious unreliability was plain for all those wishing to see it. By contrast, his own authority was beyond reproach and in no need of justification, even on the numerous occasions when the president opined on issues well beyond his knowledge, whether the projected direction of hurricanes, the blame for global economic instability or possible treatments for Covid-19. It is tempting to see this phenomenon of 'post-truth' as unique to an especially unusual US president, whose disinterest in the conventions of political process was matched by his lack of interest in checking his facts against the evidence. But this would be naïve. Trump's distinctive style has mirrored that of other populist political figures across the globe. Jair Bolsonaro, elected president of Brazil in 2019, is an open admirer of Donald Trump; his similarity in style and policies has led some to call him the 'Trump of the Tropics'. As with Trump, evangelicals are among Bolsonaro's strongest supporters, sharing his conservative opposition to abortion, same-sex marriage and secularism (Webber 2020). In the traditionally more restrained world of British politics, Prime Minister Boris Johnson has been subject to multiple accusations of lying while in office. The rules of the UK's House of Commons bar Members of Parliament from openly accusing one another of lying, which is judged 'unparliamentary language'. But Johnson's behaviour has provoked some of his colleagues into challenging these archaic regulations, Green Party MP Caroline Lucas making the pointed remark: 'We need new rules for this Trumpian era of British politics' (Harding, Elgot and Sparrow 2021).

There is plenty of evidence to suggest the 'post-truth' tendency predates Trump and that it has emerged as a social development with global momentum independent of his presidency (Harsin 2015; Nichols 2017). Precedents can be found in the United States' 'culture wars', the polarization of public debate around conservatives and liberals that emerged in the 1970s. In his book on the topic, James Davison Hunter describes how moral debates escalated to fractious levels, with 'artificially contrived enmity' used as a means of securing funding from partisan supporters or ensuring media coverage (Hunter 1991: 169). Distorting public debate to ensure maximal exposure goes back much further than Donald Trump. Consider also the cases of climate change denial, anti-vaccine campaigners, as well as the numerous claims about 'deep state' conspiracies among those suspicious of government intervention. The blatant use of disinformation within political campaigns (e.g. Trump's 2016 election, Brexit in the UK) reflects a global phenomenon involving state authorities and private sector firms. Research at the Oxford Internet Institute found that in 2020, organized campaigns to manipulate information via social media could be traced to eighty-one countries across the world, sixty-two of which involved state agencies using such methods to shape public opinion (Bailey 2021). The spread of disinformation by conspiracy theorists about the coronavirus – from its purported link to G5 technology to claims it does not exist at all – has caused public panic, disorder and death (Spring 2020). The notion of a 'post-truth' era is starting to look more and more believable.

'Post-truth' as a social phenomenon might be summarized as a heightened tendency to reject or dismiss truth claims based on established authority. It is not the same as what has traditionally been understood as scepticism, as it is not interested in critical debate. It has been associated with anti-intellectualism (Hofstadter 1964) and with a populist hostility to elite groups traditionally viewed as the gatekeepers of authorized knowledge. Importantly, what distinguishes the 'post-truth' of the twenty-first century is not the use of false claims in political debate – this has a much longer history – but 'the fact that these claims continue to retain their political force despite being extensively debunked by multiple and authoritative sources' (Mavelli 2020: 68). Some have suggested we live in an *age* of 'post-truth', one that represents a crisis for liberal democracies. If traditional sources of knowledge are dismissed out of hand when their claims are inconvenient, what does that mean for the process of evaluating evidence? If that is no longer important, what's to stop mass manipulation of the public via lies and deception? Others view these developments as crucial to the democratic process, signalling the empowerment of populations to challenge established authorities (Fuller 2018). Does the destabilization of knowledge enable a healthy questioning of traditions and powers that might otherwise go unchallenged, inspiring an uprising of voices that were previously unheard and ignored?

The campaigns within higher education to 'de-colonize' the curriculum serve as a powerful example of the moral arguments *for* destabilizing the structures of received knowledge. Critiquing established assumptions about the production of knowledge is becoming increasingly commonplace within universities in the global north, as they seek to foster a more inclusive learning experience and a more critical approach to the cultural conditions that frame scholarship (Bhambra et al. 2018). Knowledge does not emerge from nowhere, and its destabilization can be understood as a necessary part of uncovering injustices of the past and retrieving voices that were previously excluded from public debate. To treat knowledge as contested also has a strong legacy within the sociology of religion. Peter Berger and Thomas Luckmann's definition of knowledge was 'everything that passes for knowledge' in society (Berger and Luckmann 1966: 15), implicitly acknowledging that claims to knowledge are subject to contestation and inviting their critical scrutiny. While their significant influence has not produced a developed social constructionist approach within the sociology of religion (Hjelm 2018), an enduring interest in 'plausibility structures' has kept questions about the social underpinning of religious beliefs centre stage.

But what does all this mean for the status of religion? Any social movement that disrupts widely held notions of truth has potentially massive implications for the status and power of religious identities. A scepticism towards mainstream education, knowledge and power makes sense if you believe your tradition to be correct while the rest of society is in error. This is not to suggest that all religious people are sceptical in this way, but it does go some way towards explaining why scepticism of the kind we associate with the 'post-truth' era and religious conviction might be closely related. But what exactly is this relationship, and does the post-truth age herald fresh challenges or opportunities for religious expression? If 'post-truth' signals a cultural change in how truth claims are managed, how have religious identities been caught up in this process? The present chapter explores these questions and attempts to ascertain what the implications of the 'post-truth' tendency might be for the sociology of religion.

The destabilization of knowledge

The scepticism associated with 'post-truth' is fed by various kinds of doubt. It can be a tendency to doubt mainstream science or institutions of knowledge, representatives of political elites or those who are spokespersons for powerful organizations. It can be a general wariness towards claims made by those who represent power or influence. Back in the 1970s, an age of 'postmodernity' was declared, one in which the big stories are not believed anymore. While debates about postmodernity have been overtaken in recent years by other concerns, the postmodern destabilization of traditional forms of knowledge has persisted and been popularized, finding expression via the language of 'fake news', 'alternative facts' or 'post-truth'. The notion that there is a single truth to which we can all point and which offers grounds for confidence in one's perspective seems less credible or realistic than it used to. This intuition has found its way into common parlance, with 'truth' now used not in a singular form – 'the truth' – but as a personal possessive – 'my truth'. The light-hearted, mass authored online *Urban Dictionary* defines 'my truth' as a 'Pretentious substitute for "non-negotiable personal opinion"', citing its usefulness as a means of avoiding arguments or challenges to unpopular points of view. More seriously, it has been invoked to mark the special status of a narrative previously silenced or marginalized. In her now infamous exposé interview with the Duke and Duchess of Sussex, broadcast in March 2021, Oprah Winfrey invited Meghan Markle to share 'her truth'. While postmodern thinkers often presented the de-centring of truth as a liberating experience, many critics of our contemporary 'post-truth' age are much more despairing.

Phenomena associated with the category of 'post-truth' share a suspicion of conventional authorities, scepticism towards established expertise and a tendency to affirm 'alternative facts' based on a range of unconventional, unstable or highly tendentious sources. The denial of climate science, the manipulation of political rhetoric for blatant partisan gain, the use of media platforms to peddle what are widely acknowledged to be falsehoods – all signal an era in which truth appears to be in crisis. The use of social media to disseminate such claims on a mass scale makes the issue global in scope. While advocates of 'conspiracy theories' have been around for many years, their claims have traditionally been dismissed by the public majority as fringe oddities. The case of former British footballer and well-known conspiracy theorist David Icke is a telling example. Icke famously claimed the earth had been hijacked by a race of reptilian beings, who manipulate events in order to keep humans in fear and feed off their negative energy. This, among a series of other bizarre claims, published in over twenty books and promoted via speaking engagements across the globe, has attracted widespread ridicule as well as accusations of anti-Semitism. Icke has become emblematic of conspiracy theory as a vehicle for the absurd, the irrational, the baseless and paranoid. In November 2020 he was permanently suspended from Twitter for contravening its rules on Covid misinformation.

But what was once marginal and without credibility is now apparently the stuff of more mainstream discourse. In some cases – for example Donald Trump's frequent dismissal of his critics' accusations as 'fake news' – such strategies are used to reinforce political agendas and influence the terms of public debate. The deliberate use of disinformation for political gain obviously has sinister connotations, recalling totalitarian regimes in Nazi Germany and the Soviet Union, for example. But the twenty-first century is very different, not least as the internet has – in many parts of the world – made information much more freely available. Consumers of the web have a range of sources at their disposal, from online news outlets, blogs, podcasts and the various interactive opportunities presented via social media. The phenomena associated with post-truth do not depend on the straightforward censorship of public knowledge, as with the state-led propaganda machines of the past. Instead, the abundance of information accessible at the click of a mouse reflects a different set of circumstances, including fresh opportunities for the democratization of knowledge *and* for its manipulation in the service of political or commercial interests.

The apparent mainstreaming of conspiracism is not ubiquitous, but it does span cultural boundaries. According to a March 2021 survey conducted by the Public Religion Research Institute, 15 per cent of US citizens believe that 'the government, media, and financial worlds in the U.S. are controlled by a group of Satan-worshipping paedophiles who run a global child sex trafficking operation'. Among Republican Party supporters the proportion increases to 23 per cent (PRRI 2021). This conspiracy theory, commonly associated with the QAnon movement, has been widely ridiculed, and yet it appears to command the support of almost fifty million Americans. Similarly contentious claims are sometimes channelled into the mainstream via influential public figures, as when Donald Trump lent his support to the 'birther' conspiracy that questioned the legitimacy of Barack Obama's candidacy for US president. Questioning of the president's eligibility was largely restricted to fringe conspiracists until such campaigns were endorsed by Trump, who thereby enhanced his public profile in advance of his own presidential campaign. The rumour that Obama was not a 'natural born' US citizen was given further oxygen in Arizona. Ken Bennett, secretary of state with responsibility for election procedures, and Joe Arpaio, sheriff of Maricopa County, both went to great lengths to ascertain the validity of documentary proof, held by authorities in Hawaii, that Obama was indeed born there (Barkun 2013: 187).

The picture here is of tenuous claims being granted a platform via their passage from the margins to the political centre of society. Their association with public officials or celebrities gives them credibility and, most importantly, mass exposure. Social media plays an important role in building momentum, something Donald Trump fully exploited during his time in office. But there are also social-structural factors that play a role and which illustrate how conspiracism can achieve an enduring place at the centre of the social order. In his study of the role of conspiracy theories in contemporary Turkey, Julian de Medeiros cites David Coady's work in proposing three social conditions that militate *against* conspiracy theories gaining traction. These are effective freedom of information legislation, a diversity of media ownership (and independence from government influence) and relative independence of different branches of government (de Medeiros 2018: 9). Conversely, it is the absence of these conditions that enables conspiracy theories to become established as part of an enduring post-truth politics, as in the case of Turkey under the AKP government. Both presidents Trump and Erdoğan have pursued a populist strategy which has included the destabilization of public knowledge for political gain. They have also arguably exploited the capacity of 'post-truth' as a transnational development, one given momentum via neoliberal consumerism. It is not so huge a leap from 'the customer is always right' to 'the consumer always deserves to have their truth validated'. We will return to this link later on in this chapter. Before then, let us consider how insights from the sociology of religion can shed light on the 'post-truth' tendency.

Religion, deviant knowledge and public dispute

The relationship between religion and wider cultural claims about knowledge or truth is rarely straightforward. On the one hand, increased access to knowledge has, through history, often been accompanied by religious resurgence. The modern changes that have placed religious texts directly in the hands of ordinary people have disrupted inherited authorities, especially those that rest on a hard distinction between religious leaders and their followers. In this respect the democratizing effects of the internet are part of the much longer process marked by the emergence of the printing press, mass production of paperback books and the introduction of the affordable home computer. All enabled empowerment through knowledge among the mass populace. The consequences for religious movements can be charted across the globe. For example, the late-twentieth-century resurgence of Islam was characterized not just by conservative Islamist groups but also by the 'pluralization of religious authority' among those who benefitted from mass education and the ready availability of print and online Islamic media (Hefner 2009: 158). Access to new sources enabled ordinary Muslims to bypass religious elites in their engagement with religious knowledge.

Other cases suggest a relationship of tension. Indeed, some religious movements have been distinguished by a worldview that challenges, refutes or undermines assumptions considered to be foundational by their surrounding culture. The sociology of religion has a long history of researching sectarian groups distinguished by strict rules of conduct and hard boundaries between themselves and wider society (e.g. Troeltsch 1931; Wilson 1970). A range of 'world-rejecting' sects have upheld convictions at radical odds with values embraced as the social norm. Early Mormons practised polygamy, what they called 'plural marriage'. While the mainstream Mormons discontinued this practice formally in 1890, fundamentalist Latter-Day Saints are known to continue this practice to the present day. Jehovah's Witnesses have traditionally resisted blood transfusions on the grounds of biblical teaching. Early members of the Church of Jesus Christ Scientist (or 'Christian Science') – founded in New England by Mary Baker Eddy in the late nineteenth century – believed all physical illness was an illusion that could be cured by prayer alone, rather than medical science. Within the context of a culture increasingly turning to modern medicine as a means of living a longer, more comfortable life, Christian Scientists were promoting a 'deviant body of knowledge'. Sociologically, this can be both marginalizing and empowering at the same time. For a movement to contest a central assumption of society is to present itself more convincingly as unbound by society's rules and conventions. It is to be free from the habits of normality and bold enough to affirm a completely different way of life.

However, we find closer analogies to today's 'post-truth' in religious groups that, rather than withdraw from society, have sought to engage in public dispute with the guardians of mainstream knowledge. One striking example is the Church of Scientology, which is rooted in explanations about the origins of the world and about the nature of human identity that are profoundly at odds with mainstream Western science. Scientology owes its worldview to its founder, American former science fiction writer L. Ron Hubbard. Hubbard's 1950 book *Dianetics: The Modern Science of Mental Health* proposes a science of the mind that explains the origins of a range of human illnesses. According to Hubbard, humans' capacity to use the full potential of their 'analytic mind' is hampered by the 'reactive mind's' tendency to retain damaging memories called 'engrams'. These 'engrams' cause problems and ill-health later in life, unless addressed via a special form of counselling Hubbard calls 'Dianetic auditing'. Progressing through different stages of this auditing process can lead individuals to a status of 'clear', distinguished by a superior IQ and enhanced physical and mental health.

The claims of Hubbard and of successive representatives of Scientology have attracted widespread hostility and scepticism from mainstream scientists, many of whom dismiss Dianetics as a pseudo-science without foundation or merit. Especially fraught has been the conflict between the Church of Scientology and the psychiatric profession, so that, in sociological terms, the latter has been a major 'outgroup' against which Scientology has defined itself (Smith 1998). Indeed, at its inception, Dianetics was claimed by Hubbard to be as effective, if not more so, at addressing mental health problems as psychiatry. After being snubbed by numerous guardians of the psychiatric profession, the Scientology movement switched its strategy from a quest for scientific legitimacy to a campaign against psychiatry, which was presented as the main cause of humanity's decline, its misguided treatments leading to crime and human suffering. Subsequent mutual hostility led to Hubbard's 'determination that Dianetics and psychiatry were rivals in a struggle over the fate of humanity' (Kent and Manca 2014: 7). Scientology's campaign against psychiatry has been maintained over many decades, well after Hubbard's death in 1986. And while the Church of Scientology now engages in a range of relief initiatives (e.g. at major disaster sites), internal documents suggest they are framed by a quest to undermine and discredit the efforts among mainstream mental health professions to respond to the same crises (Kent and Manca 2014).

The case of Scientology is especially striking because of its concerted attack on psychiatric medicine stretching over many decades. It has possessed an enduring determination in promoting ideas outside and against the scientific mainstream. It has done so publicly and through the courts in a way that underlines the difference made when religious groups are financially well resourced. Thus, while still constituting a deviant body of knowledge in sociological terms, Scientology's ability to accumulate financial wealth, not least via celebrity endorsements and by charging clients for its services, means it has managed to sustain its campaign. It is also an example of defending deviant knowledge by going on the attack. Using the terms of a well-known framework formulated by Peter Berger, Scientologists have engaged in a process of 'cognitive rejection', grounded in its opposition to norms and values associated with wider culture. Not content simply to preserve the integrity of its own boundaries, however, Scientology has sought society-wide change, determined to bring the social order into line with what it considers to be the truth (Berger 1992: 41–5). It channels its efforts into a specific sub-sphere of knowledge: professional psychiatric medicine. This is not to suggest Scientology's aims are in any way parochial or specialist, for it lays at the door of the psychiatric profession some of the most serious problems afflicting humanity. The eradication of psychiatry and its replacement with Scientology as the basis for addressing mental health is understood to be the route to humankind's salvation.

Debates surrounding so-called deviant science (Dolby 1979) encompass a wide range of cultural movements, from acupuncture and feng shui to the 'auditing' of Scientology and the 'anti-vaccine' campaigns that have resurged in the wake of the Covid-19 pandemic. There are indications that the distinction between orthodox and deviant knowledge is now less clear than it has been for some time. We live in an age in which approaches to truth and knowledge emerge in a plural market of possibilities, even if some command more status than others. Michael Barkun makes sense of this differential treatment of knowledge as a symbolic economy of information. In his book *A Culture of Conspiracy: Apocalyptic Visions of Contemporary America*, he asks what makes certain conspiracy theories appealing. More specifically, what makes them credible for those attracted to them? One persistent pattern relates to their status as 'rejected knowledge' that leaves a 'stigma applied by mainstream institutions'. According to Barkun, the sense of cultural rejection that accompanies knowledge that is refused validation by 'official' gatekeepers – whether mainstream media, government or universities, for example – is a 'powerful force' which carries the 'thrill of the forbidden' (Barkun 2013: 223, 24). According to the logic of conspiracism, any widely accepted belief must of necessity be false, because it is tainted by association with the forces that shape the 'official' version of reality, the forces attempting to deceive us. Therefore, rejected knowledge is accorded particular validity; its rejection by the guardians of cultural orthodoxy signals its proximity to the truth.

Similar logic can be found among some of the most prominent religious movements of the twenty-first century. This is not surprising, given the similarities between conspiracy theories and the supernaturalist or theistic claims made by religious people. As Brian Keeley points out, both tend to explain worldly events with reference to intentional agents 'not readily available for interrogation' (Keeley 2007: 139). In this sense, we may expect epistemological tendencies to be shared by UFO seekers, believers in the 'deep state' and mainstream Christians, Jews and Muslims. This is true up to a point. Some religious writers have merged Christian fundamentalism with the methods of secular conspiracy theorists. US televangelist Pat Robertson published a book in 1991 entitled *The New World Order*, a capacious account arguing a plot to establish a one-world government was being guided by Satan and signalled the imminent end times. Indeed, it is the appeal to an opposing force with which one must contend and compete that is the most important parallel. Whether conceived as 'the world', pluralism, white Christian conservatism, liberalism or the secular state, having a citable nemesis is a powerful means of shoring up religious identity boundaries. For this reason, the parallels between conspiracism and religious movements increase with the level of tension with what are considered to be mainstream social values and assumptions about reality. For the Church of England, the US Episcopal Church and Sunni Islam in Saudi Arabia, the parallels are likely to be weak and rare. Among more sectarian groups, oriented around a wariness towards mainstream society, parallels with conspiracist thinking are more likely to be evident. Conspiracism aligns with a perception that one's worldview and values are under attack (Castelli 2007). This sometimes corresponds to a situation of material deprivation but not always. Spokespeople for the US Christian Right (many of whom supported Donald Trump) often present themselves as victims of persecution even when they are part of the white majority: relatively wealthy, well represented in government and with a vibrant right-wing media that wholeheartedly supports their position (Marti

2020: 209). Their perception of themselves as unfairly marginalized appears to be closely related to a tendency to make sense of things in conspiracist-type terms.

Citing a powerful, opposing 'outgroup' also helps demarcate where legitimate and illegitimate knowledge is to be found. It signals who can be trusted and who cannot. A long-term example is the creationist movement, which has since the early twentieth century shaped its public campaigns around its rejection of Darwinian evolution (Numbers 2006). Over this period, especially in the United States, creationist campaigners have sought to advance opportunities to promote their perspective in the public sphere. Education has been a key target sector, with the development of curricular resources for schools but also via museums and theme parks structured around a creationist worldview (Bielo 2018). In a process that could be described as 'cognitive bargaining', creationist advocates have, over time, adjusted their strategies in line with broader cultural norms in order to improve their chances of success. With the emergence of 'creationist science', for example, the strategy was to adopt the norms and language of mainstream science in order to lend contentious knowledge credibility among a broader audience, much like the Scientologists had done in the 1950s. Hence Whitcomb and Morris's 1961 book *The Genesis Flood* argued that the great flood was a historical event not because it was mentioned in the Old Testament but because there was geological evidence for it. The intelligent design (ID) movement was an extension of the same process, taken a step further by avoiding any explicit reference to the Bible or God. Instead, ID was about using conventional academic tools to establish the likelihood that a supreme being lies behind the complexity of the natural world. In claiming for itself academic credibility, the creationist–intelligent design movement also emphasizes the 'theoretical' status of evolution, attempting to secure a status of equivalence. In other words, they shore up their own position by attempting to destabilize their opponents'. A related strategy is described by its critics in terms of 'false balance': claiming equal status between two sides of a debate when the vast majority of experts support one 'side' of the issue. This strategy can be found in debates on a variety of topics, from climate change to evolution to Covid-19. It is a means by which conspiracy theories can secure a platform on grounds that appeal to liberal-democratic values (such as fairness, equality and free speech). Therefore, while emerging boundaries between the mainstream and the marginal are often presented as rigid and absolute, it would be more accurate to describe them as contours that frame a negotiation between religious movements and their cultural environments.

If the Church of Scientology has reinforced its campaign against psychiatry by making the stakes of the dispute about a shared human priority, i.e. health, creationist evangelicals have done something similar with evolution, but in this case, the stakes are about education and free speech. In the former case, Scientologists claim that to get the issue wrong is to jeopardize the future of human health and well-being. In the latter, creationists call for vigilance in order that the next generation of young people avoid being corrupted by a school of thought that will draw them away from the Bible or by a secularist agenda that lacks moral substance. Both rest on a dualistic framework and define their mission over and against a form of established knowledge they reject as erroneous, malign or both. Both appeal to issues of the human good that have universal resonance. While there are many who do not see things in these terms, the strategy adopted by both movements makes sense as a means of maximizing appeal to a broad audience. They also engage concerns that carry weight in legal contexts, and it is not incidental that both Scientology and creationists have been involved in numerous legal disputes over the past few decades, as they have sought to defend and promote their point of view.

Religion, power and legitimacy

Despite these commonalities between particular religious movements and elements of the post-truth tendency, there are important differences as well. One important quality of the post-truth tendency has to do with power. I had a friend at university who claimed he was a direct descendent of King Solomon. He was eccentric and often said strange things. No one believed him. But then again, he had no power. He was not in a position to steer public opinion or for his views to have an influence over people's lives. When Donald Trump rejected the claims of experts or dismissed the very idea of expertise itself, the consequences were, clearly, much more significant. Much of the debate about the 'post-truth' phenomenon has focused on the behaviour of politicians and their advisors, in other words: those with power. This is not just a case of pointing out unreliable statements made by politicians, which is – sadly – a long-established tradition. Rather, it is to observe a tendency to treat knowledge in a political fashion. This relates to what Tom Nichols calls the 'politicization of expertise' (2017: 225). In other words, the increasingly normalized willingness to manipulate public discourse in a way that serves a given agenda. The phrase *increasingly normalized* is important here. Some readers may see this as an obvious point. Of course people in power behave in this way; it was ever thus. This may be true, but there has been a shift in strategy in recent years that does, I would argue, represent a step change. A number of different social forces converge to bring this distinctive arrangement about.

The first and most obvious point is about *information overload*. As Tom Nichols puts it, in despairing tones, 'I fear we are witnessing the death of the ideal of expertise itself, a Google-fueled, Wikipedia-based, blog-sodden collapse of any division between professionals and laypeople, students and teachers, knowers and wonderers – in other words, between those of any achievement in an area and those with none at all' (Nichols 2017: 3). Not all commentators are as pessimistic as Nichols, but the explosion of information to which he refers is undeniable. Within the global north, and in increasing waves elsewhere, an abundance of data, opinion and knowledge – across a vast spectrum of quality – is available with unprecedented ease to an unprecedented proportion of people. With such volume comes confusion, as established authorities are just one among many voices. Voices that were previously marginal or esoteric can build new communities of support. The 'post-truth' tendency is, in part, a by-product of excess information.

Another factor is a type of *heightened relativism*. In their influential book *Habits of the Heart*, Robert Bellah et al. (1985) wrote about expressive individualism as the idea that identity is formed by personal experience, rather than inherited or shaped by one's circumstances or family. This has been extended in the twenty-first century. There is now a widespread assumption – especially among younger generations – that identities can be treated with greater flexibility than in the past, whether in terms of gender fluidity, body modification or the curation of multiple identities online (Katz et al. 2021: 75–81). All identities are changeable, and personal reinvention is a positive thing to be affirmed and supported. In fact, to suggest that there are limitations is a moral infringement on individual autonomy. The dramatic shift in debates about gender identity over the last decade is a striking case in point. To say one's gender identity is biologically determined and unchangeable would have been, twenty years ago, a truism. It was not a claim that would have been challenged by most people. To say the same thing in the second decade of the twenty-first century would be to invite criticisms of intolerance and even outrage. The pace of change has been dramatic. Identity is malleable and subject to personal choice. With this privileging of individual agency comes a correlative scepticism towards external authorities, especially those perceived to impose on that agency. This is sometimes cynically dismissed as the hyper-sensitivity of the 'woke' generation, preoccupied with the quest for 'safe spaces' as shelter from the 'microaggressions' of a world in which they struggle to cope. Some commentators have written of a rise of 'victimhood culture' (Campbell and Manning 2018). And yet this emphasis upon individual agency is not necessarily a sign of self-centredness. The same underlying assumption shapes young people's reluctance to tolerate judgementalism or hostility to minority groups (Perrin 2020). In my own research, it has been discernible in attitudes of Christian university students, who are uncomfortable with evangelism as they do not feel they have the right to speak with authority into others' lives (Guest 2015). Whether self- or other-directed, the emphasis is on respecting individual agency over and above external voices. Within the context of 'post-truth', such individualism provides a rationale for rejecting established authorities.

The third social force instrumental in this pattern was introduced in the last chapter in terms of a *strategic orientation to authority*. I used this concept to interpret some of the distinctive characteristics of populism, especially in those cases where it intersects with religion. This orientation, distinguished by a willingness to engage tactically, selectively, in order to maximize advantage over one's perceived opponents, was identified among those wishing to harness power in the public realm. We see it plainly in the behaviour of populist politicians like Donald Trump, Jair Bolsonaro and Recep Tayyip Erdoğan. But these national leaders model an approach that can be seen in much wider circles. As I argued in the last chapter, this can be seen as part of a migration of neoliberal ideas about competition into non-economic spheres of life. It reflects a utilitarian form of individualism driven by self-interest and transactional exchange. It prioritizes winning the game over any rules of the game and teaches us that bending the rules is fine if it gets us to where we need to be. Insofar as this tendency shapes public discourse, it heightens the circulation of post-truth tendencies by legitimizing lying and manipulation when it serves our interests. A point about exposure is important here. While Donald Trump's behaviour is of moral concern for numerous obvious reasons, it is of sociological interest because we, and everyone else who turned on the TV at least once during his four years in office, knows about it. In the age of 24-hour news and social media, political corruption is plain for all to see. What was so shocking about Trump's presidency – and numerous other examples of 'post-truth' before and after him, if we are being entirely honest – is that lying and manipulation of truth were so blatant and unapologetic. And if they treat this as part of the game, why shouldn't we do so too?

Sustaining post-truth in a neoliberal age

Post truth, while clearly sounding echoes from the distant past, is a quintessentially neoliberal phenomenon. As such, its effects on religious movements provide an important part of the picture in explaining how neoliberal conditions have furnished a new contextual framework for religious expression. There is no doubt that the 'post-truth' era has generated opportunities that some religious actors have used to their advantage. It could be argued that the conditions of neoliberalism have enabled religious expressions of 'rejected knowledge' to gain global traction and public support as never before. This is not simply a matter of the World Wide Web democratizing access to information, providing a platform for contentious and subversive claims and in so doing unsettling the epistemological norms of the mainstream. This is part of the picture, but also important are the consumerist affirmation of personal opinion, social media as a relatively unregulated site for generating mass followings and the cynical rejection of established authorities reinforced by populist political movements.

But how should these changes alter how we do the sociology of religion? Specifically, what kind of changes to our conceptual apparatus might be required if we are to make sense of religious phenomena apparently caught up in the post-truth shift?

Sectarian groups have remained interesting to sociologists of religion in part because they represent concerted attempts to maintain purity of belief and practice within contexts that exert multiple pressures to accommodate to wider social norms. Sects have traditionally done this by maintaining distance – geographical or social – from wider society as a means of more effectively filtering their members' exposure to polluting influences. The Mennonite Amish maintain geographical distance from non-members within rural areas of the United States. The Plymouth Brethren maintain hard boundaries with the outside world by restricting their reading, not watching television or listening to the radio and not eating with non-Brethren. Their doctrine of separation demands this. One twenty-first-century compromise has seen Brethren using networked laptops as part of their work, but even these are subject to technical modifications that filter access to information on the World Wide Web. A similar religious argument for technological modification emerged among ultra-Orthodox Jews in Israel in 2004. Religious leaders' campaign for a 'kosher cell phone' was motivated by concerns that 3G mobiles granted young people easy access to morally dubious web content (Rashi 2013).

We tend to conceive of these measures as 'top down' phenomena, that is strategies of control imposed by religious hierarchies, sometimes reinforced with the threat of expulsion or public sanction. But they also, of course, have an important voluntary dimension. Members of sects choose to limit their own exposure to malign influences and engage in an active effort to avoid experiences, ideas or people they believe will undermine their religious identities. Such voluntary life management is compatible with the pillarization that was historically the norm in some European countries like Belgium and the Netherlands. Pillarization is characterized by the segmentation of society into groups which identify with a common worldview, with each 'pillar' possessing its own institutions – for example schools, universities, trade unions – tied to their identities as Protestants, Catholics or Socialists, for example (Houtman 2020). It is also common in analogous form within twenty-first-century everyday life. Indeed, maximizing exposure to ideas, influences and people likely to reinforce one's pre-existing beliefs is arguably a highly popular strategy for dealing with the cultural pluralism of the neoliberal age. Negotiating diversity is hard work and often requires reconfiguring one's appreciation of social normality: what's conventional, commonplace, legitimate or acceptable. What better way to deflect these challenges while having one's prejudices and values validated than to populate one's social life with like-minded associates?

In the previous chapter, we discussed Pippa Norris and Ronald Inglehart's impressive study *Cultural Backlash*, about the rise of authoritarian populism across the world. They argue this development may be interpreted as a counter-reaction to the 'silent revolution' that has propelled liberal values into a position of dominance in many societies. It is this shift in values, they argue, that triggered the rise of populist parties discussed in the previous chapter. At the individual level, there are various ways in which people have reacted to this. They may adapt to the new reality, rail against it via authoritarian populist politics or stay silent in a strategy of self-censorship. A further option Norris and Inglehart describe is especially interesting for the present chapter. They write of 'a retreat to social bubbles of like-minded people, the great sorting, now easier than ever in the echo chamber of social media and the partisan press, thereby avoiding potential social conflict and disagreements' (Norris and Inglehart 2019: 16). Norris and Inglehart's description captures a distinctive feature of twenty-first-century neoliberal culture. It might be summarized as a confluence of social forces that enable the easy exclusion of dissenting voices. In simpler language, we are talking about like mixing with like and the facilitation of this via particular social arrangements. This pattern is commonly described in terms of 'echo chambers', when all those involved in a conversation are affirming the same viewpoint. The lack of dissent prevents underlying assumptions and overt errors or misjudgements from being called out.

Post-truth and commercialized knowledge

Norris and Inglehart's analysis is relevant to the current chapter because it offers a way in which we might explain how post-truth tendencies achieve voice and maintain momentum. However, what we are confronting here is not a form of social organization – like the church or sect theorized by Ernst Troeltsch or Bryan Wilson – but a style of social engagement, made possible, attractive and normative by commercial forces. Insofar as these forces function according to the logic of market preferences, they also have a tendency to reaffirm the consumer's pre-existing cognitive biases or values. We get what we like and so are rarely challenged to change our habits. This is especially acute on social media, where the algorithms used by platforms such as Facebook, Twitter and TikTok ensure content is flagged based on a user's prior engagement, alongside commercially sponsored material that is filtered according to presumed market preferences. As Luca Mavelli puts it, the 'algorithmic personalization of information means that we are more likely to receive in our social media feeds stories, news, and perspectives that confirm our established beliefs' (2020: 69). According to Jayson Harsin, this corresponds to a 'decline of institutional enclosures' and a 'hyper-segmentation of society', undermining previously stable societal structures of meaning-making (Harsin 2015: 330). What keeps information in circulation is not its truth or authenticity but its appeal to consumers. With each click the story gains more momentum. At the same time, the competition for public engagement incentivizes providers to heighten sensationalism and hone their ability to meet consumer demands. The speed and ease with which information is accessible in the neoliberal age have changed the expectations of individual consumers. As Tom Nichols comments in his book *The Death of Expertise*, laypeople may be interested in expert knowledge, but they 'are mostly interested in experts who are accessible without much effort and who already agree with their views' (Nichols 2017: 222). In this respect the economic characteristics of a neoliberal age are instrumental in enabling the exchange of information along post-truth lines.

This argument can be taken further by reconceiving post-truth not merely as a tendency or orientation to reality but as a regime or market. Jayson Harsin builds on Michel Foucault's argument that all claims to truth are not simply measurable against an established body of verified reality but are subject to the *regimes of truth* operative within a given context. Each society, according to Foucault, has its own regime of truth, which dictates the discourses it takes as reliable, the dominant criteria cited in establishing truth, the status of those charged with sanctioning truth and the mechanisms for distinguishing truth from falsity. In other words, truth is framed by a political arrangement and is closely related to the distribution of power (Foucault 1980). But as Harsin points out, we live in very different social conditions to those in which Foucault was writing in the 1970s. And if there has been a regime (of truth) change, then this is characterized by the multiplication of media, the shift away from chronologically scheduled news delivery and the consumption of information via an expanding multitude of technologies configured to consumer convenience. As Harsin summarizes it:

> the geography of news and truth has shifted as has the temporality of news
> consumption: no longer delivered in morning and evening, or broadcast at six

or eight – it is composed of millions of beeps and vibrations, revolving tickers that shape-shift and/or disappear by the second, and news unfolds in a highly affectively charged attention economy of constantly connected cognition. (Harsin 2015: 329)

Harsin's idea of an 'attention economy' is crucial here. It highlights the ways in which the exchange of information has been restructured around a commercial impetus to maximize consumer engagement, often financially incentivized via advertising revenue. If the commercial providers are competing for our attention, then the exchange of information is very much functioning like a market. Insofar as truth is traded within such contexts, what ultimately counts as true may well be 'a function of the extent to which a "truth" is marketable, transferable, usable, and consumable' (Mavelli 2020: 59). Truth becomes a commodity, achieving heightened profile by virtue of its consumer appeal and irrespective of its authority in non-market terms (Lyon 2000: 80). Part of its consumer appeal involves the invitation to consumers to interact with the information offered – clicks, likes, retweets, new posts or blogs. We have an unprecedented opportunity to be informed, while the means to achieve this undermines any possibility of a settled or universally shared version of the truth.

The 'attention economy' is an important factor in how information is engaged online and in associated commercialized networks. How it impacts religious phenomena is far from clear, and future research will need to consider how 'social bubbles' function as sites of social and religious engagement, identity and community. Online gatherings have been undertaken of necessity during the coronavirus pandemic; they may persist with renewed significance after Covid-19 has been brought under control, in light of practical advantages and accessibility for less mobile religious practitioners. What the present moment indicates, perhaps, is that online possibilities of engagement appear generative of new opportunities to speak and be heard. This, in turn, incites new opportunities for subversion, even while being channelled through commercial platforms. One example that has recently come to light is that of Abraham Piper, described on Wikipedia as a 'serial entrepreneur and artist', who is living in Minneapolis, Minnesota. He is the son of influential US conservative evangelical John Piper, co-founder of the Council on Biblical Manhood and Womanhood. The younger Piper has had a rocky relationship with his evangelical upbringing, being ex-communicated from his father's church after abandoning his faith aged nineteen. His estrangement from the evangelicalism associated with his father came to a head when he went public with his criticisms of this tradition. At one time, these would have been shared among a small group of friends, perhaps a network of post-church supporters. In 2021, it was announced via a series of videos on TikTok, the social media platform based around the sharing of short video content. Abraham Piper has, at the time of writing, 1.7 million followers on the platform. If the post-truth age has introduced a public mood characterized by popular scepticism and emotive reasoning, it has also been accompanied by the introduction of new platforms for the expression of dissent and subversion.

Assessing the post-truth age

The phenomena associated with 'post-truth' have provoked serious concern among a variety of commentators. There is a strong argument that they pose a danger to democracy itself; as Tom Nichols argues, 'a stable democracy in any culture relies on the public actually understanding the implications of its own choices' (2017: 231). The undermining of trust in expertise and conventional sources of knowledge has worrying implications for political governance as well as for the education of citizens. Others are less worried. Sociologist of science Steve Fuller addresses 'post-truth' as a lens through which knowledge production as a matter of power is laid bare and the interests of so-called experts rendered open to critical challenge. As he comments, 'There is more to knowledge than the consensus of expert opinion, and even what the experts take as knowledge need not be interpreted as the experts would wish' (Fuller 2018: 181). This might resonate with Scientologists and creationists who remain sceptical of 'established' knowledge, especially when it appears to undermine the truth claims at the heart of their own traditions. The conditions of 'post-truth' constitute a benign arena for religious groups comfortable engaging with new technology but wary of established or official 'expertise'. They are able to inhabit online spaces that provide platforms from which individuals can hit back, launch counter-narratives and find others of like-mind (Singler 2015).

A note of caution is also necessary though. Reporting on their research into the migration of 'culture wars' debates into the UK context, Duffy and Page (2021) note the radical disconnect between the mass media and the public. In the main UK newspapers and news sites there has been a massive expansion of content on the UK 'culture wars' in recent years – just 21 articles in 2015; in 2020 there were 534. By contrast, the language associated with these 'culture wars' appears entirely alien to large proportions of the populace. In their survey, Duffy and Page found that 38 per cent didn't know what 'woke' meant, a figure that increases to 50 per cent among those aged over fifty-five. Almost 49 per cent had never heard of 'cancel culture'; the figure was 54 per cent for 'microaggressions', 34 per cent for 'trigger warnings', 35 per cent for 'identity politics'. While these terms are not the same as 'post-truth', they form part of the same cluster of developments in public discourse, characterized by the heightened relativism described earlier. We need to take care that we do not take media reporting to be the same thing as social reality. We must also avoid uncritically projecting the priorities of particular strata of people onto the entire population.

But there is nevertheless a dimension of the 'post-truth' phenomenon that has society-wide reach, one we might abbreviate as the *metric exception*. The risk of growing public disillusionment with 'experts' is that politicians will surround themselves with advisors who tell them what they want to hear. Knowledge will be manipulated by those who govern in the interests of placating the public and consolidating their power. We have already witnessed examples of this within some of the populist regimes that were discussed in the previous chapter. One element of this step change involves the co-option of a particular kind of expert into government agendas. Academic observers of the neoliberal age have noted the significance of private think tanks in steering political discourse and government policy (Davies 2017: 134–7; Peck 2010). The role of think tanks is not straightforward, but it does represent a layer of intellectual culture closely associated with governing powers. As private providers, think tanks also have an incentive to provide the ideas, the thinking and the data that is palatable to those in power. Knowledge is here politicized within its own industry, as an established part of the political process, especially in Anglo-American contexts. This change of political culture has introduced new participants into the power play of liberal democracies; some are focused on economic concerns – such as the promotion of competition in neoliberal terms – while others have a social democratic profile. Many attempt to combine the two, and in so doing clothe sociopolitical agendas in economic language. An important dimension of this relates to what David Beer (2016) calls 'metric power', i.e. the privileging of numerical data as a measure of value. We see this in the pre-eminence of statistics in the justification of public policy, as well as in systems of accountability in public services. We see it in the privileging of quantitative evidence within government and think tank reports. We see it in the importance of maximizing the number of 'likes' we get on Twitter, friends on Facebook or subscribers to our blogposts. We see it as we track our credit scores, our loyalty card points or our performance in league tables. If it can't be counted, we learn, it doesn't count. The neoliberal age does not, therefore, involve the destabilization of *all* forms of knowledge. Metric power is apparently exempt from post-truth scepticism, up to a point anyway.

Beer argues that metric power is a core element of neoliberalism and a principal means by which neoliberal influence is extended. As he states, in a neat summary of its internally reinforcing logic, 'Measurement and competition run hand in hand, in terms of having the capacity to justify one another' (Beer 2016: 23). Taken as a form of knowledge, metrics carry a number of important social consequences that are relevant to the 'post-truth' era. First, they sideline the need for personal trust and familiarity. Such 'subjective' considerations are secondary to the 'objective' truth of numbers, which are portable and communicable beyond the perspectives of individuals. Second, the privileging of metrics de-values the notion of considered judgement, preferring instead the immediate, obvious and blatant. There is no need for interpretation, for the meaning is plain. Moreover, metrics constitute a universal measure that transcends cultural difference; its mathematical form gives it a universal quality that places it beyond reproach. This pattern is reinforced by the desire for immediate gratification fostered by consumerism. Other forms of knowledge are easily crowded out. As Beer puts it, metric power operates by 'chipping at the boundaries of discretion and thoughtfulness' (2016: 178). In assessing how religious movements have been shaped by the post-truth era, one important question will be how have they engaged with these privileged forms of knowledge and with what consequences.

Further reading

There is an emerging, cross-disciplinary literature on the phenomenon of 'post-truth' and its social contexts. For a journalistic, but highly thought-provoking, discussion, see

Matthew D'Ancona's *Post-Truth: The New War on Truth and How to Fight Back* (2017). For more focused studies of the phenomenon of conspiracy theories in today's world, see Barkun (2013), Medeiros (2018), Robertson (2016) and Singler (2015); excellent discussions that engage broader debates about the status of knowledge in the 21st century can be found in Mavelli (2020) and Nichols (2017). For a characteristically provocative and insightful treatment, see Steve Fuller's *Post-Truth: Knowledge as a Power Game* (2015).

CHAPTER 5
SECURITIZATION: NEW FORMS OF STATE ENGAGEMENT

Introduction

The relationship between neoliberalism and religiously inspired terrorism is not straightforward. On the one hand, neoliberal economics is one of the engines that have enabled the extension of Euro-American power across the globe. As such it is an obvious focus of opposition among those whose faith inspires them to resist what they see as the forces of the late modern age. It was Iran's Ayatollah Khomeini who in 1979 described the United States as the 'Great Satan', accusing it of imperialism and corruption. Many conservative Islamic voices have, in subsequent years, echoed this message, lamenting the economic influence of the United States as well as its globally exported culture, attacked as materialistic, individualistic, decadent and secular. Insofar as fundamentalist Islam is defined against this image of US power, Islam-inspired terrorism might oppose the forces of neoliberalism for similar reasons. The forces of neoliberalism are also sometimes associated with sinister powers believed to be collaborating in their attempts to control the world. The global banking system, the IMF, the US military-industrial complex, the United Nations, NATO – all get cited as part of a transnational conspiracy driven by 'Western' interests (see Chapter 4). Violent resistance to such forces is not, of course, limited to Islamic groups. Acts of religious terrorism have been justified in similar terms by very different religious parties, for example the syncretistic Japanese religious movement Aum Shinrikyo, which famously released the chemical weapon sarin on the Tokyo subway system in 1995, killing thirteen and injuring many more. Aum Shinrikyo drew its inspiration from the Christian Bible, Hindu and Buddhist philosophy, the teachings of French astrologer Nostradamus and conspiracy theories about power concentrated in the hands of Jews (Juergensmeyer 2003: 110). If there is a link between religious ideology and opposition to neoliberalism, it is not a simple one.

While neoliberalism emerges as a symbolic focus of opposition, terrorist networks have also made strategic use of methods and resources commonly associated with neoliberal cultural conditions. In their insightful study of the rise of the Islamic State (IS) terrorist organization, Jessica Stern and J. M. Berger highlight their use of the relatively unregulated world of social media – especially Twitter – to recruit supporters and wage a propaganda war against their opponents. Twitter also enhanced the capacity of IS to manage its campaigns for the hearts and minds of Muslim communities the world over. IS advocates were no longer at the mercy of TV networks to gauge levels of support across their global affiliates; instead they used social media for a form of 'focus group testing' of grassroots Muslim support. The adoption of this 'feedback loop model' enabled IS to advance its militant cause using tools more commonly associated with Silicon Valley (Stern and Berger 2016: 70–1). The initial reluctance of Facebook, Twitter, YouTube and other social media platforms to regulate online spaces – whether in the name of corporate autonomy or freedom of speech – also enabled extremist groups to take advantage of this new, global town square. In other words, neoliberal economics generated novel opportunities for terrorist groups, even while their message often attacked the cultures that gave rise to these possibilities.

As far as religious attacks on neoliberalism are concerned, 9/11 remains an era-defining reference point. It was on 11 September 2001 that one of the most iconic symbols of the neoliberal age – the Twin Towers of the World Trade Centre in New York City – was reduced to rubble. The two passenger airliners that crashed into them were flown by members of the Wahhabi militant organization Al-Qaeda, who had hijacked them mid-flight. Two other planes formed part of the coordinated attack, one flying into the Pentagon while the fourth crashed into a field in Pennsylvania following a struggle between passengers and the hijackers. In total, there were 2,977 fatalities, while another 25,000 sustained injuries because of the attacks and consequent structural damage. Most of those who died were civilians. In subsequent communications, Al-Qaeda's leader, the Saudi-born Osama bin Laden, claimed the attacks had been motivated by the United States' support for Israel, occupation of various Muslim nations in the Middle East and proximity of its military to the holiest sites of Islam. In 1979, the Iranian Revolution, which replaced a westernizing secular government with the authoritarian rule of Islamic clerics, reminded the world that religion could exert political power. In 2001, the events of 9/11 reminded us that this power could take the form of horrific violence.

In retaliation for the 9/11 attacks, US president George W. Bush – supported by allies including the UK – launched the 'War on Terror', invading Afghanistan and later Iraq. Opinions vary on whether these and other targets were chosen for claimed links with Al-Qaeda, other terrorist threats, or to further US economic power abroad. 9/11 and its aftermath have cast a shadow that has re-emerged on repeated occasions over the past twenty years as further acts of terrorism committed in the name of Islam have occurred across the globe. In 2004, bombs on commuter trains in Madrid killed 193 and injured around 2,000. The 7/7 London bombings in 2005 killed 52 and injured more than 700. In 2015, an attack in Paris, including shootings and the detonation of a bomb in the Bataclan theatre, left 130 dead. Other incidents occurred across the world, claimed by or believed to have been committed by individuals inspired by a militant form of Islam. Identifying specific motives is more complex, but oft-cited issues include complicity in US-led invasions of Afghanistan or Iraq and other military incursions into the Middle East.

One of the most enduring legacies of this wave of terrorist activity is its use as a justification for anti-Muslim prejudice and hostility. Research within Europe and North America indicates patterns of Islamophobia predated 9/11, including a stereotype of Muslims being prone to fanaticism or aggression (Al Atom 2014; Runnymede Trust 1997).

9/11 exacerbated existing tensions, but also marked a turning point as emerging prejudices were channelled into more formal measures of state control.

The resulting anti-Muslim prejudice has filtered into a series of influential developments across the world within the spheres of politics, culture and the law. This has coincided with a new sensitivity surrounding the visibility of religious identities. Within the United States, the United Kingdom and other nations in the global north, Muslims constitute a small minority. Associated with immigrant populations originating in the Middle East, Far East or Africa, the 'Muslim' as a public persona has taken on stereotypical qualities which are bound up in visual identity markers as much as character traits. Skin colour, style of clothing, facial hair, head coverings – all contribute to the consolidation of a damaging stereotype that has coincided with a rise in Islamophobic incidents.

These processes have also paralleled a heightened regulation of religion, justified by politicians on the basis of public safety and national security. While the explicit focus is on militant Islam, the consequences of this process extend across a much wider remit, so that *securitization* can now be viewed as a tool of the state used to advance political agendas and reinforce cultural boundaries. The range of regulatory devices is wide and complex and incorporates multiple layers of state action and bureaucratic governance. Just considering the example of Islam, we can observe across a range of societies the heightened regulation of Muslim communities through such measures as the banning of headscarves, surveillance of communities, exclusion of speakers labelled 'extremist' from public platforms or even whole countries, withdrawal of state representatives from dialogue with Muslim organizations, disempowerment of Muslim organizations in the civic sphere, calls for the mandatory training and accreditation of imams, increased police counter-terrorism powers, and heightened scrutiny of Muslim institutions of education (e.g. Brown 2008; Busher et al. 2017; Chong 2013; Dahab and Omori 2019; Eroukhmanoff 2015; Fernandez 2018; Humphrey 2009; Mavelli 2013; Scott-Baumann et al. 2020; Thorleifsson 2017). While diverse in practice, such measures all contribute to what has been described as the securitization of Islam.

Writing in the field of politics and international relations, Philippe Bourbeau defines 'securitization' as 'the process of integrating an issue into a security framework that emphasises policing and defence' (2014: 187). In cases where religious groups are integrated into this kind of framework, they are presented as a risk to the public, one that demands intervention by the state. In practice, this involves new legislation and policy framed in terms of counterterrorism and public order. Securitization has also made its way into the management of public services, as schools, universities, prisons and other state-funded bodies are co-opted into government security initiatives. Issues of security have become part of the broader state regulation of religion, sometimes extending well beyond its original rationale.

This chapter addresses how the securitization process has developed in several national cases. It also considers the social consequences of securitization for religious groups. In this sense it moves beyond the approach, maintained by the Copenhagen School of security studies, that treats securitization as a kind of speech act issued by representatives of the state, thereby ascribing particular groups the status of threat. This approach conceives securitization as a state-authorized declaration that justifies treating an issue outside of the realm of politics and within the realm of security. The declaration by President George W. Bush of a 'War on Terror' following 9/11 is a powerful example. However, while part of the process of securitization, this is not the whole picture. The discussion that follows is informed by Stuart Croft's critical response to this approach; in particular, we note three ways in which Croft moves beyond the theoretical framework of the Copenhagen School. First, taking seriously the intersubjective way in which ideas are communicated, Croft extends securitization so that it includes not just speech but image and silence. His is an 'intertextual' approach that attributes the securitization process to a range of media. Second, acknowledging the importance of the state, Croft includes 'the role of all socially powerful agents both in producing and in reproducing securitizations' (Croft 2012: 82). It is important to consider the influence of media and think tanks, for example, on securitization, factors especially germane in the case of Islam (Scott-Baumann et al. 2020: 27–30). Finally, Croft pushes the Copenhagen School's emphasis on extraordinary measures taken by the state into a much broader response. Such extraordinary measures are not simply a matter for the state – or indeed other powerful forces – but involve the performance of new behaviours by a range of social actors. In Croft's words, '[t]he audience thus co-produces the new social reality' (2012: 85). Securitization becomes part of everyday life, through which ordinary people become complicit in how a new 'threat' is perceived and handled.

The following discussion, while treating securitization as a global phenomenon, also recognizes that there remain important differences at the level of the nation state. Contrasting cases reveal variations in how securitization shapes religious identities and their relationship with their social contexts. A final section therefore explores the social consequences of securitization and how best to make sociological sense of these given the evidence available. We open, though, with a close examination of a particular case, that of the counterterrorism Prevent Strategy in the UK. Having been subject to development over almost two decades, steered by the priorities of several different governments, Prevent offers a powerful illustration of how counter-terrorism measures both change the construction of religion at the regulatory level and influence the lives of particular religious minorities.

The UK's Prevent Strategy: From community intervention to universal surveillance

While the governing structures of the UK retain elements of religious establishment – for example, Church of England bishops sit in the House of Lords, part of the nation's legislature – they function mainly along secular lines. Up until the turn of the millennium, the state related to religious bodies largely as repositories of heritage (e.g. historical church buildings) or of culture (e.g. as aspects of a diverse population). An increase in regulation since then has emerged from two quarters. First, equality legislation has both restricted and empowered religious groups as they negotiate their relationship with wider cultural values (McIvor 2020), a theme explored in Chapter 8. Second, regulatory measures were extended and emboldened by the association in policy circles of radicalization with Islam (Fernandez 2018: 175). The Prevent Strategy mirrors other state counter-terrorism measures in seeking to anticipate and prevent violent acts before they occur. In this sense it is concerned with the management of risk and reflects a policy perspective that views the twenty-first century as an age of new dangers that demand new responses.

Prevent originally emerged in the years immediately following 9/11, as part of the Labour government's counter-terrorism strategy, 'Contest'. Contest was conceived as comprising four elements, which have been retained by the UK government ever since: 'pursue' (concerned with stopping terrorist attacks), 'protect' (protecting the public from terrorism), 'prepare' (mitigating the impact of an anticipated terrorist attack) and 'prevent' (preventing individuals from becoming involved in terrorism in the first place). The first three 'p's largely fall within the remit of the police and security services. 'Prevent', on the other hand, has been conceived as a set of responsibilities stretching across a much wider range of organizations, although its governance and modes of delivery have changed over time. During its first iteration, overseen by the Labour governments of Tony Blair and Gordon Brown, Prevent was applied as a series of community engagement projects, targeted at particular regions. The policy linked counterterrorism with community cohesion, channelling funding into communities with the highest proportion of Muslim residents. In this sense the assumption that it was Muslims who were most vulnerable to 'radicalization' was explicit. Much of the Prevent funding was handled by local government, making its way into a variety of projects including educational initiatives aimed at raising awareness of Islamic beliefs and culture and fostering greater integration of Muslim communities, such as English language tuition and training in active citizenship for Muslim women (HM Government 2011: 28). From 2007, Prevent also incorporated 'Channel', a de-radicalization initiative coordinated by the police and aimed at individuals judged to be at risk of being drawn into terrorism. Channel was modelled on strategies used to safeguard people at risk of involvement in drug crime, gang activity and domestic violence, and partnered with other local specialists and stakeholders, including Muslim community leaders recruited as mentors.

Subjected to a review following the formation of the Conservative-Liberal Democrat coalition government in 2010, Prevent was reconceived with the emphasis placed less on community intervention and more on vigilance across public bodies. Previous Prevent initiatives were criticized for channelling resources into too wide a range of projects, to the detriment of distinctively counter-terrorism policy goals, and some partner organizations were criticized for affirming views 'not consistent with mainstream British values' (HM Government 2011: 58).

The revised Prevent guidelines – issued in 2011 – explicitly extended its remit while narrowing its application. While identifying the UK's most serious terrorist threat to be from 'Al Qa'ida, its affiliates and like-minded terrorist organisations inspired by violent Islamism' (HM Government 2011: 13), it broadened Prevent to cover all forms of 'terrorist ideology' (HM Government 2011: 45). This reflected a shift in focus from preventing violent extremism to countering those *attitudes and values thought to lead to terrorism*. In other words, it signalled a reorientation, from acts of terrorism to 'challenging extremist (and non-violent) ideas that are also part of a terrorist ideology' (HM Government 2011: 6). At the same time, the new guidelines separated issues of cohesion from counterterrorism, effectively rejecting the previous government's policy of addressing the latter by reinforcing the former. Prevent was in the process of becoming leaner, more centralized and with a smaller pot of funding, subject to stricter controls.

John Holmwood and Therese O'Toole have characterized this shift in the Prevent Strategy as one from a 'hearts and minds' approach to one of 'muscular liberalism' (2018: 45–63). David Cameron, the UK prime minister from 2010, was keen to differentiate himself from his Labour predecessors. The following year, at the Munich Security Conference, he called for an end to tolerating 'segregated communities behaving in ways that run completely counter to our values' (quoted in Holmwood and O'Toole 2018: 51). A hardening of political rhetoric on counterterrorism was matched with statutory reform in 2015, with the introduction of the Counter-Terrorism and Security Act. This new piece of legislation imposed a legal obligation on 'public authorities' – including schools, universities, hospitals, prisons and local government – to have 'due regard to the need to prevent people from being drawn into terrorism'. While the letter of the law remains moderate and non-specific, the act was accompanied by new Prevent guidelines, which were much more expansive about how the new approach should be implemented.

The 2015 guidelines reinforced the need to challenge ideas, not just actions, reaffirming the purview of Prevent to include 'all forms of terrorism and with non-violent extremism, which can create an atmosphere conducive to terrorism and can popularise views which terrorists then exploit' (HM Government 2021). In other words, a direct correlation between extremist ideas and a proclivity to commit acts of terrorism was assumed. Consequently, an emphasis was placed on the requirement among public authorities – part of what was now called the 'Prevent duty' – to maintain monitoring systems capable of identifying cases of potential radicalization among their employees, pupils, students, inmates or patients. The Home Office would assume overall responsibility for compliance, devolving the task of holding local bodies to account to sector level authorities. In practice, a vast network of bureaucracy was generated, demanding annual compliance documents from each institution and mandatory Prevent training for hundreds of thousands of employees, now called upon to play their part in monitoring their co-workers and clients on an ongoing basis. Advocates view this as a heightened vigilance appropriate to an age of global terrorism. Critics see an insidious embedding of a universal surveillance system, prone to eroding trust and stoking suspicion among British citizens.

It was in these guidelines that the aims of Prevent were attached to the defence of 'British values'. The document defines 'extremism' as 'vocal or active opposition to fundamental British values, including democracy, the rule of law, individual liberty, and the mutual respect and tolerance of different faiths and beliefs', also incorporating 'calls for the death of members of our armed forces, whether in this country or overseas'

(HM Government 2011). The same definition was used in guidance issued in 2014, requiring publicly funded schools to 'actively promote' these 'fundamental British values' (Holmwood and O'Toole 2018: 66). This reflects a government move towards affirming cultural and moral boundaries defined around 'Britishness'. The articulation of anti-terrorism using the language of 'British values' has led some critics to suggest the new policy reinforces a pre-existing bias against Muslims and the emboldening of nationalist groups, some of which promote an anti-Muslim message. While defenders of Prevent have repeatedly highlighted its focus on all forms of extremism – including far-right groups – the statistics of Prevent referrals support the claim that Muslims have been disproportionately targeted (Scott-Baumann et al. 2020: 149).

Prevent has always been controversial, provoking opposition among academics, politicians, lawyers, civil society groups and Muslim communities. Research has exposed how it has diminished trust in UK authorities among British Muslims (Awan and Guru 2017), encouraged an evasion of sensitive topics within UK universities and a disengagement from higher education among Muslim students (Scott-Baumann et al. 2020), encouraged suspicion of Muslims within British schools (Busher et al. 2017; Holmwood and O'Toole 2018) and compromised the likelihood of Muslims cooperating with counter-terrorism measures (Choudhury 2017). It has also been subject to legal challenges. In 2019, the Court of Appeal ruled that a paragraph within the Prevent duty guidance issued to higher education institutions in England and Wales was unlawful (Gayle 2019). This followed an action taken against the Home Secretary by Dr Salman Butt, a Muslim writer and speaker who had featured in a previous government press release, which labelled him an 'extremist'. Butt claimed this act had been tantamount to defamation and had had an adverse impact on his career as a public speaker, including at universities. While the court dismissed most of Butt's claims, it upheld the accusation that the Prevent guidance was insufficiently clear on the issue of inviting public speakers onto university campuses. According to the ruling, the wording ought to have included the need to balance the different duties of universities according to the Counter-Terrorism and Security Act: to have *due regard* to the risk of individuals being drawn into terrorism and to have *particular regard* to the need to ensure freedom of speech, as well as regard to the importance of academic freedom (HM Government 2015). The offending paragraph has now been removed from the Prevent guidelines.

A notable feature of the UK's Prevent Strategy post-2011 is its allocation of responsibility for the monitoring of shared spaces to the individual citizen. In this sense, the policy reflects an important dimension of neoliberalism: the shifting of responsibility from the government to the individual (Fernandez 2018: 171). This does not amount to a wholesale devolution of responsibility as a form of empowerment, however. Rather, the state maintains overall authority by defining the policy and the rules of compliance. It also, via its devolved departments, exercises bureaucratic oversight of public bodies whose compliance is monitored on a regular basis. The cost of compliance is passed on to public bodies and the responsibility of on the ground surveillance handed over to ordinary staff members who are obliged to complete the 'Prevent training', including guidelines – widely criticized for being vague and unhelpful (Jones 2020: 130–1) – on how to spot cases of radicalization. But the state retains overall scrutiny, reserving the right to intervene more directly should it choose to do so.

In this sense, Prevent – and the securitization measures it conveys – signals a use of state power that has potentially major implications for religious groups viewed as controversial, subversive or deviant. The breadth of the definitions used to define terrorism, extremism and 'British values' means it is capable of labelling a wide range of groups as problematic, even though the community most affected so far has been Muslims. While Prevent has assumed different emphases at different points in time, and despite the controversy it has provoked, it remains in place with strong support from central government. At the time of writing, a long-awaited review of Prevent is under way. However, critics have raised concerns about its limited remit and the fact that it is being led by Sir William Shawcross, a former chair of the Charity Commission for England and Wales, who has gone on record with highly critical views of immigration and multiculturalism in Britain, and of Islamic influence in Europe. Many Muslim groups, academics, charities and human rights groups have, in protest, boycotted the review, refusing to engage with its consultation process.

Prevent represents a very specific case of securitization, one that has had a major impact on the lives of Muslims in Britain. However, it is by no means unique, and many other nations have initiated counter-terrorism measures that appear to have had similar consequences. Existing scholarship has, for example, highlighted the use of counter-terrorism measures to securitize the Muslim population in Australia (Chong 2013; Humphrey 2009: 147), Germany (Humphrey 2009: 143), India (Egorova 2018) and the United States (Eroukhmanoff 2015). Examples beyond Islam have also been noted, including the securitization of Tibetan Buddhism by the Chinese state (Topgyal 2012) and the securitization of Jehovah's Witnesses within Russia (Knox 2019).

To make proper sense of these developments sociologically, we need to go back into recent history and to a set of global developments that reshaped how religion was understood among intellectuals in Europe and North America, including in the sociology of religion. Revisiting these changes, and tracing how they lead us to the present moment, will help us understand the significance of the securitization of religion.

The construction of religion as risk

By the early 1970s, the discipline of sociology had – like other social sciences in the 'Western' tradition – largely consigned religion to the dustbin of history. Where it was acknowledged to exist, it was assumed to be a residue from pre-modern times, destined to fade away as successive generations gradually caught up with the more progressive forces of the twentieth century. It was certainly not a force to be reckoned with. In prosperous economic nations, it was believed to exist only among the marginal communities who clung to past loyalties out of insecurity or in the private lives of more traditionally minded citizens. At best, it was benign but moribund, a spent force on the way out. These assumptions were especially embedded among those Peter Berger would later describe as the 'knowledge class', a group that is relatively small but influential on account of controlling 'the institutions that provide the "official" definitions of reality, notably the educational system, the media of mass communication, and the higher reaches of the legal system' (Peter Berger 1999: 10). Exactly how embedded became clear after the Iranian Revolution in 1979. The toppling of a secular, pro-Western government by an Islamic clerocracy (i.e. rule by religious scholars) revealed religion to be a political force capable of bringing about dramatic social change. The widely held assumption that modernization was the inevitable and inexorable carrier of secularization needed to be reconsidered. But if religion was not a spent force, how could existing sociological theories explain why it endured in certain contexts and not in others? And what were the social conditions that led to religion becoming mobilized as a power capable of revolutionary change? The events in Iran unsettled policymakers thousands of miles west of the revolution because it didn't fit into their expectations of the modern age, and if these were wrong, what else had they got wrong? And what other religious surprises might be around the corner?

In truth, the Iranian Revolution coincided with a number of other events that challenged the understanding of religion as a benign, apolitical survival of the past. The New Christian Right was gaining momentum in the United States, soon to abandon its support for 'born again' Democrat Jimmy Carter for the Republican Ronald Reagan. Reagan's victory in the 1980 presidential elections marked the emergence of Christian conservatism as a powerful political movement closely aligned with the new president's small government, free market agenda (Smith 2006: 325–63). Protestant–Catholic tensions in Northern Ireland had achieved new levels of social discord and violence, spreading from Ulster to the British mainland. From the vantage point of relatively secularized England, the republican Catholics and unionist Protestants looked equally fanatical, embodying a religious militancy difficult to imagine in the rest of the UK. Two years before the Iranian Revolution, the Peoples Temple – a communalist, racial justice-oriented Christian sect led by former Disciples of Christ minister Jim Jones – had migrated from California to French Guyana to establish a self-sufficient agricultural community. A year later, 'Jonestown' was struggling to sustain its members and Jones's behaviour had become increasingly erratic and paranoid. A visit from California Congressman Leo Ryan on behalf of concerned parents reinforced Jones's conviction that their utopian dream was doomed and that the only option left was to commit collective 'revolutionary suicide'. In total, over 900 died, the largest loss of US citizens' lives at a single incident before 9/11 (Juergensmeyer 2003). The 1970s overturned the idea that religious movements could be ignored by those in power as marginal, ineffectual and harmless.

The events at Jonestown have filtered into Western popular culture. The expression 'to drink the Koolaid' – shorthand for blindly accepting the authority of a dominant personality – is named after the powdered soft drink laced with cyanide and sedatives that was ingested by Peoples Temple members. Whether their deaths can be attributed to coercion, credulity or a free choice to end their lives remains an open question that will never be definitively answered. But the notion underlying the 'drink the Koolaid' expression reflects much about how unconventional religious groups were viewed in the aftermath of the 1970s. The 'cult controversies' that James Beckford wrote about in his 1985 book of the same name very much centred on ideas of insidious deception and the manipulation of vulnerable individuals. Beckford's book is about the social responses to the so-called New Religious Movements (NRMs) that came to public attention in the decades following the Second World War, the most prominent being the Unification Church (or 'Moonies'), Scientology, the Children of God and the International Society for Krishna Consciousness (ISKCON). From this response emerged the popular use of the term 'cult', used to refer to groups considered 'small, insignificant, inward-looking, unorthodox, weird, and possibly threatening' (Beckford 1985: 13). Despite sociological attempts to highlight the problems of this use of the term – not least its expansive application to any religious movement that 'looks dodgy' – it remains commonplace to this day. Its persistence reflects a tendency for public interest in religion to focus on the sensational, prurient and controversial, a tendency only heightened in recent years following various abuse scandals within mainstream and marginal religious communities.

Beckford's analysis of the social response to New Religious Movements is a helpful reference point as we address this chapter's theme of securitization. The processes it describes are echoed in more recent cultural developments in which religious activity is understood as a security threat. Both cases conceive religious phenomena as suspicious, with a particular concern for young people and their socialization into unusual ideologies. Both also emerge as sites of impassioned contestation, as different parties exchange claims and counterclaims about the religious movements involved. In both cases disputes have made their way into the courts, so that religious matters enter into legal and regulatory regimes as oppositional groups seek suppression, control or incarceration of religious actors, and religious groups in turn seek redress and the protection of their rights. And both cases have generated the formation of bodies of self-appointed 'experts', which have claimed to hold the key to understanding the religious movements in question and the key to solving the social problems for which they are blamed (Kundnani 2012: 3). The anti-cult movement in the 1970s and 1980s was able to gain influence because of the fears and anxieties of parents, whose children had joined New Religious Movements. Anti-cult 'experts' not only validated parents' anxieties but also often claimed to be able to rescue these young adults and restore them to their families. They claimed their 'de-programming' methods – maintaining a veneer of credibility by leaning on dubious psychological research – would undo the sinister 'brainwashing' that had led NRM converts to make such misguided decisions in the first place. By the post-9/11 era, the language used to address these matters had – to some degree – changed, but many of the underlying assumptions about religion and social deviance remained. Whether addressing the issue of 'cults' or 'radical Islam', critical 'experts' find the root of the problem in ideology, the site of the problem in individual psychology and the solution in a form of re-education.

Beckford argues that the rise of 'cults' cannot be understood independently of societal reactions to them. This is partly because public perceptions are for the most part grounded not in direct experience but in a circulation of impressions shaped by the mass media. A similar process can be observed with respect to so-called radical Islam in the twenty-first century. Here, though, representations (and misrepresentations) of the subject matter are channelled not just by journalism and online commentary but by state interventions. Beckford notes that while cases of litigation had occurred across Western nations, and piecemeal sanctions had been applied in particular cases, no Western state had, by the mid-1980s, 'enacted legislation designed to control NRMs' (Beckford 1985: 283). The same cannot be said for 'radical Islam', which has been cited as the justification for new counter-terrorism legislation across a range of nations. The recent securitization of Islam has been galvanized by the introduction of new laws, state-sponsored initiatives and political rhetoric as governments of various political persuasions respond to what they consider to be a security threat. This chapter attempts to address securitization as a sociological phenomenon. Accusations of 'radicalization' and attempts to conceive of Islam as a security threat cannot simply be treated as claims or counterclaims measurable against an external 'truth'. These are social phenomena, framed by a particular era in global politics and emerging in public in a complex process of mutual reinforcement.

From fundamentalism to 'radicalization'

Much can be learned about episodes of religious controversy by tracing the development of the terminology used to describe it. An instructive example is the word 'fundamentalist'. Originally coined during the second decade of the twentieth century, 'fundamentalist' was a term self-ascribed by conservative Christians in the United States who wished to signal their rejection of modern values and affirmation of the 'fundamentals' of Christianity. The term was popularized via *The Fundamentals*, ninety essays in twelve volumes, published between 1910 and 1915, all written by Christian ministers and theologians seeking to defend what they saw as the essential truths of the Christian faith. While the emergent term 'fundamentalist' was initially used as a positive self-description among conservative Christian leaders, it developed more negative connotations over time. The famous 'Scopes Monkey Trial' of 1925 led the print media to portray anti-evolution Christians as backward, uneducated and ignorant, and 'fundamentalist' took on these pejorative associations (Marsden 2006). However, it was not until the Iranian Revolution in 1979 that the term was applied beyond Christianity to indicate a form of religion that was political, militant and aggressive.

Twenty years later, we again were faced with a fresh application of a pre-existing term to a Muslim constituency. This time it signalled a heightened securitization of religion and the term was 'radicalization', which emerged in policy discourse following 9/11. In a review of literature, published in 2013, Alex Schmid argues that 'radicalization', while popular in political circles, suffers from a multitude of definitions and so no scholarly consensus on what it means, as well as a lack of empirical investigation into its explanatory power (Schmid 2013). Some scholars have suggested the term emerged in response to the demand for an explanation of 'home grown terrorism' (Truong 2018).

When perpetrators of terrorist acts were known to not be exclusively foreign fighters – for example, the UK's 7/7 bombers were from Leeds in Yorkshire – then a concept was needed to account for why individuals might attack their own society.

It is worth noting that, historically, the term 'radical' has often been used to refer to progressive causes. Its conflation in the twenty-first century with ideas of reactionary extremism is significant, especially when we consider how it functions as a verb. 'To radicalize', while traceable to the nineteenth century (Williams 1976: 251–2), has more recently acquired a meaning to do with a supposedly manipulative process that leads to the embrace of a new, perhaps extreme, ideology. In this sense the word 'radical' has achieved a status analogous to that of 'cult' in the 1970s in indicating a problematic, dangerous or socially subversive religious movement. This analogy can be extended insofar as both terms emerged in the context of moral panics about counter-cultural religious groups and about the presumed vulnerabilities of those attracted to them. It is true that recent uses of the term 'radicalization' do not usually imply a loss of agency to the degree that was imputed to 'cult converts' four decades ago, although the 'brainwashing' accusations expertly debunked by sociologist Eileen Barker (Barker 1984) remain a feature of discussions about Islam in higher education, as found in recent research among university students and staff (Scott-Baumann et al. 2020). In fact, official UK Home Office guidance issued by the Research, Information and Communications Unit recommends 'brainwashing' or 'indoctrination' as synonyms preferable to 'radicalization', the latter now viewed as carrying unhelpful associations with Islam in the public mind (RICU 2007: 7–8). This language is by no means neutral. Significantly, 'radicalization' shares with the earlier 'cults' controversy suggestions of a loss of control, of manipulation and of a movement to a religious orientation at odds with the prevailing social order. It is also seen as a plausible causal factor in explaining political violence, a conceptual shift that occurred among American and European policymakers in the wake of 9/11, 7/7 and other terrorist attacks (McGlynn and McDaid 2019: 561). In this respect, 'radicalization' is commonly used to convey simultaneously a sense of power and powerlessness, of subversion but deferred agency.

It is also, within policy discourse at least, commonly associated with a particular set of assumptions about how religious identities become 'radical'. Variously referred to as the 'pathway' or – less charitably – the 'conveyor-belt' model (Holmwood and O'Toole 2018: 55), 'radicalization' within policy discussions has tended to be viewed as linear in process, ideological in its triggers and psychological in its site of operation. Simply put, those who are 'radicalized' typically encounter an ideological source – personal or online – which gradually changes their perspective to one in which violence is justifiable and required, leading them to commit acts of violence. That is, unless this process is disrupted and the subject is re-educated. Presenting 'radicalization' in this way has enabled governments to justify interventions at the individual level and the targeting of specific religious traditions because of particular texts or teachings – however obscure, contested or marginal.

Embedded in this perspective is the assumption – pervasive in counter-terrorism discourse – that acts of terrorism by Muslims can be understood as a direct outworking of their Muslim beliefs. This despite scholarship that suggests this connection is tenuous at best. Indeed, many Muslim terrorists – while claiming to act in the name of Islam – are religious novices, often new converts, with limited socialization into the textual and practical traditions of Islam (Stern and Berger 2016: 82–3). Religiosity as an established and embedded practice appears to protect against violent radicalization (Fernandez 2018: 172–3). And yet so much of the emergent public debate links 'Islam' with violence. Religion is assumed to be a determinative and dominant aspect of identity among those who commit terrorism in its name, quite irrespective of its broader social and religious contexts. According to Clara Eroukhmanoff (2015), this is sometimes exacerbated by assumptions made by security professionals about radicalization being an objective, observable, independent process that can be 'tackled'. In her research into US security services, Eroukhmanoff identified a tendency to understand suspected radical Muslims using a consequential logic akin to rational choice theory. On this basis, awareness of a suspect's desires and of how they might be realized is sufficient for the security services to intervene, because terrorist behaviour is assumed to be an *inevitable* consequence of this combination of factors. No room is left for contingency, hyperbole or a change of heart, and the urgency of pre-emptive action is used to justify this reasoning. Violence becomes an expected consequence of radicalization. Conversely, there is no room for those who have radical beliefs but do *not* act violently. Effectively, the belief itself becomes criminalized and becomes the justification for punitive action. Eroukhmanoff goes on to identify a further problem in the approach of security specialists. In keeping with the assumptions of rational choice theory, 'actors are viewed as autonomous agents in the world, and their practices are thus disconnected from each other. Since Muslim individuals "choose on their own" to radicalise, their choice is separate from the choices and the actions of people around them, including the police' (Eroukhmanoff 2015: 255).

This allows pre-emptive interventions by security professionals – including documented cases of entrapment – to be fully justified, as 'radicalization' is conceived in terms of a 'remote other', that is wholly separate from counter-radicalization forces. Such thinking also allows the latter to dehumanize suspects, who are assumed to think and behave in a wholly different way to themselves. In treating the terrorist suspect as a rational, autonomous individual whose decisions and actions emerge independently of their social context, security services are also echoing notions of the self that are consistent with neoliberalism. In a striking distortion of narratives that emphasize self-generation as self-empowerment, these same narratives are here revealed to be instrumental in *disempowering* Muslim subjects. For it is by this logic that their presumed inclination towards violence is effectively reinforced.

It is difficult to think of a more compelling case for the sociological approach to religion. For such simplistic and dangerous generalizations are only possible if religious phenomena are abstracted from the social settings from which they emerge. Scepticism about this model of radicalization has been expressed from various quarters. Fabien Truong, in his ethnographic study of Muslims in Paris, traces how 'radicalization' emerged in the wake of 9/11 and argues that the term's over-psychologization reductively papers over important social factors and presents a notion of 'ideas' as overly deterministic

(Truong 2018). Terrorism experts with close links to the security services have also expressed reservations. Former CIA operations officer and terrorism consultant Marc Sageman, in his book *Leaderless Jihad: Terror Networks in the Twenty-First Century* (2008), argues that radicalization cannot be treated as a simple, linear process, which can be plotted on a straight line with clear causes and consequences. Sageman, basing his research on over 500 biographies of terrorists, presents radicalization as a collective, rather than individual, process, in which kinship and friendship networks are important elements. Other academic critics have focused on geopolitical factors, including the foreign policies of Western powers in the Middle East (Coppock and McGovern 2014: 246). The conveyor-belt theory allows the motivations behind terrorism to be imagined as atomized within closed enclaves of 'extremist' individuals, separated from experiences of alienation and marginalization that could be attributed to the state and its representatives. At the same time the capacity of these individuals to 'infect' wider systems and 'vulnerable' populations is inflated via alarmist public (including media) discourse, further heightening suspicion. This is expertly illustrated by John Holmwood and Therese O'Toole in their analysis of the so-called 'Trojan Horse' controversy, when a moral panic was ignited around the influence of Muslim governors on a group of schools in the UK city of Birmingham. Stoked by alarmist news media and government officials keen to appear tough on 'radicalization', the ensuing response led to major disruption to what were previously high achieving schools and the undermining of several teachers' careers. Most strikingly, this occurred despite enquiries finding no evidence of the alleged 'extremist plot'. The anonymous letter to Birmingham City Council that triggered the controversy (and which was leaked to the press) is widely believed to have been a hoax (Holmwood and O'Toole 2018).

'Radicalization' and 'Islamization'

Anxieties about Muslims within a range of societies predate the post 9/11 drive towards securitization. But pre-existing prejudices – from the blatantly racist to arguments about cultural incompatibility – have fed into the security panic so that emerging anxieties are leant extra plausibility. Imposing restrictions on Muslim communities is easier to justify when public unease is reinforced by embedded prejudice. The power of 'radicalization' as a concept lies not in what it captures about identity change among would-be terrorists – as discussed earlier, its utility in this sense is quite limited – but in its ability to evoke anxiety and fear about dangerous ideologies. As its use has fostered strong associations with Islam, the term 'radicalization' has also been a major vehicle for the securitization of Muslims at the popular level. In turn, this has reinforced anxieties about Islam as a cultural incursion into liberal-democratic societies, with emerging stereotypes highlighting assumed incompatibilities of belief, values and lifestyle.

This tallies with what Talal Asad argues about Islam being Europe's religious 'other', which, he argues, is rooted in narratives of history that impute to Islam an 'ingrained hostility to all non-Muslims'. Islam emerges as an important reference point in the definition of 'Europe', because this 'alleged antagonism to Christians . . . becomes crucial to the formation of European identity' (Asad 2003: 169). According to Asad, in so-called Western discourse, the ideas of 'civilization' and 'secularity' are framed by this narrative. The latter we will return to in Chapter 8; the former has more immediate relevance, because it illuminates how the treatment of Islam and Muslims as a threat builds on a long history framed by assumptions about social order, liberal morality and the proper place of religion in society. The heightened individualism typical of neoliberal cultures reinforces this tension, as Muslims are often viewed – whether fairly or not – as affirming values at odds with the prevailing social order. This presumed dissonance frequently focuses on the violation of individual freedoms, especially the treatment of women (Guest et al. 2020: 27; Stolz et al. 2016: 141). Luca Mavelli (2013) goes as far as to argue that the twenty-first-century securitization of Islam rests on the assumption that Islam transgresses a norm that has become essential to Western secularity. Mavelli argues that Islam is deemed threatening because it aspires to function within the political realm and so contravenes the notion that religion should remain confined to the private sphere and subordinate to state power. While such a representation of Islam overlooks huge complexity and unhelpfully essentializes 'Islam' into a singular phenomenon, this does accord with dominant *constructions* of Islam within many Western societies.

Insofar as this captures something axiomatic to common perceptions of Islam and Muslims, it is not surprising to find the verb 'Islamization' used in a decidedly negative sense. According to Lene Kühle,

Islamisation plays a similar role to that played by the concept of 'brainwashing' as understood by the ACM [anti-cult movement]. . . . In the case of 'cults', the alleged brainwashing techniques entail the use of abduction to free the persons from other influences, and in the case of Islamisation, where it is not individual persons but the country that is being changed, the solution is to actively combat the presence of and accommodation to Islam as well as the acceptance of 'parallel societies'. (Kühle 2018: 225)

'Islamization', then, emerges as the description of a process at the societal level. It signals the erosion of 'indigenous' ways of life and the corruption of established moral norms, imagining 'Islam' to be a foreign force seeking pre-eminence. Some right-wing rhetoric cites this danger in civilizational terms, like the Danish organizations Kühle describes as focused on stopping the 'Islamisation of Europe' (Kühle 2018: 223). Securitization of Islam can here be seen as reinforcing political agendas, legitimizing the fear of Islamic influence and exaggerated claims about the scale of it. The same tactics can be observed among those cases that invoke the defence of national identities, cases often distinguished by a resurgence of populism (see Chapter 3). The very notions of 'Islamification' or 'Islamization' coined by far-right groups conjure up the image of a social order tainted, corrupted or distorted by alien influence. The social order most often hinted at is nationalist and affirms a vision of British, American, Austrian or Hungarian national identity, for example, in which Islam has no legitimate place. This is a common pattern within the expression of popular xenophobic or racist prejudice, as it inscribes a cultural boundary in legitimizing the inclusion of some and the exclusion of others. As Talal Asad (2003) and others have repeatedly pointed out, this othering of Islam has a wide cultural purview, with Muslims discursively constructed as 'other' in relation to a range of nationalist discourses across Europe (Miera and Pala 2009; Nielsen 2010) and in relation to a pan-European identity as well. As a pattern it stretches beyond the populist fringes of Western societies, informing government responses to the challenges of immigration, security and social cohesion. Turkey's application for membership of the EU officially rests on economic, social and political criteria, but the barriers to its acceptance are widely assumed to be bound up in Turkey's Islamic culture, filtered through the experiences European populations have with Turkish migrants (Humphrey 2009: 141–2). Other cases illustrate how the securitization of Islam has informed how states handle matters of citizenship. The British government's decision to deprive Shamima Begum of her British citizenship following the fifteen-year-old's move to Syria to fight with the Islamic State terrorist group provides a striking example. National identity emerges not just as a tendentious symbolic marker of propriety; it is also weaponized as a means of excluding those who transgress cultural boundaries.

And yet motifs of nationalism are far more free-floating and contested than is often assumed, including among those who deploy 'Britishness' as a tool with which to mark out a cultural other as unwelcome. Indeed, in his illuminating ethnographic study of the radicalization of Muslim men in urban France, Fabien Truong cites the case of one individual whose experience of the Hajj, while intended to reinforce the unity of the universal 'ummah', actually threw into relief differences of culture that were deployed as markers of difference. In his account of his experiences in Mecca, 'Radouane' spoke of how the French stuck together, remarking on the cultural conventions that made French pilgrims better mannered than some Muslims from other parts of the globe. As Truong comments, 'Islam from below is rooted in ever-shifting histories and personal geographies; Islam from above floats in a void of first principles' (Truong 2018: 90). So attempts to mark out difference and 'distinction' using the language of nationality occurs among Muslims as well, as does the projection of markers of collective identity as tools of power and exclusion. 'Islam', 'France' and 'Britain' may be invoked with varying meanings and by various actors, but their exclusionary power works in analogous ways.

Another dimension of exclusionary language relates to inter-religious difference. Egorova and Ahmed (2017) discuss mutual perceptions among Jews and Muslims in the contemporary UK, drawing on interview and ethnographic data to highlight how these perceptions are often framed by British attitudes towards 'minority communities', including anti-Semitic and Islamophobic stereotypes, and mediated by local experiences. Essentializing tendencies are observed moving in both directions – exhibited among Jews referring to Muslims and among Muslims referring to Jews – but the patterns the authors trace are suggestive of important differences as well. First, there appears to be more political momentum behind negative stereotyping of Muslims, for example in 'the political Right portraying Jewish people as potential "allies" of European Christians in the fight against the "Islamisation" of Europe' (Egorova and Ahmed 2017: 293). Second, while fear of the 'other' is a common trope, including fear of persecution and hostility, stereotyping of Muslims includes their portrayal as likely perpetrators of violence. So, Muslims are doubly 'othered', as alien to both a pan-European identity and a security concern that renders their presence a threat to the social order. The comparison with the UK's Jewish community is instructive in highlighting common assumptions about assimilation and national loyalty. The global Jewish diaspora arguably has as strong an image of transnational community as the global Islamic *ummah*, and yet public discourses of British identity rarely call into question the loyalty of British Jews. Strong supporters of Israel and its defence of its borders are not labelled 'unBritish'. By contrast, a set of associations that links Islam with both violent extremism and a racialized 'other' are often used to place the Muslim community outside of the boundaries of British identity. Even the far right, rarely apologists for the Jewish community, have made a decisive shift in recent years away from a less discriminate colour racism, instead adopting an affirmation of British identity that assumes Islam as its essential 'other'. In 2015, the far-right group Britain First reached out to the Jewish community of Golders Green, London, offering their support to a population suffering from the 'Islamization' of the UK. Representatives of the Jewish community strongly rejected the offer (Ghert-Zand 2015).

Securitization and state power

Some aspects of securitization are arguably mirrored across all societies aligned with neoliberal economics and culture. For example, the tendency to privilege mathematical data as especially objective and reliable (Beer 2016) informs the use of algorithms in the identification of risk. Within the context of counter-terrorism initiatives, this manifests in the use of surveillance technology to anticipate sites of violence and pre-emptively identify those vulnerable to radicalization. There are clearly serious problems in determining security risks in this way. Surveillance technology is only as good as the data inputted into it, and if that already reflects patterns of racial and/or religious bias, we can expect that bias to skew the technology as well. Such systems also effectively treat citizens, according to Heath-Kelly, as 'compilations of abstract risk factors' (2016: 65). Aspects of religiosity are here incorporated into a distinctively neoliberal method of constituting the subject. Transnational forces are also essential to the securitization of migrant populations, as policies are coordinated into 'a common language to connect diverse Muslim communities as threats' (Humphrey 2009: 137). In this respect relations *between* nation states exert an important influence on how securitization measures play out within different societies.

While undoubtedly empowered by the global response to 9/11, securitization measures are also framed by the politics of nation states. A securitization of Islam has, for example, been bound up in the rise of the populism addressed in Chapter 3. In 2018 seven mosques were closed and forty imams expelled by the Austrian authorities, after they were shown to have links with an organization close to the Turkish Erdoğan government. The Austrian chancellor, Sebastian Kurz, had run an election campaign the previous year that invoked anxieties about immigration and Muslims. His formation of a coalition government with the far-right Freedom Party reinforced this aspect of his agenda (Heinisch, Werner and Habersack 2020: 164). So as Turkey continued to pursue its quest for membership of the European Union, Kurz affirmed his strong opposition, defending a vision of European cultural identity in which Islam has no place. The year 2020 saw Kurz proclaim his intention to outlaw 'political Islam' (Jones 2020), although the wording of the nation's counter-terrorism legislation was eventually changed to 'religiously motivated extremism' (Kiyagan 2020). But the methods of securitization extend beyond Islam. In 2017, the Russian Supreme Court upheld a ruling that labelled Jehovah's Witnesses as 'extremist' and banned the religious movement on Russian soil. This was possible because Russia's anti-extremism law – passed in 2002 in response to Moscow bombings attributed to Chechen terrorists – adopted an especially broad definition of extremism. Incorporating the 'stirring up of social, racial, ethnic or religious discord' (Knox 2019: 149), it has enabled the outlawing of groups with no history of violence or evident intent to cause harm. The subsequent imprisonment and alleged torture of Jehovah's Witnesses by Russian authorities have been met with fierce condemnation across the globe. Critics have suggested these actions – against a patently peaceful Christian sect – reflect a cynical use of the language of risk and radicalism to vilify minority religions that dissent from the Russian Orthodox Church, which has been strongly supported by the Putin government. Securitization emerges, then, as a tool of the state used to defend cultural boundaries and secure political capital. It also emerges in transactional relationships between states, such as when policies on migration are framed by the language of security in order to align more closely with transnational agendas. Small states like Macedonia are keen to advance their case for membership of the EU and NATO integration, and echoing the foreign policies of more powerful nations helps their case (Rexhepi 2018: 2230).

Securitization also has softer expressions, so that concerns about social integration, welfare provision and education reflect assumptions about Islam more forcefully affirmed via foreign or defence policies. An example can be found in how different nations uphold different strategies for distinguishing between acceptable and unacceptable forms of Islam. Muslims are often accommodated by societies and governments only insofar as they demonstrate their adherence to a state-approved 'moderate Islam', thereby becoming complicit in a process of 'domestication'. Domestication constitutes a state-managed strategy that accords social inclusion based on certain conditions; inclusion becomes conditional and something that can be revoked. Michael Humphrey (2009) identifies different approaches to domestication in Britain and France, for example. On the one hand, the British tradition of multiculturalism presupposes the possibility, in principle, that different religious groups can coexist harmoniously, so long as they adhere to a common orientation to citizenship. Writing about changing understandings of citizenship within a comparative study of European nations, Carolina Ivanescu (2016) roots this process in the politics of immigration and race relations after the Second World War. As the British government sought to manage the consequences of the dissolution of the British Empire, immigration from Commonwealth nations was initially welcomed for economic reasons. Restrictions were imposed by the 1962 Commonwealth Immigrants Act, although its announcement the year before had the opposite of its intended effect, with rates of immigration rising sharply as families attempted to 'beat the ban' (Ansari 2004: 158). Further waves of immigration occurred during the 1970s as the cultural profile of Muslim immigrants diversified and included refugees fleeing conflict, famine or persecution. Eventually, the racial tensions of the 1980s became overlaid with anxieties about Muslim communities, first in the aftermath of the Rushdie Affair when many Muslims mobilized in public protest over Salman Rushdie's novel, *The Satanic Verses*. The book was viewed as insulting to the Prophet Muhammad and led the Iranian leader Ayatollah Khomeini to issue a *fatwa* (i.e. a legal ruling, even though it was popularly reported as a threat, judgement or death sentence – Modood 1990: 129). While the 1990s saw the establishment of civic society organizations that sought to channel and legitimize a range of British Muslim voices, the stereotype of militant Islam – characterized by male aggression, intolerance and suppression of free speech – re-emerged most forcefully as a concern following 9/11. What emerged in political rhetoric in subsequent years was a construction of 'moderate Islam': civically engaged, without being subversive; religiously observant, so long as emergent values were broadly in line with the liberal norm; serious and committed in its tradition but without compromising its loyalty to Britain. Similar assumptions surrounded policy initiatives aimed at mobilizing Muslim women as moderating influences within Muslim communities (Brown 2008; Jones 2020: 129). The strategy of distinguishing the 'good Muslim' from the 'bad Muslim' (Birt 2006) emerged as a means of developing a critical narrative about terrorism but without appearing to undermine the British tradition of multiculturalism. It was becoming clear that Islam had a place within British public life, but that this only applied to a particular form of Islam.

By contrast, the French tradition of 'domestication' is much closer to a form of assimilation. French culture takes precedence over religious identities, so that the latter are expected to be practised mainly in the private sphere. The French secular tradition – called *laïcité* – treats religious symbolism as problematic in public spaces; the wearing of conspicuous religious symbols has been banned in public schools since 2004 and the full face covering was banned from all public spaces in 2010. These examples reveal how French laïcité is defined not merely by the differentiation of public and private spaces but also by the upholding of values taken to be integral to French identity. Given that face veiling was interpreted by policymakers as a means of oppression, forced upon Muslim women by men and reflective of their second-class status, 'the headscarf represented a symbol of female oppression and an expression of the Islamist attack to the cohesion of the French social body' (Mavelli 2013: 175). While French laïcité applies, in principle, to all public expressions of religion, the history of immigration from North Africa and its associated racial tensions within the French context have meant Islam is especially vulnerable to prejudice and demonization. Given that, since the 1980s, most North African migrants have come to France on a student visa (Virkama 2017: 94) and bearing in mind the strong tradition of leftist secularism on French campuses, we might expect Islam to be a focus of some tension among university students. Interestingly, in her ethnographic study of African migrants studying in Paris, Anna Virkama found these Muslim students tended to practice their faith in private and were keen to adjust to the conditions of mainstream French society; they also showed 'little interest in claiming more rights as Muslim subjects' (Virkama 2017: 106). In other words, they had internalized the domestication expected of them by the French system.

The social consequences of securitization

Some of the social consequences of securitization have already been discussed in this chapter. The stigmatization of Muslims, weakening of civil liberties and erosion of trust among public sector workers have all been noted. The consequences are most profound for Muslims, whose citizenship has become a matter of contention in various social contexts. As Islam has become largely associated with security issues in policy discourse, so Muslims have been called upon to demonstrate their rejection of extremism. Indeed, their status as acceptable citizens is presented as conditional upon this. This tendency to view Muslims through a securitized lens, heightening associations with aggression, violence and fanaticism, reinforces a momentum towards an othering of the Muslim subject. Already vulnerable to racial othering, Muslims are thereby rendered potentially dangerous as well, positioned, as Michael Humphrey puts it, 'at the social margins, at the limits of citizenship' (Humphrey 2009: 137).

Without seeking to underplay these concerns, there are several further issues that arise from the securitization process of a distinctly sociological character. As these are not so frequently noted, I will conclude this chapter by outlining three such issues and their implications for the sociology of religion. All relate to questions of the social contexts in which the impact of securitization is felt and may be summarized as *misrecognition*, the *overspill into private spaces* and the *retrieval of agency*.

Some of the most worrying effects of securitization are unintended but are no less important for being so. One consequence is the risk of *misrecognition*. As Islam and Muslims have been increasingly associated with security concerns in the public imagination, so anxieties have been projected onto broader racial and cultural categories of people who have been mistaken for Muslims (Carr and Haynes 2015). Williams and Vashi suggest that, generally speaking, in the US context, it has been those religious groups that have the most visibly distinctive practices that have been subjected to the most discrimination. In this sense, the street parades of Italian Catholics, sabbath observance of conservative Jews and hijab wearing Muslim women fall into the same category (2007: 271). That being so, evidence suggests that when the category of 'Muslim' is the lens through which minority groups are viewed, then a particular set of associations become salient. Reports of retaliation attacks against 'Muslim-looking' people increased significantly in the weeks following 9/11. Four days after the September 11 attacks, 42-year-old Frank Roque went on a shooting rampage in Mesa, Arizona, murdering gas station owner Balbir Singh Sodhi. Sodhi was of Indian descent and had migrated to the United States ten years earlier. He had a beard and was a turban wearer, in accordance with his Sikh faith (Lewin 2001). When he was arrested, in a chilling foretaste of the Trump era, Roque apparently shouted out 'I stand by America all the way'. Subsequent research has identified multiple patterns of misrecognition in a variety of cultural contexts. In a study of young people from diverse cultural backgrounds living in Scotland, Hopkins et al. found cases of Sikhs, Hindus, South Asian, Black and Caribbean individuals who had been assumed to be Muslim because of their physical appearance. The authors attribute this to the portrayal of geopolitical events in the media, the homogenization of the 'Asian' community in the public imagination and the lack of visibility accorded to non-Muslim ethnic minority groups (Hopkins et al. 2017). In her ethnographic research into Jewish-Muslim relations in contemporary India, Yulia Egorova finds patterns of mutual recognition are often distorted by ethnic or racial tropes, which confuse perceptions about the cultural-religious 'other', their loyalties and security risk (Egorova 2018: 140–2). Misrecognition is not just an innocent error of judgement but is indicative of limited religious-cultural awareness among the general public and of the racialization of 'Muslim' as a category of identity. It illustrates how the prejudicial and exclusionary readings of Muslim identities impact on a much broader public. Close attention, therefore, needs to be paid to the way in which 'Muslim' as an identity marker is both operationalized by sociologists of religion and constructed among those in a position to exercise judgements about their peers. For this reason, it was encouraging to see the UK's All Party Parliamentary Group on British Muslims define Islamophobia in a way that included 'Muslimness and perceived Muslimness' within its remit (APPG 2018: 11). It was less encouraging to find the UK government refusing to adopt the definition.

Securitization has been accompanied by a heightening of targeted surveillance of particular communities. In 2010, the now infamous 'project champion' in Birmingham made use of funding from the UK government's counter-terrorism budget to deploy surveillance cameras in two predominantly Muslim residential areas, before local opposition led to the initiative being discontinued (Karner and Parker 2017). The rise of a surveillance society has also highlighted how a securitization of religion claimed to focus on public spaces also makes its way into more *private* domains.

Part of this process is driven by the democratization of surveillance power. For example, the scrutiny of the home for evidence of religious danger is enabled by mobile technology in the hands of intrepid journalists. Shereen Fernandez recounts the case of the San Bernardino, California shooting in 2015, when husband and wife Syed Rizwan Farook and Tashfeen Malik killed fourteen and injured twenty-two others at a Department of Public Health training event and Christmas party.

After the shooting, a media frenzy ensued as journalists were granted access to Farook and Malik's home by their landlord. Journalists, mostly using their mobile phones, seized this opportunity and documented the interior of the house, focusing primarily on the Islamic objects found within it. . . . Everyday Islamic objects, such as prayer beads and prayer mats, were the focus of journalists, despite these items being quite characteristic of what would typically be found in many

Muslim homes. This home, once occupied by a Muslim couple was transformed by the media into a 'reliable' depiction of a Muslim terrorist's home, with heavy emphasis placed on religious objects, thus forging a link between everyday Islamic practices and acts of terrorism. (Fernandez 2018: 178–9)

Here, journalistic representation becomes part of the technology of 'risk documentation and management' (Fernandez 2018: 179); the private material elements of the home are made public in a way that makes them symptomatic of terrorist potential.

There is also a state-driven push towards scrutiny of the Muslim home. This is partly driven by the move, among policymakers, to put pressure on Muslim parents to monitor and report on suspicious behaviour by their children (Awan and Guru 2017), echoing a call for children to be removed from 'extremist' parents (Fernandez 2018: 183–4). This extension of 'pre-crime' space into private realms is reflected in a tendency among Muslims to modify their behaviour so as to avoid any risk of being labelled as a security concern (Lyon 2018: 183). For example, while the UK's Prevent Strategy functions within *public* institutions – schools, universities, prisons, hospitals and so forth – there is always a risk that conversations in the home may migrate into public spaces, especially when children are involved, and misunderstandings easily occur. In June 2021, in a class discussion, an eleven-year-old boy called for 'alms' to be given to the oppressed; his teacher mistook 'alms' for 'arms' and he was referred to the police via the Prevent duty. Other cases have seen a nursery worker mistake a four-year-old's drawing of a cucumber for a 'cooker bomb' and a ten-year-old's description of his 'terraced house' misunderstood as 'terrorist house' because of a spelling error (Taylor 2021). Prevent's own referral statistics suggest Muslims have been over-reported by public sector workers, reflecting a tendency to perceive risk when there is none and to view Muslims through the lens of the terrorist threat (Guest et al. 2020: 41). As Muslims become more aware of this, it is understandable that they would engage more concertedly in self-surveillance and self-censorship out of fear of being stigmatized as a potential terrorist (Fernandez 2018). Within educational contexts, this is especially concerning, as Prevent could be leading some to avoid having conversations about terrorism when open conversations are exactly what is needed if critical reflection on radicalization is to be fostered.

Misrecognition is hereby closely connected with stigma. In his influential study of the same name, Erving Goffman defined stigma in terms of attributes that are defined as 'discrediting', leading to the disqualification of individuals from 'full social acceptance' (Goffman 1963: 13; 9). The stigmatization of Muslims as suspicious or even dangerous has been enabled by securitization measures like Prevent, as they heighten anxieties about a threatening presence among us and encourage public sector workers to express their anxieties in referrals to the authorities. The fact that so many of these referrals are taken no further by police suggests the process is highly vulnerable to pre-existing prejudices based on Islamophobic stereotypes, rather than highlighting reasonable grounds for suspicion. But this process of stigmatization is also granted added legitimacy via the UK government's definition of terrorism in terms of opposition to 'fundamental British values'. Terrorist threats are not just dangerous to society; they also represent a threat to a shared way of life. We have to ask whether a deeper consequence of securitization might be a kind of secularization of Islam. For example, if Islam is perceived to be acceptable only if it is confined to the home and only if it assumes a passive, politically quietest form (Birt 2006), avoiding conflict with the state (Brown and Saeed 2014), to what extent is securitization becoming a vehicle for a form of secularism closer to the French model? Does it imply, as Wendy Brown (2008) suggests, that Muslims living in the West are being asked to choose between loyalty to the state and loyalty to Islam? Further research is needed to elucidate in greater detail the wider impact of such policy initiatives, recognizing that policy always has a social life including unintended, and often unacknowledged, consequences.

It is this social life of policy that frames my final point. A difficulty with many existing analyses of securitization is their tendency to underestimate the *agency* of individuals, constructing Muslims as passive recipients of either radical ideologies or government initiatives. Both arguably re-inscribe an orientalist narrative that constructs Muslim subjectivity as credulous and submissive. In her comparative study of Islam and citizenship in the Netherlands, UK and France, Carolina Ivanescu (2016) includes a case study of Leicester, one of the most multicultural cities in the UK. Addressing the impact of the Prevent Strategy on the city's sizeable Muslim population, she notes its capacity to demonize Muslims as objects of suspicion, but also finds Muslims who approach Prevent as an opportunity. It is a way in which the community may receive government funding and a channel through which they can build links with local authorities, even if they are often required to 'situate themselves in relation to issues of national security and the perceived Islamic danger: radicalization' (Ivanescu 2016: 125). Other research has uncovered ways in which Prevent has been harnessed by Muslims as a means of empowerment, whether to secure funding for chaplaincy or reinforce an institutional case for Muslim representation (e.g. Aune, Guest and Law 2019; O'Toole et al. 2016). This is not at all to suggest the negative impact of initiatives like Prevent is counterbalanced by positive consequences. Nor is it to suggest the construction of Muslims in terms of risk is a price worth paying for any consequent visibility granted to their needs as a community. Rather, it is to call attention to the problem of assuming such securitization processes are uncritically and passively accepted by those whose lives are most impacted by them. To assume this is to reinforce a model of Muslim subjectivity that is as problematic as that identified by Clara Eroukhmanoff among US security personnel. It assumes surveillance cultures elicit responses that are uniformly compliant, as if power only moves in one direction (Lyon 2018: 49). This is as untrue of Muslims as it is of other religious groups. Even among those who feel most constrained by securitization measures nevertheless engage in a process of negotiation with the pressures imposed on them. How we can best make sense of this kind of religious selfhood in sociological terms is the topic of the following chapter.

Further reading

Much of this chapter arose out of research I conducted as part of the 'Representing Islam on Campus' project, which ran from 2014 until 2020. Covering the securitization of

Islam in UK universities, the project's findings were published in a book-length study – *Islam on Campus: Contested Identities and the Cultures of Higher Education in Britain* (2020), by Alison Scott-Baumann et al. – and a report – *Islam and Muslims on UK University Campuses: Perceptions and Challenges* (2020), by Mathew Guest et al. – which is freely available online.

The impact of securitization within broader social contexts is explored in a number of excellent published studies (e.g. Brown and Saeed 2014; Fernandez 2018; Karner and Parker 2017; O'Toole et al. 2016). Comparative analyses – whether examining securitization in different cultures (e.g. Humphrey 2009) or across the experiences of different religious communities within the same culture (e.g. Egorova 2018) – are especially illuminating.

For a theoretically subtle, insightful analysis of the securitization of Islam within US counter-terrorism initiatives, see Clara Eroukhmanoff's (2015) prize-winning article in the *Critical Studies on Terrorism* journal.

CHAPTER 6
RELIGION AND THE ENTREPRENEURIAL SELF

Embracing the entrepreneurial

In 2009 I attended a convention of the 'Global Leadership Summit' (GLS). What sounds like a very grand affair, perhaps something akin to the World Economic Forum in Davos, attracting world leaders and experts to grapple with global affairs, was actually a day-long training conference held at a local church in England, attended by maybe 100 people. The Global Leadership Summit is an initiative that was established in 1995 by the Willow Creek Association, closely linked to Willow Creek megachurch in Chicago, the famous church at which, until 2018, Bill Hybels was senior pastor. Willow Creek is famous for its church growth programmes (see Chapter 2) and had already made a name for itself as a standard bearer of the church growth philosophy long before the Willow Creek Association branched into leadership training. The GLS began as a mass conference held on Willow Creek's South Barrington campus, attracting aspiring pastors from across the United States with its impressive programme of expert speakers. Eventually, the initiative was extended to reach a global audience and was exported via a franchise model to local churches across the world. By 2009, 812 churches across the UK and Ireland were members of the Willow Creek network, receiving a monthly leadership audio resource, a quarterly publication on church leadership, access to free downloads and a range of discounts on Willow Creek events and resources. The 2009 Global Leadership Summit was convened at 14 venues across the UK and Ireland, together attracting over 3,100 delegates.

Curious to know more about this phenomenon, I found myself in St Albans, a leafy town in the English home counties. Located on what appeared to be an industrial estate, in a converted warehouse, was the town's Vineyard Church, part of the network of charismatic churches co-founded by John Wimber in the early 1980s. The St Alban's Vineyard had converted its industrial unit into a high-tech auditorium with impressive conference facilities and was hosting the GLS for interested church leaders from the area. The talks were played on DVDs projected onto a large screen at the front of the church, small group discussion followed specially devised workbooks and the event book shop sold publications by the guest speakers as well as other writers on the subject of leadership. They included *Leading the Revolution* by Gary Hamel, described on his website as 'one of the world's most iconoclastic and influential business thinkers'; *How the Mighty Fall, and Why Some Companies Never Give In* by former faculty member of the Stanford Graduate School of Business Jim Collins, who was listed by Forbes as one of 2017's 100 greatest living business minds; and *The 360 Degree Leader: Developing Your*

Influence from Anywhere in the Organization by pastor, multi-million selling author and leadership guru John C. Maxwell, co-founder of EQUIP, which claims to have trained six million Christian leaders in more than 185 countries. The GLS speakers for 2009, whose talks were projected onto the screen for the St Alban's delegates, included Tim Keller (senior pastor of Redeemer Presbyterian Church in Manhattan, NY), Jessica Jackley (co-founder of Kiva, the world's first peer-to-peer micro-lending website) and Chip and Dan Heath (business consultants and authors of *Made to Stick: Why Some Ideas Survive and Others Die*, also on the bookstall). Everything was emblazoned with the GLS Willow Creek brand. The church itself had a commercial-style coffee shop, as well as a comfortable 'green room', well stocked with complimentary refreshments for the organizers and worship band, who had opened proceedings. And while some of the guest speakers were church leaders, most were not, and some were held up as examples of great leadership because of their success in the corporate world.

The Global Leadership Summit provides a fascinating insight into how religious initiatives and ideas from commercial business sometimes converge in the twenty-first century. This is a convergence of ideas and methods, but it is also a convergence of resources, with church leaders turning to private business for models of success and vitality. To be precise, the GLS does not represent a simple embrace of the profit motive, baptizing material wealth as divine blessing like advocates of the prosperity gospel. In fact, the speakers included cautionary advice, calls for corporate responsibility and were not uncritical supporters of free market capitalism. Rather, the overall message of the GLS is more akin to what William Davies describes as 'social optimization', the fusion of instrumentalist market thinking with a recognition that people are often motivated by altruism, loyalty and shared identities. Whether this represents a humanization of capitalism or the instrumentalization of the social in the interests of power and profit is open to debate (Davies 2015: 184). But this amalgam of social awareness and a hard-nosed focus on goal-oriented efficacy has an obvious appeal for churches motivated by growth and the expansion of their influence. They aspire to achieve presence, vitality and impact on an ambitious scale. The message emerging from the GLS emphasizes the power of human potential, harnessed through determination, inventiveness, relationship-building and an entrepreneurial approach to problem-solving (Guest 2010: 272–3). This latter idea – of the *entrepreneurial* – reflects the event's promotion of creative thinkers and bold pragmatists. In heeding lessons from business, the charitable sector *and* church, it embodies a neoliberal assumption that all problems can be reduced to practical factors that can be addressed using learnable skills and a 'can-do' attitude, regardless of the sphere of life in which they occur. Pastors can learn lessons from business because they essentially face the same kinds of challenges in church, amenable to the same logic. But this logic is mastered via an application of an entrepreneurial approach: bold, unintimidated by failure, pragmatic and ambitious. GLS teaches pastors to heed the lessons of those who have overcome the challenges life has thrown at them by dogged persistence and a willingness to think outside of the box.

This chapter discusses several ways in which religious movements have embraced an entrepreneurial approach within the neoliberal age. It considers a range of examples to illustrate how religious entrepreneurialism reflects the embrace of market norms addressed in Chapter 2. In their indebtedness to a neoliberal model of entrepreneurialism, they illustrate how empowerment and agency are not mobilized outside of existing social structures but through them. But beyond sound marketing, the entrepreneurial also represents an orientation to self-formation; by drawing on sociological theories of identity it is possible to examine how religious movements turn to entrepreneurial strategies of engagement as a means of working on the self. In so doing, they generate powerful mechanisms for maintaining relations of power, even while appearing to free the individual from those very same bonds.

Celebrity, entertainment and the spectacular

It was the icon of 1960s 'pop art' Andy Warhol who became associated with the idea that we will soon live in a time when everyone will get their fifteen minutes of fame. The phrase can be traced to an exchange between Warhol and a photographer; seeing the crowds of people wanting to be part of the picture, the artist is reputed to have said, 'Everyone wants to be famous.' The photographer's reply – 'Yeah, for about 15 minutes, Andy' – hints at the cost of fame, the adoration counterbalanced with the discomfort of public exposure. It speaks to the complex tension between private and public identity that has become a characteristic of late modern culture – the paradox of personal recognition granted via public visibility. Warhol's phrase also resonates with sociological accounts of modernity that emphasize the collapse of traditional hierarchies of representation. The question of who gets to be famous is one bound up in processes of detraditionalization, as the old authorities become destabilized and fame becomes more available to a wider range of people. If we were to ask which figures were most famous – best known to the general public – in early 1950s Britain, we would be faced with a list of royalty, politicians and radio presenters: all white, upper class and mostly men. By the 1960s this had begun to change, and the growth of pop music, alongside the increasing availability of television, brought a new host of 'celebrities' to the attention of the public, some even with regional accents. This democratization of public space changed the nature of 'fame', as it altered the range of cultural resources available to ordinary people.

Around the turn of the millennium, a fresh set of innovations sparked further resonances with Warhol's well-known phrase. Two are especially important. First, the emergence of reality television in the 1990s extended the democratization of fame inaugurated earlier, placing members of the public at the centre of a range of TV series. Formats vary, including house and garden makeover shows, knockout series in which contestants compete on the basis of a given skill (cooking, singing, dancing, sewing) and endurance-based competitions in which participants strive to coexist within a contrived environment (e.g. a desert island, tropical jungle or a locked house). Reality TV remains hugely popular, if often controversial, and it is tempting to view it as the ultimate realization of Warhol's prediction. It has massively expanded the number of individuals in the public eye and transformed the idea of 'celebrity'. Fame is no longer contingent on a particular talent (whether in sport, journalism, acting or popular music, for example); instead, it has developed to include fame as a consequence of fame itself. The 'celebrities' that often appear on TV panel shows are now famous for having been on reality TV shows.

Second, the creation of the internet marked an unprecedented expansion in the range of information available, introducing new – and inexpensive – opportunities for global connectivity. The emergence of social media heightened interactive possibilities further. Platforms like Facebook, Instagram and Twitter can be described as free in the sense of incurring no direct financial cost to their users and of being relatively unregulated spaces for the exchange of information, images, video and comment. In recent years, the successful exploitation of such platforms has generated a new breed of celebrity. 'Influencers' who generate enough 'followers' make their material – whether concerned with children's education, beauty products or fashion – attractive to commercial sponsors, leading to lucrative income streams. Because the web is largely a visual medium, it is perhaps not surprising that the most successful and popular influencers are concerned with matters of image.

There is a particular style of evangelical Christianity that has drawn inspiration from this set of cultural developments. In one sense it builds on a tradition of cultural borrowing put in the service of communicating a compelling message. As societies are perceived as drifting into a secular or morally bankrupt state of normlessness, so the evangelical desire to speak in culturally compelling terms becomes more urgent. While some fundamentalists have responded by speaking more loudly, most have come around to the idea of speaking *differently* and in a language more people might hear. But this cultural sensitivity has, I would suggest, taken a particularly interesting path in recent decades. An example will help to show what this path entails.

I once attended a dedication service for a child of a friend of mine. It was held in his church, an independent evangelical church on the outskirts of the north-eastern English town where I lived at the time. This was a church that had been established decades before, but, with the help of tithing, fund-raising and collaboration with local businesses, established a brand new premises in 2010 that doubled up as a conference centre, located on a nearby industrial estate (not unlike my St Alban's experience). A high and spacious foyer gave way to bright, airy function rooms, with a Starbucks coffee shop established within the same premises, a result of a franchise arrangement. As I made my way to the back of the foyer, directed to the service itself, I saw we were heading into a large auditorium. At the front was a stage, on which a worship band were playing very loud praise songs using professional equipment that wouldn't have been out of place at a rock concert. A huge sound desk stood at the back of the hall, from where a sound engineer controlled the PA system. In between were many rows of movable chairs, most empty because the majority of those present were standing up, singing along to the songs, waving their hands in the air, greeting familiar co-worshippers with smiles, hugs and slaps on the back. During a brief lull in the sung worship, the pastor – a cheerful looking man in jeans and a jumper, speaking with a local accent – offered a brief welcome. And then, something unexpected happened. We moved into what I only later realized was this church's version of 'notices'. All churches have this: a moment in the middle of the service when someone gets up and makes a few announcements – details of that week's Bible study, news of a new creche facility, a guest speaker is coming to talk about their new book, Dave and Judy are having another baby and so on. They are delivered with varying degrees of enthusiasm, often read from sheets of paper, and amount to a few brief bits of information in which the congregation might be expected to have some interest. Five minutes, ten at most. In this church, 'notices' was a series of professionally produced video trailers, with soundtracks, edited together and projected onto a huge screen at the back of the stage. For a minute, I thought I was watching a set of advertisements for commercial products, the stylistic similarity to a TV commercial break was so striking. When I realized the 'products' were youth-oriented Christian events, I deduced that this must be a set of events happening nationally and that the church was promoting festivals and gatherings from their wider network, events their own members might be interested in attending. But this was not the case. What I was witnessing was the church's own events. I really *was* witnessing their version of 'notices': locally set, in-house, church-organized opportunities for congregants to gather together. They had recast their locally based church life using the methods and imagery associated with Hollywood moviemaking. The production quality was superb; the audio-visual synchronicity was professional standard; the overall look was expensive, vibrant, dynamic, youthful and exciting. I was being sold a very particular kind of Christianity, which used a very distinctive set of tools to promote itself.

Churches like the one described above can be found across the global north. They are often independent, but sometimes they situate themselves within organized networks. Like regional supermarkets keen to spread their commercial scope while retaining a distinctive brand, those that are most successful expand into multiple sites, establishing a vibrant presence in different residential locations while preserving a singular style, and often the same overall pastor, and so build a corporate brand identity. These churches are for the most part evangelical, often charismatic, often attracting a congregation that is younger than average, with a corresponding emphasis upon qualities and experiences associated with younger generations: energy, determination, creativity, dedication, a zest for life and an enthusiasm for God. The energy is home-grown, but the model of church is often learnt from elsewhere.

One of the most paradigmatic churches in this tradition is Hillsong, founded in 1983 by senior pastor Brian Houston and his wife Bobbie in New South Wales, Australia. From its foundation until 2018, Hillsong was formally part of the Australian branch of the Pentecostal denomination the Assemblies of God, but in practice has for many years functioned as an independent network of large churches, now based in fourteen nations across the world. As such, it has developed its own brand of church, appealing to young people by echoing their experience and priorities as global citizens of the twenty-first century. Worship music is professionally produced (and can be consumed outside church via CDs and downloads), lives are affirmed rather than challenged and the images that adorn Hillsong promotional material reflect a vibrant, youthful existence in which everyone is beautiful, healthy, happy and exuberant. It currently claims to attract around 100,000 individuals to more than eighty churches across the world. These constitute a global network concentrated in urban centres, including major cities such as London, Paris, Amsterdam, New York City, Los Angeles and Cape Town. Beyond its own churches, Hillsong has – like several of the biggest, most successful megachurches – achieved the status of 'influencer', effectively setting the agenda and standard for many other churches that seek to emulate Hillsong's appeal and success.

These neo-Pentecostal churches share a number of common features, possible to summarize in terms of *performance*, *professionalism* and a distinct style of leader, described by some as the *pastorpreneur*. Performance captures the 'theatre-style church services that offer intense multisensorial experiences', emulating popular music styles and hence 'blurring the boundaries between entertainment and Christian religion' (Klaver 2015: 149). Scale is important, and there is a mirroring of the megachurch tradition, whereby worship spaces are modern and adaptable to maximize capacity and also accommodate the latest technology. This leads on to the professionalism that marks a shared aspiration to maintain the same standards of media production associated with the entertainment and movie industries. This translates into high levels of spending, often funded via tithing by the congregation, but sometimes supplemented by commercial opportunities generated by the possession of state-of-the-art buildings and facilities. Hillsong's main church building, situated in the north-western suburbs of Sydney, is a vast complex, purpose-built at a cost of A\$25 million and includes a 3,500-seat auditorium. Like the church described earlier, it invests in high production value, and its digital audio system alone cost A\$4 million (Connell 2005: 320–1). At a practical level, this reflects a desire to maintain a spectacular church experience, impressive by broader secular standards of performance and entertainment. Symbolically, it reflects a desire to appear credible in mainstream commercial terms (Bielo 2019). To establish and maintain this kind of church requires entrepreneurial leadership. Neo-Pentecostal churches are mostly independent and so – at least in the beginning – cannot depend on cross-subsidy from others in the same denomination or network. They are also materially ambitious – their services demand expensive technology, advanced skills in operating it and a ready stock of human capital in the form of volunteers from the congregation, willing to invest lots of time and energy to make it all work. Demanding affordable but spacious accommodation, these churches are often situated in out-of-town locations, in buildings that look more like conference centres than traditional churches. Consequently, they also need to deploy strong marketing and promotion, including via online media. Those who oversee all of this are required to have skills in facilitation, people management, fund-raising, public speaking, networking, and the ability to motivate and inspire an energetic, largely unpaid team of workers. It is therefore fitting that those successful in this role have been dubbed 'pastorpreneurs'.

Hillsong is notable for affirming a message and style of Christianity that favours the tackling of life's challenges via individual effort rather than social-structural change. In this, it sits within a long-established tradition in the evangelical movement, emphasizing the experience of being 'born again' and the personal journey with God that is unique to each believer. From an early embrace of a 'prosperity' message, Hillsong has since tended to borrow from the language of popular psychology, focusing on human flourishing, on realizing our full potential and on the empowerment one can enjoy upon embracing a godly life. It mirrors the values of late modernity in affirming, as Matthew Wade puts it, 'the inviolable integrity of the individual and the right and responsibility to realise his/her own ideals for perpetual reinvention' (2016: 673). In taking seriously the challenges of building a coherent sense of self within an uncertain world, Hillsong has obvious appeal to young adults. It also embodies the neoliberal prioritization of the self-directed individual, so that the successful life is the life in which the individual is enabled and empowered to realize their full potential. But Hillsong remains firmly evangelical and so inhabits a tradition that retains particular religious and moral assumptions, including about the proper role of men and women. In this context, how is the neoliberal self-empowered while also being formed in the model of gender traditionalism? We will return to this question in the next chapter.

An inclination among evangelicals to borrow tools from the entertainment industry is nothing new. During the 1920s and 1930s, the famous Pentecostal preacher Aimee Semple McPherson had, according to Linda Ambrose, an 'unmatched flair for the theatrical', which was reflected in her highly dramatic sermons, featuring stage props, special effects and an overall feel for the spectacular (Ambrose 2017: 108). One sermon featured Sister Aimee bringing a motorcycle on stage, whose siren was sounded loud and long to convey to the audience the urgency of the need to be saved. McPherson's church was Angelus Temple, located in Los Angeles, not far from Hollywood, and remains a popular megachurch to this day. By 2008, Richard Flory and Donald Miller were describing a megachurch event in California featuring the 'WORRRLD CHAMMMPION MOTORCROSS RIDERS FOR JESUS!', performing daring stunts before a stadium of enthusiasts as a warm-up act for evangelist Greg Laurie (Flory and Miller 2008: 59). While not all evangelical churches feature motorcycle stunts, the flair for the spectacular extends well beyond the more colourful corners of the United States. Birgit Meyer writes of the 'spectacularization' evident among Pentecostal megachurches in Ghana, for example, a pattern she links to the turn to democracy in various African countries, which has typically been accompanied by the 'liberalization and commercialization of hitherto state-controlled media' (Meyer 2007: 19–20).

The congregational size of these churches is contingent on their immediate cultural context, but their aesthetic style, social ambition and thirst for professional standards of presentation can be found across the world. The church where I attended the dedication service of my friend's child, described earlier, while reasonably large by UK standards, still only had a congregation of 2–300, a fraction of the Australian and American megachurches it sought to emulate. Megachurches like Hillsong, Saddleback, Lakewood and Planetshakers have established a certain slick, glitzy, stadium rock professionalism that has become a template for evangelical churches the world over (Figure 6).

One way in which to interpret this phenomenon sociologically is as a strategy for attracting new converts, aping the look and feel of elements of popular culture as a means of heightening appeal. Evoking the market analogy discussed in Chapter 2, churches are functioning like commercial businesses in order to maximize their attractiveness to a

Figure 6 The interior of Lakewood Church, Houston, Texas, during a worship service in 2013. The auditorium has a capacity of 16,800. *Source*: Wikimedia.

given market niche. But there is another dimension that has more to do with aesthetics, performance and professionalism. I want to suggest that this tendency, characterized by a turn to the cosmetic – or *cosmeticization* – is worth considering in its own right, rather than simply as effective marketing. It is worth considering because it brings with it implications for how the religious self is performed and how particular forms of identity are privileged as a consequence.

Cultivating the religious self

Given sociological accounts of modernity have often foregrounded a turn towards individualism, it is not surprising that those same accounts have inspired new theorizations of the self. One approach can be found in Anthony Giddens's book *Modernity and Self-Identity*, which presents identity as a reflexive achievement, the personal construction of a narrative lending coherence to life when external circumstances remain unstable or uncertain (Giddens 1991). This emphasis upon self-empowered identity formation has filtered into discussions of religious innovation, including a turn to the subjective or spirituality, that conceives of religious traditions as sources for the self (Heelas and Woodhead 2005). Australian sociologist Adam Possamai goes further in arguing that the circumstances of neoliberalism demand a redefinition of religion, which is best conceived as a 'social tool' that works to further, heal or entertain the self (Possamai 2018: 202). However, this approach risks emphasizing the empowerment of the self while overlooking the social conditions that shape it. We discussed in Chapter 2 the work of Véronique Altglas, which challenges the assumption that alternative spiritualities reflect an unfettered individualism, instead highlighting how such choices are framed by social status, not least by social class (Altglas 2014). To retrieve a sociology of the entrepreneurial religious self that reflects the circumstances of the twenty-first century, there is a need to acknowledge the internalization of entrepreneurial norms into constructions of religious identity, as exemplified in the cases from evangelical Christianity described earlier. But it is also important that notions of individual empowerment that emerge from this remain contextualized in relation to the social and religious circumstances in which they are set. This is especially important insofar as these circumstances reflect a particular configuration of power.

A helpful means of bridging this divide can be found in the work of Canadian sociologist Erving Goffman. Goffman never wrote about religion and yet his numerous publications on the self and social identities have been hugely influential across the social sciences. It is Goffman's 1959 book *The Presentation of the Self in Everyday Life* that is most relevant for our present purposes and is the work to which his influential perspective on the self is most often traced. Breaking from previous social theorists who conceived of social identities as determined by pre-existing social structures, Goffman views the self as active, and as capable of adapting to and performing in a variety of situations. This is reflected in the dramaturgical metaphor for which Goffman is well known. Individuals behave differently according to the different roles they are playing, including those which are 'backstage' in contrast to those which may be described as 'front-stage'. The imam assumes a different style of speech, gesture and deportment depending on whether they are addressing their community at Friday prayers, advising a regular at the mosque about spiritual matters or discussing the latest news with their partner over dinner. Importantly, Goffman does not treat these personas as situational masks that conceal our 'true selves'. Rather, the very fact that we selectively adopt and shift into these personas is a reflection of who we are. The observation that selves are acts of presentation is hardly novel; what Goffman is arguing is that 'the very structure of the self can be seen in terms of how we arrange for such performances in . . . society' (1959: 244).

Goffman is especially helpful in challenging dominant paradigms in the sociology of religion because he begins with the self, rather than tradition, community or movement. His approach is especially apposite within a neoliberal context because it can accommodate the possibility of multiple identities and identity change. When identity is conceived as a complex process of performance, responsive to situational change and role allocation, its entrepreneurial dimension is brought to the surface. Individual agency remains central, with roles things to be inhabited and negotiated, rather than inherited or determined by external structures. Goffman's approach highlights dynamic processes of identity enactment, important in understanding the significance of religious identities that are treated as ongoing projects. Finally, Goffman argues that people are involved in an ongoing process of *impression management*, evident when we 'try and make the invisible visible in order to dramatize our roles' (Lawler 2014: 121). The Bible study group member who places their well-thumbed Bible on the coffee table, multiple post-it note bookmarks visible as a sign of regular, committed usage; the Muslim woman who refuses to shake hands with a man but makes a slight bow while placing her hands on her heart as a sign of piety *and* politeness. Goffman sustains attention on how identities are performed for the benefit of a social group. Remaining attentive to these human tendencies enables us to understand better how the entrepreneurial and the religious become fused within neoliberal contexts.

Aesthetics, emotions and the religious self

In the twenty-first century, entrepreneurial religion commonly includes an appeal to the cosmetic. Identities are performed with reference to a set of cultural resources derived from the worlds of media and entertainment, and as such take on a distinct visual quality. The pattern here is well illustrated by returning to the neo-Pentecostal churches described earlier. All of these churches are – broadly speaking – Protestant, associated theologically with personal faith and the authority of the Bible. And yet the descriptions of Hillsong and similar churches illustrate the importance they attach to image, embodiment and performance. The theological legacy of the Reformation has encouraged a presentation of Protestant churches as focused chiefly on the interior life of faith. Materiality and ritual have often been excluded on the assumption that these constitute the Catholic heritage against which Martin Luther was reacting in the sixteenth century. And yet, as a number of anthropologists have observed, there are striking aspects of Protestant religion bound up in material and ritualized expression (Coleman 1996; Meyer and Houtman 2012). These are overlooked if observed through a lens that prioritizes interiority and personal faith as the axes of Protestant identity. What I am arguing here is this conception of Protestantism as material religion is developed a step further once the cosmetic dimension is fully acknowledged.

The phenomenon can be described as an aesthetic style which, transmitted both in person and online via global networks, emerges as a template that other leaders and churchgoers can emulate (Klaver 2015). Christian identity is modelled via chiefly visual imagery and predominantly via the human body. The public image of these churches is conveyed via the exuberant, inspired bodies of those who have embraced the experience available within. And these images are tailored for circulation and re-appropriation within a global network, an imagined community of like-minded and like-bodied Christians. Addressing the example of Hillsong, Miranda Klaver observes how this aesthetic style takes the form of a 'product' that is standardized and portable across national borders, an arrangement necessary if the emerging package is to appeal to a transnational audience: 'Use in Hillsong network churches of the same inspirational videos, identical lighting schemes and smoke effects, and even replication of bodily gestures and language expressions on stage leaves little room for experiment or improvisation on the part of the various Hillsong churches' (Klaver 2016: 152).

These developments point to a shift in the cultural landscapes within which religious identities are formed and expressed. A turn to the cosmetic – or a 'cosmeticization' –

mirrors the emphasis upon a crafted, aesthetic self that valorizes norms of beauty and youthfulness. But if one element of this is the circulation of images and visual tropes that mirror celebrity culture, another is the cultivation of embodied emotional states that convey credibility or status within religious contexts. The work of Amy Wilkins – undertaken at the interface of sociology and social psychology – is especially insightful here. It explores how particular emotions are interpreted among evangelical communities as indicators of Christian faith, virtue or wholesomeness. Wilkins's comparative study *Wannabes, Goths and Christians* (2008a) breaks new ground in its identification of *visible happiness* as an evangelical identity marker. Based on qualitative research into the lives of evangelical students at a US college, Wilkins's work focuses on happiness not as an internal state but as 'an emotional culture learned and given meaning through social interaction' (2008b: 283). Here she is drawing on Goffman's work on how identities emerge via performance and on the work of sociologists like Arlie Russell Hochschild on how emotions are subject to processes of conscious management (Hochschild 1983). Among the evangelicals that Wilkins studied, happiness is assumed to be both desirable and achievable, and an experience that distinguishes Christians from non-Christians. Happiness, as Wilkins puts it, is compulsory, and the performance of emotions that suggest its absence – anger, sadness, disappointment – implies a Christian faith that is incomplete or inauthentic. By contrast, evangelical Christians learn to interpret their own happiness as evidence of their intimacy with God and their moral correctness. This impulse to manage the presentation of the self illustrates how a sociological understanding of religious identity can move beyond more discursive emphases on beliefs, creeds and scripted rituals. But it also uncovers a potential among religious actors to accredit emotional states with particular meanings, in turn highlighting how religious identity is a matter of recognition as well as self-identification. It is not enough to proclaim one's own evangelical status verbally – although this may be expected as a precondition of acceptance, especially when 'testimonies of faith' are important. It is also necessary to embody that identity in a way that's convincing among the existing group, and this may have as much to do with emotions and moods as it does with words and ideas.

Wilkins's study, however, goes further than this, proposing an approach to understanding the relationship between thought and emotion. Specifically, she finds among evangelical Christians a complex connection between *feeling* happiness and *learning to talk and think* about it in a particular way. It is in this sense that Wilkins writes about 'emotional culture' (2008b: 282), a set of meanings and practices modelled by existing members via their interactive styles of evangelism, the wording used in promotional literature, conversion stories shared at meetings and direct instruction on introspective methods based around solitary reflection, prayer and Bible reading. All reinforce a shared culture that cultivates a set of skills for managing emotions. This includes an element of what Arlie Russell Hochschild (1983) calls 'deep acting', as participants learn to recognize and replicate the shape of an inner feeling or emotion. As they learn to recognize what the right kind of emotions feel like for that group, so they also develop strategies for holding themselves to account for feeling those emotions and hence feeling like a legitimate and *authentic* Christian by the group's standards. This is echoed in anthropologist Tanya Luhrmann's book *When God Talks Back*, which explores how evangelicals in the United States learn to recognize when God is present and when he responds to them. Her book focuses on the Vineyard Christian Fellowship, the charismatic network of churches which hosted the GLS event I described at the beginning of this chapter. Its founder, John Wimber, embodied a form of Christianity that assumed God to be intimately present; those with genuine faith have access to his power just as they may hear his words. Luhrmann shows how members of the Vineyard learn that God speaks to them within their own minds. They learn the importance of developing 'the ability to recognize thoughts in their own mind that are not in fact their thoughts, but God's' (Luhrmann 2012: 39). This may sound like a peculiar line of analysis for a social scientist; it appears to address questions of divine presence ordinarily within the remit of theology. And yet following Goffman's approach to identity as performance, and Wilkins's recognition that emotional management can be an important dimension of religious identity, these issues take on a fresh sense of sociological relevance. To ask how individuals recognize God to be present is not to ask *whether* God is present but to explore the process whereby internal dialogue becomes ascribed with divine significance. It is also to explore how this process is learned as a skill within a given socio-religious context.

One way in which contextual norms become central here is in the association of emotional expression with cultural identity, so that a cultural performance of religion can signal a form of belonging. For example, happiness can feature in attempts by religious groups to acclimatize to the standards of a more neoliberal culture to which they have migrated. Williams and Vashi describe how a second-generation migrant experience means many Muslims in the United States are constructing an American Islam, reflecting their liminal status between two realms. They describe a class at a masjid, at which an out-of-town sheikh addressed an audience about Islamic marriage practices. Distinguishing between traditions that are Islamic and those that are particular to Arab and Pakistani culture, he questioned the wisdom of arranged marriages, emphasizing instead the importance of a relationship of love freely chosen and characterized by respect and happiness (Williams and Vashi 2007: 278–9).

The skills and capabilities that are important to the performance of religious identities are not detached from other markers of identity. Wilkins's study focuses on a campus-based Christian organization that she calls 'Unity', its members primarily from white middle-class backgrounds. The relational styles of expression favoured by them are also those commonly associated with the middle classes – good cheer, friendliness, warmth and personality. What are presented as expressions of religious commitment can serve as behavioural identity markers that link religious groups with a particular social demographic. Wilkins finds that the emotional states that are promoted here are also taken as indicators of moral character. To be happy is associated with being a good person, while bad feelings are viewed as the universal outcome of the immoral behaviours from which they abstain, such as pre-marital sex and drinking. As Wilkins concludes, 'the desire for good feelings motivate, explain, and naturalize other moral choices. These choices, in turn, allow Unity Christians to think of themselves as strong, grounded, purposeful, and self-controlled' (Wilkins 2008b: 297).

Research among middle-class Christian university students in the UK reflects some analogous patterns. Taking her lead from Weber, Gerrard (2014) argues that UK universities are characterized by a pervasive 'learning ethic' that re-inscribes the logic of neoliberal capitalism. As students learn to be rational, worthwhile, successful subjects they also internalize their role as consumers of higher education, chiefly understood as a means to economic advancement. This emphasis has been apparent in government policy and internal university management following the sector's accelerated marketization since 2010 (Brady 2012). Within this context, do Christian students imagine their futures in terms of neoliberal models of success, or does their faith lead them to develop a more resistant identity? Invited to comment on their aspirations for the future, Christian students affirm different strategies for negotiating between their religious values, an uncertain future and the neoliberal pressures of the university. Some imagine a future structured around Christian resistance to capitalist injustice, with their careers viewed as channels for the furtherance of moral good and the dissemination of Christian truth. But these expressions of conviction are heavily influenced by middle-class mores, as well as a privileged status free from the risk of economic precarity. Here, 'aspiration emerges as an imagined site for positioning oneself as different from a perceived norm, i.e. a narrative of western capitalism that foregrounds moral failings to do with selfishness, superficiality and materialism' (Guest and Aune 2017: 8.3). In other words, neoliberal themes can inform an entrepreneurial religious self by serving as a focus of opposition and protest.

Experts and enablers of the religious self

If the lens of the entrepreneurial self illuminates how religious identities are worked on, consciously developed and form part of the wider negotiation of life in neoliberal times, this process also has its own external resources. To treat identity in terms of its resources is to invite consideration of a range of familiar entities, all of which may play an important part in shaping the ways in which individuals embody their religious convictions. Places of worship, sacred texts, religious officials like ordained priests, local imams or rabbis – all often play important roles in religious identity formation. Within neoliberal cultural conditions, another source emerges that is of particular interest: the expert in identity development. The emergence of fields of expertise in enhancing human potential – often in the service of commercial markets – is brilliantly charted in William Davies's book *The Happiness Industry: How the Government and Big Business Sold Us Wellbeing*. Davies traces the ways in which sub-disciplines within psychology, economics and business management evolved in dialogue with industry in the developed world. New methods for understanding human identity and behaviour were often shaped by the desire to maximize labour efficiency and private profit. As this body of 'expertise' took on new forms throughout the twentieth century, the focus of its application shifted.

Whereas previously, business consultants, marketing gurus and time and motion analysts advised business managers on how to troubleshoot problems of efficiency, these same 'experts' were later called upon to intervene in the workplace, addressing these problems directly with the individual worker. What emerged was a range of coaching programmes and training courses brought in by both private business and public sector organizations, sustaining a new industry in motivational consultancy which tended to imagine workplace problems as limitations located within the attitude of the individual. Interventions aimed to restore the individual's 'self-belief and optimism with ruthless efficiency' (Davies 2015: 111).

The focus here is the individual subject. The problem is not the business, its structures or the inequalities of wealth inherited by those who are struggling to stay focused; it is Pete's fault for having the wrong attitude. This constitutes a powerful channel through which neoliberal assumptions about individualism remain socially embedded. Jeremy Carrette and Richard King find the discipline of psychology to be important in this respect, influential because its notion of the psychological self appears to have been naturalized, achieving the status of common sense. How else are we to understand who we are and how we behave? They go further, arguing that psychology 'is the regime of knowledge that dovetails with capitalism because its attempt to stabilise the self for the services of society is useful for law, order and the market' (Carrette and King 2005: 63).

A popularized form of this strand of psychology has been highly influential within some religious circles. A long line of self-appointed experts have merged insights from this discipline with Christian teaching. Crucial here was Norman Vincent Peale, who first published *The Power of Positive Thinking* in 1952. Happily embracing one critic's description of him as 'God's salesman', Peale pursued a lifetime of Christian ministry distinguished by the use of popular media to reach as large an audience as possible. He was the pastor of Marble Collegiate Church in New York for over fifty years, and it was here that Donald Trump and his family encountered Peale's message in the 1970s. Trump would later describe Peale as a mentor, and while the future president's involvement in his church was, to all accounts, perfunctory, he would certainly come to embody Peale's message of self-belief. Marble Collegiate Church became a valuable conduit for Peale's teaching, located on Fifth Avenue in the heart of Manhattan. However, most of his influence was channelled via the Foundation for Christian Living, based in the rural town of Pawling, 70 miles upstate, which was the nerve centre of his independent ministry. This ministry – distinguished by international speaking tours and a mailing list with close to one million subscribers – was made possible by the substantial royalty income generated by his multi-million selling self-help books. By far his most significant was *The Power of Positive Thinking*, which combined elements of evangelical Christianity, the New Thought tradition associated with Christian Science and popular notions of the American Dream. Peale saw his book as a practical guide to living, grounded in orthodox Christianity, although his critics were less convinced, accusing him of syncretism, heresy and establishing a cult of personality. The book's mass appeal, though, was undeniable and was rooted in its direct, problem-solving message, using anecdotes from Peale's speaking tours to illustrate how everyday challenges of ennui and depression can be dealt with using a simple three-stage formula: 'picturize' a desired goal, engage in prayer about it to seek God's guidance and then take practical steps to realize it. Historian Carol George summarizes the rationale for Peale's approach as 'premised on two modest assumptions: that there were significant numbers of people who thought they were sick, in need of care, and incapable of being full productive contributors to society; and that they were sufficiently interested in being restored that they were willing to try his therapeutic message of practical Christianity, and not incidentally, buy the book' (George 1993: 137) (Figure 7).

Peale's influence can be felt to this day, shaping an accessible philosophy that merges evangelicalism, popular psychology and well-being culture, and the conservative assumption that society's problems are best addressed not via structural change or government but through the self-directed transformation of individuals. Peale's commercial success also enabled him to conduct his ministry with relative autonomy from the religious organizations to which he owed allegiance. This captures something about his influence and its sociological bases: it was founded on a form of charisma developed because of its relative independence, rather than because of his position as a pastor or church official. In this Peale mirrors the pastorpreneurs mentioned earlier, who draw their status not from denominational appointment or training but through a 'performative style' that authenticates their position in the eyes of their followers (Klaver 2015: 153). It is perhaps significant that Peale's impact as an international public speaker was the foundation for his work as an author, rather than the other way around.

While drawing on a tradition of Christian self-help and motivational speaking indebted to Norman Vincent Peale, the twenty-first century's 'experts' in religious selfhood adopt

Figure 7 Norman Vincent Peale during the 1940s. *Source*: National Portrait Gallery, Smithsonian Institution, photo by Oscar White.

a much more technologically ambitious approach. Perhaps the most striking, influential example is Texan author and megachurch pastor Joel Osteen (figure 8). The youngest son of pastor John Osteen, Joel worked for seventeen years on the production side of his father's TV ministry. His skill in managing the delivery of a well-marketed message via multimedia platforms has undoubtedly contributed to his success as a preacher and author. He took over as pastor of Lakewood Church in Houston following his father's unexpected death in 1999. The younger Osteen describes his movement into public preaching as a reluctant one but says he was told by God to accept his father's request to preach in his stead.

Osteen fuses the language of the self-help industry with that of charismatic Christianity. The charismatic emphasis on encountering God's power in the immediacy of one's everyday experience remains but is enveloped within a feel-good message of universal affirmation. According to Osteen, 'faith to me is having a positive outlook, believing that things are going to get better and expecting good things in life. God's given you the strength to endure a tough time' (quoted in Einstein 2008: 124). While Osteen's message is unremarkable in placing a slant on the positive – an optimistic, celebratory tone can be found across the Pentecostal movement, for example – it is distinctive for disavowing the traditional evangelical emphasis on sin.

His message is also marked by its stress on the pragmatic, something he inherits from Peale. Both preachers present their spoken and published message via the medium of direct, practical guidelines that their audience can easily digest and apply in their everyday lives. Osteen accentuates his personable humility – he didn't want to be a preacher because he was shy and didn't think he could fill his father's shoes; his sermons are peppered with

Figure 8 Joel Osteen preaching at Lakewood Church, Houston, Texas. *Source*: Justin Brackett/ Wikimedia Commons.

personal stories and self-deprecating jokes; he is referred to in all marketing and church promotional materials as 'Joel', always smiling, always encouraging. To underline this, Mara Einstein points to one appearance on the 'An Evening with Joel' speaking tour, where Osteen's wife Victoria took to the stage to proclaim 'Joel is exactly what you see on TV in his personal life', reinforcing his status as knowable: a familiar friend (Einstein 2008: 135). At the same time, he is the pastor of possibly the largest congregation in the United States (approximately 50,000 attendees weekly – see figure 6), is a best-selling author, a wealthy media celebrity, a successful public speaker and a loving family man with an attractive wife. He models a particular version of the American Dream, a notion not inconsistent with the prosperity message promoted at Lakewood. The Osteen brand is about success, and this is modelled as well as preached.

Osteen's ministry bridges the familiar and the exceptional, presenting an aspirational message that recognizes where people are, but also points to where they could be. The distinctive combination of ideas evident in Osteen's message highlights the evolution of particular strands in the 'operant theology' of evangelical Christianity. Perhaps more than ever, evangelicalism draws on a range of cultural sources beyond formal, espoused theological frameworks (Ward 2017); part of this involves the extended invocation of subjective experience as a site of Christian meaning-making. This is an important observation, because it reminds us that formal statements of belief – issued by a wide range of religious groups and movements – do not always function in a straightforward way (nor take conventional forms, as readers of Osteen's books might agree). Assuming belief statements serve as a blueprint for religious identity is to overlook how they *function* within the social realities of religious life. It also overlooks the performative character of religious identity, which calls for an approach that recognizes agency, a negotiation of shifting resources and an entrepreneurial orientation that seeks new inspiration among the complexities of twenty-first-century life.

These complexities include engagement with new media, and this can have unexpected consequences. For example, the case of Judah Smith, pastor of Churchome in Washington state, reveals how online media can refract broader themes of mobility and self-empowerment. Jessica Johnson comments on the ministry of Smith who, while based in Seattle, delivers his message on a global platform through tours and appearances. Moreover,

> the web site advertising his book *Jesus Is* _____ , much like Pastor Judah himself, is constantly on the move. The *Jesus Is* _____ campaign uses a participatory, user-friendly digital platform to simulate a perpetual process of branding that, in appearing seamless, democratic, and autonomous, serves to affirm his self-presentation as an approachably hip dude who is relatable despite his celebrity. (Johnson 2017: 170–1)

Johnson's study of Judah Smith's website reveals how religious, social and consumerist interests become fluid, overlapping in creative assemblages of interaction that refuse to be reduced to any one of these registers. What emerges is not solely religious nor solely consumerist but both: 'the *Jesus Is* _____ campaign has a life beyond its eponymous publication; it is as mobile and fluid in its promotional reach as Pastor Judah is in his celebrity' (2017: 173). Johnson shows how the promotional campaign invites interactive online engagement focused on who people understand Jesus to be; adopting interactive marketing techniques facilitates the expression of personal convictions while also promoting the commodity of Smith's book.

Conclusion: Neoliberal economics and religious selfhood

Based on fieldwork conducted at Hillsong churches in Amsterdam and New York City in 2013–14, Miranda Klaver suggests that Hillsong is especially attractive to a particular 'urban tribe'. She identifies core volunteers and participants as members of the 'creative class', often university educated, self-employed young adults working in the creative media industries, such as app development, photography or website design. Attracted to cosmopolitan cities for the employment and lifestyle opportunities they present, the creative class find at Hillsong opportunities to use their skills as volunteers in church and access to a diverse community of like-minded peers. Klaver argues that Hillsong churches function like 'third spaces', places that are neither work nor home but which provide spaces in which those new to a city can build relationships, extend their networks and ultimately find an experience of community (Klaver 2016). Similar conclusions are drawn by Gerardo Marti in his book *Hollywood Faith*, an ethnographic study of the Pentecostal Oasis Christian Centre in Los Angeles. Oasis has a congregation whose members include many working in the movie industry, their peripatetic and precarious employment leading Marti to characterize them as 'occupational nomads' (Marti 2008: 178). Oasis provides a sense of orientation for these individuals, not just as a haven from instability but as a channel through which that instability achieves greater meaning and purpose. Used to having to promote themselves within a precarious occupation, these creatives are typically skilled networkers. They also embody an entrepreneurial approach to selfhood that migrates into their religious identities. As Marti observes,

> there is a ready affinity between spreading the fame for themselves based on their personal skills and abilities and spreading the fame for their God based on communal values and beliefs. In other words, the occupational circumstances of workers at Oasis force them into a constant stream of self-promotion, and once they have the vision of using their influence to spread ideas and beliefs that they hold dear, they can use the same set of skills to promote the fame of Jesus Christ and his church. (2008: 179)

The imperative of having to sell oneself in order to thrive is a common cliché within the twenty-first century. Marti points out that while his case study is highly distinctive, the personal marketing, branding and self-promotion so evident in Hollywood point to a much more commonplace phenomenon in US society. Moreover, this cultural pattern is rooted in economic changes that can be found across societies that have embraced neoliberalism as a socio-economic order. The economic shifts that have led to the increasing transfer of risk from the corporation to the individual contract worker can be seen at an escalating pace across societies shaped by the neoliberal turn (Kvachev 2019). Self-promotion is part and parcel of a new form of precarious employment: unpredictable, short term, unstable and dependent on the individual worker being mobile, flexible and adaptable, and continually managing to outshine and undercut their competitors in order to secure an income. Social media platforms like Twitter and LinkedIn both enable and perpetuate this new normal. In this sense, the entrepreneurial self is not an especially empowered self but one left with no choice but to fall back on their personal gumption in order to survive.

The neoliberal age places significant pressure on the entrepreneurial self. As Marti comments, 'Within particular industries, especially when there is a need to complete short-term projects in an efficient and error-free manner, workers will be consumed with the effort to become celebrities in their own right' (2008: 182). Insofar as this reflects what has become commonplace in twenty-first-century economically prosperous nations, it is not a pressure that is experienced as an imposition but manifests as part of the everyday reality of identity development, especially for younger generations (Katz et al. 2021). If consumerism is focused around seduction, the process through which individuals are persuaded products are essential for their lives, the emergence of the entrepreneurial self marks the increasing involvement of ordinary individuals in the processes whereby symbolic goods are produced and marketed. These processes are appropriated not simply in exchange for a stable income but as a dimension of identity construction. But this process, as I've tried to emphasize throughout this chapter, is by no means unconstrained by or detached from the social circumstances in which it is expressed.

For the religious self, these patterns raise interesting possibilities for how different forms of religion achieve legitimation. It has been suggested that the global flows of power and information exchange characteristic of the late modern age destabilize the role that traditional legitimating institutions play (Lyon 2000: 90). The examples explored in this chapter suggest religious identities continue to seek legitimation but from different kinds of sources from those that were dominant in the past. Considering the organizational and individual examples addressed earlier, a sense of legitimacy appears to be produced out of interactions with cultural norms that are associated with neoliberal trends. Mirroring the neoliberal preference for forms of evaluation that refer to markets, calculation and individual choice (Davies 2017: 23), evangelical phenomena like Hillsong embody forms of authority more commonly encountered in the life of commercial markets.

In Chapter 3, we addressed how a religious engagement with populist politics may foster a *strategic* orientation to identity. Religious expression becomes steered by a desire for power or influence in the public realm, and relationships are forged on a strategic, instrumentalist basis as a way of achieving this. In Goffman's terms, this may be understood as the adoption of new personas – perhaps temporary or situational – ultimately oriented to the achievement of a new end. To this we may add two more models of religious selfhood. The *syncretic self* – or what David Lyon calls the 'plastic self' (2000: 95) – affirms a combination of sources ordinarily expected to be discrete or mutually exclusive. I'm thinking here of the individual who is born into a Jewish family and is reluctant to disavow his heritage, even after converting to Islam; the child of a Jewish father and Christian mother who refuses to compromise the richness of her religious upbringing by affirming one tradition over the other; the practitioner of Eastern spiritualities who, while rejecting his evangelical past, nevertheless has come to value the diverse influences on his religious biography. All of these are genuine examples, encountered through my own research, and reflect a reluctance to identify exclusively with one tradition. This is mirrored in a discomfort with evangelism or overly confident moralizing. These individuals' recognition of their own eclectic religious journey rules out any possibility of being a fervent advocate for conversions of any kind. The syncretic self may be passionate about moral issues, but distinctly religious concerns have been resolutely packaged as matters of private conscience.

This contrasts markedly with our third concept – the *entrepreneurial self*, which encompasses the range of examples explored in the present chapter. The entrepreneurial self is oriented towards personal growth through public engagement, actively producing and promoting resources bound up in the ongoing negotiation of religious identity. It is restless and ardent, preoccupied with religious identity as an unfinished entity but confident that the project is being well-fed by an abundance of resources: organizational, media-based and those derived directly from inspiring mentors, figureheads or identity 'experts'. In this respect the entrepreneurial religious self resonates with what Max Weber describes about Calvinist Protestants in *The Protestant Ethic and the Spirit of Capitalism*, at least in its restless engagement with self-development. Here, though, the momentum is much more positive, life-affirming and sits loosely alongside matters of religious doctrine. That said, the entrepreneurial self does not represent an unqualified liberation from tradition. Indeed, the dependence on the cosmetic that has become so important in the cases described earlier has also been used as a means of re-inscribing conservative models of religious identity. This relationship is explored in detail in the following chapter.

Further reading

Studies that link religion with market conditions have not tended to explore issues of the entrepreneurial self in conceptual terms, hence the borrowing from Goffman in this chapter. However, a number of excellent publications provide case studies that repay ongoing consideration, not least Jenkins and Marti (2013), Johnson (2017), Klaver (2015), Marti (2008, 2010) and Wilkins (2008a, 2008b). On the technologies of work and psychological well-being in the neoliberal age, William Davies's *The Happiness Industry* (2015) is superb.

CHAPTER 7
POWER AND RELIGIOUS DIFFERENCE

Introduction

Including 'power' as a major theme in a book about neoliberal religion is important for several reasons. First, as Penny Edgell argues, the sociology of religion has, in recent times, neglected 'religion's role as a source of conflict, division, and inequality in favor of an emphasis on its positive and prosocial aspects' (Edgell 2012: 249). There are questions of power and submission that it needs to address as a subfield because these have been overlooked. Second, attending to questions of power helps place in critical context the phenomena of choice and consumption central to accounts of the neoliberal. When these ideas are so often associated with freedom and self-empowerment, it is especially important to scrutinize the cultural conditions in which they are embedded and the forces that constrain them. Third, there are far too many blatant examples of the *misuse* of power within religious contexts for this issue to be ignored.

This last point has special resonance as we move into the third decade of the twenty-first century. It was 2006 when activist Tarana Burke initiated the #metoo movement to highlight sexual harassment and abuse; #churchtoo began trending on Twitter in 2017, calling attention to the same issues within organized Christian contexts. The following year, a group of evangelical women launched #silenceisnotspiritual, a global network raising awareness of gender-based violence against Christian women and the role of institutionalized silence in enabling its continuation. Accusations of physical and sexual abuse by clergy and church leaders have come to light at an escalating rate since the 1990s, with the exposure of abuses of power stretching across the Roman Catholic, Anglican and other denominations across the globe. Extensive media coverage as well as several high-profile feature films, including the 2015 Academy Award-winning *Spotlight*, which tells the story of the *Boston Globe*'s investigation into sexual abuse in the Catholic Church in Massachusetts in 2001–3, have heightened public awareness. In the UK, the Independent Inquiry into Child Sexual Abuse (IICSA) was established in 2015, covering historical and more recent institutional failings, and has published several investigative reports on abuse within church settings. Research is bringing to light the abuses that occurred earlier in the twentieth century, through programmes of forced child migration, in which state and ecclesiastical authorities were complicit (Lynch 2015). In the UK, following the Second World War, around 4,000 children were removed from their parents and sent to live in institutions or foster homes abroad, mainly in Australia, New Zealand, Canada and Southern Rhodesia (now Zimbabwe). More recent cases of clerical abuse highlight how such issues endure into the present. Influential conservative evangelical

Jonathan Fletcher, former minister of Emmanuel Church, Wimbledon, was the subject of an investigation by Thirtyone:eight, an independent Christian charity concerned with safeguarding children and adults at risk. Its report, published in March 2021, recounts cases of coercion and control, bullying and the use of physical punishment in church settings. Some of those subjected to Fletcher's behaviour described their experiences in terms of 'spiritual abuse' (Thirtyone:eight 2021: 5), reflecting how the character of the abuse was closely tied to the religious contexts in which it occurred. The same term has been used to describe experiences of LGBT+ people excluded from churches because of their sexual identities (Sherwood 2020).

These alarming cases highlight both the capacity for abuse of power within religious organizations and the power they exercise in concealing it. Whether we understand this as a *distinctively religious* form of power or simply a pattern we find across all kinds of institutions, there is no denying the fact that religious organizations have power and that this power often has serious consequences.

Addressing power in relation to religion sociologically requires we attend to how power emerges within shared contexts, on what basis and how it is exercised in practice. Power has a long theoretical legacy within mainstream sociology. For Marx and the Marxist tradition, it is bound up in economic interests and the social class structure; power, closely related to wealth, is wielded by the ruling classes to exploit the working classes. Max Weber was more subtle, conceiving power in terms of social action at a more elementary level. For Weber, power is the capacity to realize one's own will in the face of resistance from others (Gerth and Mills 2009: 180). It is not solely driven by the desire for economic reward but is connected to a range of desires, including the desire for honour or social prestige. Ruling power, whether religious or non-religious, implies recognition of the legitimacy of the basis upon which power rests (Swingewood 2000: 109–10). Weber delineates three ideal types of legitimacy: traditional authority (that which is inherited from traditions of the past), legal-rational authority (based on position within an administrative or legal system) or charismatic authority (based on special qualities ascribed to individual personalities).

Despite Weber's influential legacy, the sociology of religion has not always paid as much attention to issues of power as it might have done. One reason has to do with the politics of the sub-discipline. In university contexts in which religion is a contentious subject, there is arguably pressure on scholars to distance themselves from the normative claims of religious groups. At the same time, openly hostile perspectives risk undermining the integrity of the sub-discipline itself, suggesting an approach that is reductive and simplistic. Avoiding issues of power circumvents this conundrum. From a theoretical point of view, the significant influence of Peter Berger and Thomas Luckmann's *The Social Construction of Reality* (1966) may also be germane. Berger and Luckmann foregrounded the capacity of religion to bestow order and meaning on people's lives, with less concern for how it might be connected to dominance, resistance or marginalization (Beckford 1983). This emphasis on religion as a source of order and meaning may also explain the appeal of Berger's work among theologians, who find in it a means of rendering religious worldviews plausible in social scientific terms. However, this implicitly benign and order-focused framework has receded in the face of recent interest in experiences of misogyny, homophobia, racism and other forms of prejudice, and the role that religion plays in sustaining them. The public exposure of patterns of abuse has only heightened interest in the relationship between religion and power, and in the role of the sociology of religion in addressing it.

Titus Hjelm calls for the development of a 'critical' sociology of religion, 'critical' in this sense conveying a commitment to examining 'the role of religion in creating and sustaining inequalities' (Hjelm 2014: 857). This is especially important when addressing neoliberal cultural conditions, given the neoliberal emphasis upon competition as a driver of value and change necessitates inequalities. As David Beer notes, 'The pursuit of inequality is a key property of neoliberal thinking' (Beer 2016: 25). If the sociology of religion is to contend convincingly with today's cultural climate, one of its key tasks must be identifying how religion contributes to these social inequalities. If religious traditions reinforce patterns of inequality or exclusion, they draw on particular symbolic resources in achieving this. Hjelm invokes Weber's approach in addressing the sociological concept of legitimation. While this might often be viewed as a matter of social cohesion – how forces that contribute to the social order are granted legitimacy – 'from a critical perspective, legitimation is a struggle for hegemony' (Hjelm 2014: 866). In other words, we are invited to consider whose interests such legitimation might serve. And which alternative constructions of reality are suppressed or marginalized in the process? These are the questions that concern the current chapter.

Power and religious classification

Many textbooks in the sociology of religion devote a significant amount of space to debates about the definition of religion. This is perfectly understandable; it helps clarify what it is we're talking about and how this relates to other, 'non-religious' phenomena. Debates about the definition of religion within the social sciences have also been helpful in illuminating the connection between the starting points of analysis and the kinds of claims that can legitimately be made. For example, if religion is defined in terms of belief, how should traditions that do not have sacred texts be understood? In relying on oral evidence gathered from 'believers', how do we handle discrepancies among them? Whose 'belief' counts as authoritative and on what grounds? Mindful of these challenges, other approaches have proceeded from a different basis. So-called functional definitions of religion define religion not in terms of assent to a particular belief or beliefs but in terms of a particular social function that is thereby fulfilled. For example, is religion that which enables individuals to find meaning in life? Or to construct a 'worldview' that has coherence over and above the conditions of its cultural point of origin? This is closer to how Thomas Luckmann approaches the topic in his 1967 book *The Invisible Religion*. It has the advantages of not privileging religious traditions which articulate clear and shared beliefs over those for which beliefs are more subdued, contested or relatively insignificant. Its difficulties include advocating a definition that is so broad that it has the capacity to include a huge range of phenomena, including many that would not conventionally be considered religious. If religions are distinguished by a capacity to facilitate meaning-making or to bring people together in an experience of common community, for example, then ought we to treat Marxism or fascism as religions? What about football, nationalism, online gaming or historical re-enactment societies? In adopting an inclusive definition like this, do the advantages of drawing attention to possible comparisons outweigh the potential problems of grouping human phenomena together that really do not belong in the same category?

I rehearse these well-worn arguments here not to advocate for any particular definition of religion but to highlight the ways that preconceived ideas can constrain and shape sociological analysis. My own preference is to follow Max Weber in treating the definition of religion as something we can expect to emerge at the conclusion of a study, rather than being predetermined at the outset. Maintaining an open mind about what 'counts' as religion and what does not enables us to see a broader range of social possibilities about how these phenomena are expressed, embodied and acted out within human experience. This is not to allow anything to count as religion, any more than being open-minded about sport means anything counts as sport. Rather, it involves remaining attentive to those phenomena that exhibit family resemblances with pre-existing entities widely considered to be 'religious'. It also means keeping this 'religious' dimension in critical perspective as their characteristics are mapped and described. The best sociological studies of religious phenomena do not, in my view, spend voluminous chapters wrestling with the definition of religion. But they do retain a close attention to how the concepts central to a movement's identity are formulated and lived out in empirical reality.

An attentiveness to classification is also useful as we consider the use of language among those whose lives we are attempting to understand. Religious identity markers are used in a variety of ways, often reflecting agendas of a moral or political kind. They indicate a process of boundary drawing that distinguishes between those who fall on one side of a significant boundary and those who fall on the other. Whether someone is 'one of us', or not. Such processes can be instrumental in legitimizing acts of social exclusion. They can also be bound up in complex networks of power and influence. Sophie Bjork-James draws attention to the ways in which the term 'evangelical' is used in the popular US media, highlighting its capacity to reinforce divisions along racial lines. Polling companies, foregrounding political differences between religious communities, tend to disaggregate white Protestants into 'evangelical' and 'mainline' – reflecting their generally divergent political sympathies – while maintaining a single category of 'African American Protestants', as their political inclinations do not tend to break down in this way. Consequently, 'evangelical' takes on racial meanings and many African Americans, while affirming identifiably evangelical beliefs, reject the term 'evangelical' as they associate it 'with white Christianity, and sometimes with racism' (Bjork-James 2021: 13).

Addressing how different identity categories interact inevitably raises the issue of *intersectionality*, which I introduced in Chapter 2 as a factor that shapes how people respond to religious diversity. It is also important for analyses of power as it highlights how the convergence or concealment of different identity markers contributes to experiences of empowerment and disempowerment. For example, Nisha Kapoor traces how the UK's Labour government responded to problems of racism during the early 2000s, a period distinguished by the securitization of the Muslim community (see Chapter 5). By highlighting the relative prosperity of different ethnic populations, the government recast the narrative from one about racial prejudice into one of class difference or, more specifically, differences in the opportunity to prosper economically. Claims that all ethnic minorities are disadvantaged were dismissed by government representatives as 'one-dimensional' and preoccupied with the problems of the past, not of the present (Kapoor 2013: 1038). The problems of the present, as they saw it, had to do with counterterrorism, and the introduction of a range of new state apparatus – extension of legal detention without trial, increased 'stop and search' powers by the police and the nascent 'Prevent' Strategy – justified exceptional treatment of Muslims as a 'suspect community'. As Kapoor argues, the UK government adopted an increasingly neoliberal approach to disadvantage, approaching this as a matter of individual circumstance rather than structural inequality. The move away from 'racism' as a broad category was one way in which the tools for addressing the problem were dismantled. At the same time, 'exceptional' security measures effectively made anti-Muslim prejudice reasonable and mandated by the state. What this example illustrates is how intersectional patterns can be used by those in power to serve a particular agenda. In other words, intersectionality can function as a top-down strategy for exercising power, as well as a convergence of disadvantage emerging at the grassroots level.

In another example, Shanon Shah explores how the lives of gay Muslims in Britain and Malaysia are bound up in intersectional relationships between multiple markers of identity – not just religion and sexuality but also ethnicity, gender and social class. Shah notes the peculiarly double-edged status of Malay citizens. Malaysia has a culturally and religiously diverse population. Malays are the largest ethnic group, with Malaysian Chinese and Malaysian Indians making up another 30 per cent of the population; just over 60 per cent are Muslim, with the remainder split between Buddhists, Christians, Hindus and other smaller religious traditions. However, Malaysia also has a Federal Constitution that both fuses Malay ethnicity and Muslim religiosity, and privileges those citizens who are Muslim Malays, affording the monarch the powers to safeguard the 'special position' of the Malay population. Malaysia's complex legal system includes Islamic laws to which Muslim citizens are subject – including the outlawing of same-sex relations and 'transgenderism' – and a penal code that applies to all citizens, including Muslims (and which outlaws what is described as 'carnal intercourse against the order of nature'). Within this context, gay Muslims hold a position of social privilege, while also living with the pressure to uphold a patriarchal, heteronormative model of Malay-ness. Deviation from this model comes with obvious risks, sanctions backed by the doubly powerful legal measures against same-sex relations. As Shah puts it, 'gay Muslims in Malaysia straddle privilege and vulnerability in their day-to-day existence' (Shah 2020: 28–29).

Intersectionality is a useful lens through which to examine religion because it helps contextualize religious facets of identity in relation to other influences on human life. Religious worldviews tend to be structured around absolutist claims about life and reality; many also make exclusivist claims on their adherents – it is difficult to imagine an official representative of any religious tradition calling for its members to maintain a partial, half-hearted or selective commitment. The Christian, Jew, Muslim or Buddhist as constructed by the 'official' discourse of each tradition has allowed their entire life to be given over to living out a body of teachings that represents ultimate truth. And yet a social scientific study of religious identity must take seriously its constituency as a social entity. How does the Christian or Jew live out their Christian or Jewish commitment on an everyday basis? What emerges from this that is recognized – and hence legitimated – as Christian or Jewish? And how does this practice relate to a theologically authorized body of tradition? Taking an intersectional approach that is attentive to how religion interacts with ethnicity, nationality, gender, age, social class and other salient factors helps us to see the social reality of religion.

With the aim of contributing to a critical sociology of religion (Hjelm 2014), the remainder of this chapter explores further dimensions of the relationship between religion and power. It asks how religion helps maintain patterns of inequality that arise under neoliberal conditions. What follows are two separate discussions, each exploring different configurations of religion and power that are influential within the twenty-first century. Each adopts an intersectional lens to highlight how experiences of empowerment and disempowerment emerge from lived relationships between religious and other identity markers. Thematically, the dual focus is on the embrace of the cosmetic as a lens on gender, and racialization and the marking of religious difference. In focusing on how religious difference takes on status according to its intersectional positioning, the aim is to highlight the processual nature of these phenomena. In other words, these arrangements are *not just there*, they are *brought about* by specific combinations of factors.

Embracing the cosmetic and gender essentialism

A sense of the malleability of the self has been especially visible in recent debates about gender and sexuality. Some sociologists have responded with attempts to unsettle notions of the gendered self as a coherent, stable or 'natural' identity (e.g. Butler 1993). They have found a rich resource in Erving Goffman's work, which emphasizes the self as performed, rather than inherited (Lawler 2014: 116–37). Once we acknowledge the self as performed, then common assumptions about gender identities can more easily be traced to particular power interests, and variations in the construction of identities are more open to scrutiny.

Considering these approaches within the sociology of religion highlights significant counter-narratives affirmed among religious actors. The malleability of gender identity has provoked predictably hostile reactions among many conservative religious groups

(Barrett-Fox and Yip 2020). In some quarters, this hostility arises from an understanding of the patriarchal nuclear family as the bedrock of Western moral order. Most explicit among the Christian Right in the United States, opposition to transgender identities is tied to campaigns against feminism, abortion and homosexuality. Gender identities are affirmed as biologically determined and conform to a traditional differentiation of roles (Gallagher 2003). Gender fluidity is confronted as a transgression against God's creation *and* a slippage in 'normality' that threatens the moral fabric of society. In several nations in the Middle East and on the African continent, same-sex relations are outlawed on the basis of an interpretation of Islamic law, in some cases punishable by death; others appeal to arguments derived from biblical texts (Kuloba 2016).

Globalization and the heightened connectivity it has enabled have brought what were previously strongly boundaried regions into much closer and more frequent contact with international social forces, including those in tension with pre-existing traditions. Neoliberal economic change – including the disproportionate volume of Anglo-American content on media platforms – has heightened the sense of 'Western' dominance and reinforced conservative counter-narratives that associate the 'rise' of non-heterosexual identities with alien, secular influences. As US conservatives blame permissive liberals, conservatives in the Middle East blame the United States as the 'Great Satan', while conservatives on the African continent accuse former colonial powers of importing homosexuality into their countries. The appeal of fundamentalist forms of religion may in part be understood as an antidote to the abundance of choice available within the identity politics of the twenty-first century (Lyon 2000: 75).

And yet some of the most striking examples of entrepreneurial religion (see Chapter 6) combine gender traditionalism with a creative appropriation of cultural resources. The two are by no means incompatible. Such examples illustrate how an entrepreneurial orientation to religious selfhood can be put in the service of restrictive identity agendas. A striking case can be found if we return to Hillsong Church in Australia, discussed in the previous chapter. Hillsong has held for some years a series of highly popular annual conferences, themed around what it understands to be the distinct needs of men, on the one hand, and women, on the other. The use of gender-tailored events is very common in the evangelical world and reflects a determination to uphold clear gendered distinctions of identity, role and 'natural' virtues. The model used by Hillsong can be seen echoed in similar conferences in the United Kingdom, the United States and elsewhere, and reflects a distinctive use of commercial resources. Moreover, these appear to shape the gender norms upheld within these contexts.

Australian scholar Marion Maddox conducted fieldwork at Hillsong's conferences between 2005 and 2010, observing the constructions of femininity and masculinity that were promoted there. Her research reveals an indebtedness to norms of attractiveness and gendered identity prominent in commercial expressions of popular culture. She describes how, at Hillsong's women's 'Colour Conferences', women are encouraged to 'diet, exercise, use makeup, get "pampered," and even resort to plastic surgery to conform to a narrow, fashion-magazine definition of "beauty"' (Maddox 2013: 12). These inducements are matched with commercial opportunities for personal enhancement available at the conference itself. Maddox describes '"pamper" stalls, decorated to resemble the cosmetic counters of an upmarket department store, offering makeup, manicures, and hairstyling' (2013: 20). Augmenting this emphasis upon physical 'perfection' is a use of 'princess' language in reference to female participants. Bobbie Houston, wife of Hillsong's senior pastor Brian Houston, is the figurehead of its women's conference and a regular speaker. Maddox cites her calling for a celebration of 'Heaven-breathed womanhood in all its beauty, softness, vulnerability and tenderness' (quoted in Maddox 2013: 16). While women are called to embody a pampered passivity, male attendees at Hillsong's men's conferences are encouraged to 'lead', 'take authority' and discover their similarities to God.

Hillsong provides clarity on gender roles in an age of gender fluidity. In this sense, it extends the anti-modern thirst for certainty that has been characteristic of Christian fundamentalism since its beginnings in the nineteenth-century United States. But it also reflects an alignment with broader commercial culture – especially notions of bodily perfection and self-empowerment common within gendered advertising and broadcast entertainment – suggesting it both resists and embraces the neoliberal context in which it functions. As Maddox comments: 'Far from acting as a boundary marker differentiating conservative evangelicals and Pentecostals from their secular communities, Hillsong's teaching on gender reproduces and intensifies the tensions inscribed in wider culture. The pressure to be – and, even more, to look – perfect, while living out complex interplays of submission, autonomy, and authority, gives a theological gloss to many women's everyday experience' (Maddox 2013: 25).

Insofar as it appears to both embrace and resist elements of mainstream gender politics, Hillsong echoes themes associated with post-feminism (Tasker and Negra 2007). In other words, it speaks the language of female empowerment, while rejecting feminism as an ideology. This apparently paradoxical position is not uncommon within evangelical circles (Aune 2006); it permits evangelicals to appear in touch with cultural change, without requiring a comprehensive reconfiguration of their religious convictions. It produces a femininity that 'promotes choice and freedom alongside conformity and constraint' (Sullivan and Delaney 2017: 854). Jenkins and Marti find a similar pattern in their study of the Oasis Christian Centre in Los Angeles. Oasis, located close to the centre of the Hollywood movie industry, runs what it calls its 'God Chicks' ministry, named after the book of the same name by influential pastor Holly Wagner. Jenkins and Marti find an age-differentiated ministry that attributes a particular role to 'older' women (by which it means those over forty). These 'older' women are called to be wise examples for younger members of the congregation. But their redefinition of 'being old' includes aspirations to remain physically attractive according to the norms of popular commercial entertainment. These women believe they must 'stay focused on looking fashionable in a healthy body as this is what allows them to prosper in the world in personal relationships and evangelical, missionary outreach' (Jenkins and Marti 2013: 246). This reflects a wider social pattern – evident in expectations projected onto celebrities – that women should grow wiser without showing any outward signs of the ageing process.

The case of Hillsong illustrates how ideas of sexual purity tied to female identity extend well beyond the United States, where purity pledges first emerged and are most culturally visible (Valenti 2010). Katie Gaddini finds similar ideas framing the experiences of single evangelical women in London, who position themselves in relation to a shared sense of the 'ideal Christian woman', distinguished by pre-marital sexual abstinence. She finds that purity norms are especially upheld by and associated with a particular kind of woman – 'the youthful, white, and middle-class ideal' (Gaddini 2020: 118) – echoing the construction of femininity celebrated at Hillsong's conferences.

Evangelical Christianity has been commonly cited as a religious movement that endorses a complementarian view of gender roles. While the language of patriarchal hierarchy has arguably been softened in recent times, the 'equal but different' approach often veils persistent inequalities (especially when men's 'natural' strengths happen to include leadership). However, existing research warns against rushing to quick conclusions about gendered empowerment and disempowerment, suggesting there is often a marked difference between what is proclaimed in church and how things work out in practice once families are at home. Research in the United Kingdom and United States has drawn attention to the co-existence of discursive patriarchy in church and more pragmatic egalitarianism in the domestic sphere (Aune 2006; Gallagher 2003). There is a difference, it seems, between models of gender difference affirmed within the official discourse of churches and the practical realities of family life. This does not resolve the ethical challenges of gender inequality of course; it merely requires us to change the kinds of ethical questions we ask.

The point of the preceding discussion is to highlight the way notions of gender difference are refracted through images of masculinity and femininity most associated with mainstream entertainment media. That religious groups should render their religious convictions meaningful using the cultural resources of the time is, of course, no new insight, but the examples earlier underline the importance of asking *which* resources are privileged and with *what kinds of consequences*?

The imagery used by Hillsong in its marketing material and conferences is markedly similar to that used in fashion magazines, and video content is populated with actors distinguished by their youth, attractiveness and apparent happiness and vigour. This I am describing, following the analysis of the previous chapter, as an *embrace of the cosmetic*, in the sense of a committed imitation of tropes used in commercial contexts to sell embodied images of men and women. These images are highly gendered and are used to reinforce a model of biological determinism, one in which men and women not only embody particular virtues and qualities but also adhere to a particular body image.

This embrace of the cosmetic may invite tensions given the frequently sexualized image of women in commercial advertising and the tradition of modesty often invoked within evangelical communities. As Dana Malone observes in her study of evangelicals on college campuses in the United States, women are judged by how they adorn their bodies, and this in turn leads to judgements about how they conduct themselves sexually. Given the pressure to conform to ideals of sexual purity, alongside the expectation that you will find a (heterosexual) partner (and marry) as a young adult, this amounts to a very fine line that evangelical women are expected to walk. They must make clear that they are available to potential partners, but never in a way that suggests they are forward or pushy, or which displaces the proactive role of potential (male) suitors. The related policing of women's bodies is exercised via expectations – and sometimes explicit sanctions – about what they wear and how they present themselves (Malone 2018: 171–2). In Hillsong, this tension is apparently tempered with calls on women to submit to the authority of men as they submit to the authority of God. At Hillsong's 'Colour conferences', women are encouraged to nurture a relationship with God that is one of devotion and submission. Some of the language used is highly evocative of conjugal intimacy. Maddox cites Donna Crouch, a Hillsong youth pastor: 'Whether you're married or single, you can know Jesus as your husband. You can have the hottest and most rocking marriage' (cited in Maddox 2013: 18). This use of romanticized language to describe women's relationship with God or Jesus can claim a theological root in the biblical notion of the church as the bride of Christ (e.g. Ephesians 5: 22–33). Its modern development into a metaphor for a distinctively female, heteronormative relationship with God has a troubling provenance. In some popular evangelical writing, for example, female submission is counterbalanced with a portrayal of God as domineering and possessive, reinforcing conjugal norms that contribute to domestic abuse (Colgan 2018).

By contrast, Hillsong's men's conferences encourage men to have a relationship with God that is more one of identification, of seeking to embody God's example, to model one's life after him. This endorsement owes much to the tradition of muscular Christianity associated with the early twentieth century, although it has enduring influence. Hillsong makes explicit use of John Eldredge's 2001 book *Wild at Heart: Discovering the Secret of a Man's Soul*, which presents masculinity in essentialized terms that emphasize heroism, adventure, risk, physical strength and courage. According to Eldredge, God created men to be wild and dangerous, and to live out three essential desires: to fight a battle, to live an adventurous life and to rescue a beauty. A later book, entitled *Captivating: Unveiling the Mystery of a Woman's Soul*, subjected women to the same kind of treatment. Tellingly, this was authored by Eldredge's wife, Stasi, alongside her husband.

The model of masculinity affirmed within Hillsong in some respects echoes the teaching of controversial American pastor Mark Driscoll. Driscoll led Mars Hill Church in Seattle until 2014, when accusations of abuse led to Driscoll's departure and the church's collapse. At its peak, Mars Hill was the largest church in Washington state and had expanded to encompass fifteen campuses. The church became strongly associated with Driscoll's distinctive style and message, which achieved national and international acclaim via his published books and popular sermons downloadable from iTunes. His style of presentation – bombastic, confrontational, unapologetically complementarian, often uncomfortably explicit in its handling of topics concerning sex and gender (Johnson 2018) – also attracted media interest and notoriety, enhanced further by his activity on Twitter. An estimated 250,000 people across the globe listened to Driscoll's sermons each week via podcast (McKinney, yet to be published: 11). Using the language of the previous chapter, Driscoll was a successful 'pastorpreneur' and one channelling a particular blend of influences. In 2006, Driscoll had been involved in the 'Together for the Gospel' conference which met in Kentucky and was instrumental in the birth of 'New Calvinism', otherwise known as the 'Young, Restless and Reformed' movement. 'New Calvinism' shared with 'old' Calvinism a commitment to biblical inerrancy and a complementarian perspective on gender, but it combined these traditional fundamentalist beliefs with a more positive orientation to contemporary culture, as both mission field and legitimate resource for communicating the Gospel message. Accordingly, Driscoll shrugged off the severe, stuffy solemnity of traditional Reformed Christianity, preferring instead to preach wearing jeans and a hoodie. His sermons included vulgar language, humorous put-downs and rants against feminism, homosexuality and men who had given in to what Driscoll viewed as the feminized, emasculated model of masculinity upheld by the broader church.

In her book *American Evangelicalism and Hypermasculinity*, Jennifer McKinney charts the rise and fall of Driscoll's ministry at Mars Hill as both a continuation of evangelical traditions of 'muscular Christianity' and the emergence of a more extreme 'hypermasculinity'. Driscoll called for the professional, domestic and sexual submission of women to men, and the belittling of those men who embody qualities deemed to fall short of Driscoll's rugged image (McKinney, yet to be published). While Driscoll's church collapsed, and his public profile and influence waned as a result, his approach to gender resonated with a wide audience. Its appeal to 'common sense' truths and the experiences of ordinary working men also anticipated the shift to a populist register that characterized Donald Trump's support base.

Mark Driscoll was by no means the first evangelical leader to draw on wider traditions of masculine identity in crafting his Christian persona. Billy Sunday, capitalizing on his image as a professional baseball player in the 1880s, was a famously imposing preacher, fusing onstage bombast with a fierce and folksy rhetoric. Even Billy Graham, that most centrist of US evangelical figureheads, crafted a public presence that was in part indebted to traditions of masculinity prominent during his long career. Graham fostered a persona of what historian Grant Wacker calls 'Christian manliness . . . masculinity disciplined by an ethic of self-restraint' (Wacker 2015: 82). In an illuminating essay, Wacker traces how Graham exhibited such 'manliness' in his energetic preaching, athletic physique, chiselled good looks and moral backbone. More Charlton Heston than Marlon Brando, Graham embodied a muscular Christianity that was wholesome and upright, while also combative and uncompromising when it mattered. In tracing the interconnections between religious traditions and the broader cultural ideas about gender which they adopt, we achieve a much clearer sense of the kinds of ideas authorized and legitimated by religious groups. Legitimation is not necessarily a conscious or deliberate process, but it can have very significant consequences that contribute to wider cultural patterns of exclusion.

The cosmetic as identity resource

Our focus on the importance of the 'cosmetic' in the performance of religious identities illuminates the role played by fashion. Religious identities are rendered visible or invisible in social contexts based on how physical markers – choice of clothing, skin colour, style of beard – are open to having symbolic meaning attached to them by observers. Degrees of distinction from the cultural norm can make some religious identities more visible – for example ultra-Orthodox Jews or Tibetan Buddhist monks – while others blend more easily into the general population. It is simply not expected of most Christians, for example, that they dress in a particular way that makes them identifiable *as Christians*. This is why restrictions on the wearing of religious symbols in public in France are viewed as a means of suppression targeted at Muslims. The most prevalent religion in France is Roman Catholicism, which has no tradition of wearing visible religious symbols, at least not among laypeople. Crucifixes worn as necklaces can easily be disguised by clothing and are anyway now often treated as fashion accessories, diluting their religious significance in the public realm. By contrast, the most significant religious minority are Muslims, and many Muslim women wear the hijab or face veil. This visibility is of course open to misperception and prejudice, something explored in greater detail in the following chapter. In countries in which Muslims are a minority, forms of traditional dress like the burqa or kameez make Muslims more visible *as Muslims* (Williams and Vashi 2007), with women in particular the target of hostility and abuse (Carr and Haynes 2015: 27). Their visibility also introduces into the public realm the opportunity for various stereotypes associated with Muslim men and women to be inscribed on their visual appearance, so that face covering, for example, is interpreted in terms of oppression. In this sense visual appearance can be a focus of hostility as well as suspicion. As Emma Tarlo puts it, 'clothes have important social and material effects which go beyond the intentions of their wearers' (Tarlo 2010: 12).

The clothing choices of Muslim women are an especially interesting example because they carry such acute symbolic resonance while also being resourced by a vibrant commercial market that presents opportunities for empowerment. In recent years, a new form of influencer has emerged – the hijabi blogger, who combines modelling with lifestyle advice delivered via social media, aimed at Muslim women who wish to be fashionable and maintain modesty in keeping with Islamic teaching. Transnational clothing styles have become merged with religious traditions in a creative fashion industry that challenges embedded assumptions about Islam and Muslim women (Figure 9). Developing a similar line of argument is Emma Tarlo's excellent study *Visibly Muslim*, which explores the choices ordinary Muslim women make about what they wear and the religious and political contexts that frame those choices. Focusing especially on the hijab (headscarf), Tarlo examines how Muslim women in London contend with the challenges of becoming *visibly* Muslim as their identities are read off their choice of clothing. Observers may also infer from this choice a range of assumptions: that the wearer must be especially pious and serious about their Muslim faith, that they are suffering oppression from the males in their family or that their religiosity has developed into fanaticism. Muslim women are aware of these projected readings and carry the anticipation of being subject to them as they conduct themselves in public. They are also conscious that their modest dress means they are viewed first and foremost as religious women and so not reduced to an object

Figure 9 The Dutch-Moroccan journalist and TV host Raja Felgata, with Amsterdam-based fashion designer Loubna Sadoq and Afghan-Dutch hijabi model and blogger Ruba Zai, after featuring in the Netherlands' annual 'Colourful Top 100' in 2014. *Source*: KleurrijkeTop100 via Flickr.

of male sexual desire, as is commonly the case in Western cultures. However, they also feel the frustrations of being reduced to their hijab, as if this is all they represent, as if their individuality is wiped out by a choice that marks them as Muslim. Tarlo comments on how these publicly imparted meanings make wearing the hijab an especially challenging experience but one that also often provokes an empowering response:

> The overloaded symbolism of hijab can therefore have extremely alienating effects on the wearer. Learning to master the hijab, to tie it in different styles, experiment with colour, combine it with fashions does, in this context, have considerable importance, for it becomes a means by which a person integrates her pre-hijab past with her hijabi present and learns to unite, or literally 'tie up', different multifaceted strands of identity and belonging. (Tarlo 2010: 76)

Tarlo's study challenges common assumptions that head covering among Muslims is necessarily an austere and solemn act of renunciation. She shows how Muslim women make highly creative, experimental choices about their attire while remaining within parameters they derive from Islamic teaching on modest dress. The hijab serves as a symbolic means of crafting their individuality while at the same time making a public statement about their Muslim identity.

Muslim women in London benefit from living in a multicultural city with an abundance of fashion outlets that serve their preferences, but they remain a minority with the vulnerabilities that accompany this status. To wear the hijab, even in creative and colourful styles, still marks an individual as marginal and visibly Muslim in a context in which suspicion and Islamophobia are not uncommon. The situation is quite different in Turkey, where a large majority of the population are Muslim and 'veiling fashion' is an established commercial industry with high-street visibility. Turkey's recent political climate, under the Justice and Development Party (see Chapter 3), means veiling fashion carries a significant symbolic load, not just in religious but in political terms as well. President Erdoğan has been a passionate defender of the right to wear the headscarf, in the face of secularist opposition, and his parallel support for market economic reforms makes for a favourable environment for commercial, but Islamically inflected, fashion. Indeed, in Turkey, veiling fashion is an industry, with high-street retail outlets, prominent advertising billboards, fashion shows and mass appeal (Gokariksel and Secor 2010: 329).

In their analysis of veiling fashion (or *tesettür*) in Turkey, Gokariksel and Secor (2010) examine the business of fashion companies in order to ascertain how their commodities are inscribed as Islamic. They identify a complex negotiation between the commercial interests of business and the desire to maintain a set of standards in keeping with what is taken to be Islamic teaching. Patterns vary across different companies, and the ethos of each varies by styles of dress sold, use of Islamic or non-Islamic banking, presentation of models in advertising and the design of staff uniforms. The degree to which observation of Islamic standards is upheld as a priority varies considerably. Perhaps even more importantly, their orientation to this challenge also differs: from the company that sees itself as engaged in the Islamicization of Turkish society by making veiling more attractive to the firm that resists any involvement in such political agendas. While selling headscarves as religious commodities, its managers view their religious significance as the responsibility of the consumer. Acknowledging the various ways in which their products are worn, they argue 'that it is up to the consumer to make the headscarf Islamic through its use' (2010: 327). These contrasting examples reflect how the inscription of Islam onto commodities is not a stable or clear-cut phenomenon. Gokariksel and Secor find a similar ambivalence among consumers of veiling fashion, whose comments on what makes fashion Islamic reveal that 'the questions of piety, modesty and the self that veiling-fashion raises are contested, debated and never fully resolved, even in its everyday practice' (2010: 328).

The contrasting cases of the UK and Turkey reveal how religious clothing conveys different potential as a carrier of identity and power depending on broader cultural contexts. Both cases are shaped by neoliberal conditions – not least the value of self-determination and commercial fashion markets – but these are refracted through the social and political circumstances of each case. 'Post-feminist' perspectives have tended, of late, to associate gender equality with the power of women to exercise free choice as consumers about how they present themselves in public. However, such perspectives have tended to associate exposure of bodies with free choices while covering bodies represents repression. This tallies with popular assumptions about Islam, which take the hijab to be emblematic of the power of Muslim men over Muslim women, in contrast to more liberated 'Western' cultures (Rootham 2015). Setting the previous examples alongside one another reveals the wrong-headedness of this understanding. The cosmetic emerges as a source of religious legitimacy operative within both Christian and Muslim contexts. Both lean on commercial markets, and both find ways of investing religious meaning in the market choices that are made. Most importantly, both reveal fusions of religious and commercial resources harnessed by women as sources of empowerment (Figure 10).

Racialization and religious difference

One of the most powerful alignments between religion and broader neoliberal culture finds expression in individualism. Individualism represents one of the most pervasive values associated with capitalist societies and is axiomatic to neoliberal developments across the global north. In broad terms, it can be summarized as the 'primacy of individual states and interests' over those of the group (Williams 1976: 165), although its expression has taken a variety of forms. A historical development can be traced from the

Figure 10 Fashion model wearing the hijab. *Source*: Ahmad Ardity via Pixabay.

143

Protestant Reformation that conceived of personal faith as unmediated by the authority of the Church to the egalitarianism that emerged from the industrial revolution as some traditional social hierarchies were broken down (Bruce 2002: 10–11). David Lyon distinguishes between expressive and acquisitive individualism, the latter conceiving identity as shaped by consumer choices (Lyon 2000: 32), and it is this idea that comes to the forefront in discussions of neoliberal cultural conditions. But individualism also emerges in distinct strands within different cultural contexts. In the United States, for example, a long-established privileging of individual rights and freedoms is often accompanied by the denial that social structures shape life chances. Prejudice and discrimination are attributed to poor judgements and bad attitudes on the part of individuals, and hence the solution to these problems is believed to lie with individuals, not government. This is how individuals are held accountable for their actions. Michael Emerson and Christian Smith (2000) describe this as 'anti-structuralism', which they argue is a major factor in explaining racial prejudice among white evangelicals in the United States. As they explain, 'because most white evangelicals perceive racism as individual-level prejudice and discrimination, and do not view themselves as prejudiced people, they wonder why they must be challenged with problems they did and do not cause' (Emerson and Smith 2000: 89). A similar pattern can be found among men who are outraged by misogyny but reject accusations of complicity from the #metoo generation on the grounds that they have not personally been a direct perpetrator of gender-based violence. This form of individualism is especially powerful because it marks a convergence between several mutually reinforcing ideas, all of which are accorded strong cultural validity in the US context. These include an evangelical view of faith as a voluntaristic personal commitment, a belief that the state's primary function is to protect individual freedoms rather than ensure universal access to services via taxation and a belief that a strong economy rests on free enterprise and a minimum of state interference. This constellation of values makes for a strong plausibility structure, what political scientist William Connolly calls the 'evangelical-capitalist resonance machine' (Connolly 2008). The evangelicals interviewed for Emerson and Smith's study do not hold openly racist views; they tend to believe strongly in equality for all Americans and that all are created equal by God. However, when faced with social inequalities, 'they refuse to accept that social outcomes could be determined by any forces other than the merit, effort, and hard work of individuals themselves' (Tranby and Hartmann 2008: 344). Their consequent refusal to address the role of social structures helps enable the continuance of racial inequalities.

This anti-structuralism also influences the scepticism and hostility directed by conservative Christians to ideas like intersectionality or critical race theory, as well as activist movements like Black Lives Matter. They are tainted by association with academia and liberalism, which represent 'establishment' perspectives. But they are also presented as ideologies (and so incompatible with Christian faith) that are socially divisive because they call attention to social difference (and so undermine the Christian call for unity). Emerson and Smith even point to cases where Black Americans are accused of inflating racism by focusing too much on problems of the past or seeing all problems through a racial lens (2000: 81–2). To draw attention to structural, shared, social prejudice is seen as stoking division. The fact that those identity markers that are dominant in the United States – white, male, straight, cisgender, affluent – are never criticized as divisive but instead are normalized reflects how this pattern is governed not by a concern for unity but by the privileging of existing elites (Barrett-Fox and Yip 2020).

Observing how prejudice is maintained *because* of individualism underlines the importance of addressing the power of institutions to perpetuate or challenge embedded inequalities. This is all the more important because the anti-structuralism of which Emerson and Smith write diverts attention away from institutional factors by rejecting their significance. The contention that institutions function as vehicles of prejudice has been reinforced via recent debates about 'institutional racism'. These have extended to include concerns about distinctively religious shades of prejudice, particularly Islamophobia and anti-Semitism, and how these might be understood as embedded in the structures of institutions. In the UK, debate about whether existing legislation is sufficient to protect minorities from religious prejudice of this kind is ongoing and unlikely to be resolved any time soon.

Recent studies of the role that religion plays in processes of racial exclusion also highlight the importance of human behaviour at the micro level. Bracey and Moore, in a study of evangelical congregations in the United States, examine how 'microaggressions' contribute to the maintenance of 'institutional whiteness', thereby reinforcing a pattern of racial segregation in the United States' churches. Their study highlights the mechanisms by which organizations become complicit in this process, showing how 'structural relations require institutional dynamics *and* human actors' (Bracey and Moore 2017: 284). In other words, we need to not lose sight of the fact that religious organizations – like all organizations – maintain ways of life, work and human conduct because of the decisions and actions of individuals. What keeps institutional cultures alive is the participation of their members.

Bracey and Moore proceed from the acknowledgement that twenty-first-century America is widely assumed to be a colour-blind era; blatant racism is thought to be a thing of the past. Far from reflecting the absence of racial prejudice, however, this dominant narrative leads white people to adopt more subtle devices for excluding those who threaten their white spaces. This does not mean the total exclusion of non-white people, but it does mean maintaining a white hegemony and a white majority. It also requires those visible minorities present in church to conform to implicit rules of conduct. This is achieved, so Bracey and Moore argue, through 'racial microaggressive activity' that protects the boundaries of white space by ensuring only those who acquiesce to its exclusionary norms remain part of the community (Bracey and Moore 2017: 286).

Bracey and Moore identify two different types of microaggression to which people of colour are subjected. First, there are those microaggressions intended to discipline new congregants into the white norms of the congregation (including not introducing the topic of race as a problematic issue). Second, there are those intended to exclude those who do not conform in the desired way. This powerful ethnographic study is striking because of its description of encounters the first author (a man of colour) had among members of majority white congregations, including the microaggressions that contribute to the maintenance of the church as a white space. The reflexive method is important here, as it is only because these churches are encountered from Bracey's perspective as a black Christian man that we are able to recognize the ways in which what might appear to be minor, incidental behaviours actually function as powerful forms of exclusion. One excerpt from his fieldnotes recounts a visit to a Bible study meeting in a rural location near a southern college town. The all-white Bible study group was meeting at the home of a couple whose house was located in woodland without any mobile signal. After some difficulty finding the house, Bracey arrived to be welcomed by a bemused woman who, he suspects, assumed on the basis of his phone voice that he was white. 'Who are you?' is her opening welcome. The only newcomer, Bracey is then shown around the house, including the couple's extensive collection of US Civil War memorabilia. Conversations about the pictures on the wall reveal the couple are strongly in sympathy with the Confederate side, historically associated with supporting the institution of slavery. Notably, Bracey did not feel safe and soon made an exit under the false excuse of having to take an emergency phone call, in spite of the fact that, as all of those present knew, there was no phone signal.

Bracey and Moore's study is a model of how ethnographic observation can generate a rich account of religious gatherings, often way beyond what could have been achieved using other research methods. It also illustrates the value of the self as a research instrument. Recognizing that identity is performed and embodied, we achieve a glimpse of the underpinning assumptions of religious groups by reflecting on their reactions to outsiders, and, in so doing, get a clearer sense of the kinds of people they take to be *most outside* of their number. It presents a strong case for how sociological studies of religion, when undertaken with critical questions in mind, cannot be artificially detached from questions of moral import. We will explore this issue in more detail in our final chapter.

Bracey and Moore's study illustrates how organized Christian contexts can serve as a means of maintaining patterns of exclusion on the basis of race. Many other studies have highlighted analogous phenomena, which may be explained as an extension of the power of white majorities to protect their own religious spaces. Gerardo Marti's book *American Blindspot* traces how this has been maintained throughout American history, with legal, cultural and religious resources used to privilege white power and ensure non-white populations are subordinated and disenfranchised. This pattern was heightened during the Trump presidency, as Donald Trump played to his supporters' hostility towards immigrants and their fear that the 'American identity' they treasured was under threat (Marti 2020: 172).

One of the recurring devices identified by Marti as instrumental in perpetuating racial prejudice is the *racialization* of various aspects of American life. Simply put, racialization refers to the process whereby a social group is homogenized into a single category and accorded qualities assumed to be innate or essential to that category. In an article revisiting Emerson and Smith's *Divided by Faith*, Tranby and Hartmann argue that the evangelicals they cite often explain their views using negative stereotypes about African Americans, suggesting 'they' are lazy, unmotivated and refuse to take responsibility for their lives (Tranby and Hartmann 2008: 345). Tranby and Hartmann argue that, on this basis, it is not sufficient to explain white evangelical views on race in terms of individualism; their embrace of disparaging racial stereotypes is also clearly a factor.

The racialization of Muslim communities presents another striking example. Carr and Haynes address the situation in the Republic of Ireland, where Muslims represent a small minority in an otherwise culturally monolithic population. According to 2016 figures, Muslims make up 1.33 per cent of Ireland's population, having grown exponentially through economic migration and the arrival of refugees since the 1990s (Carr and Haynes 2015: 22). While the Roman Catholic majority has shrunk in recent years (from 84.2 to 78.3 per cent between 2011 and 2016), it remains an overwhelming majority (Central Statistics Office 2017: 72). Carr and Haynes remark on the prejudice and hostility experienced by Muslims in Ireland, using the language of racism to describe how they are viewed through racialized discourses: 'Anti-Muslim racism operates on Muslim communities through historically informed racialized discourses that centre on assertions of Muslim homogeneity, inferiority, misogyny, atavism and incompatibility with "Western values". Muslim identities and symbols of Islam are frequently presented as synonymous with terrorism, fundamentalism, repression of women and extremism' (2015: 24).

Carr and Haynes allude to the reservations some have about describing anti-Muslim prejudice as a form of racism. A principal objection is based on the fact that Islam is not coincident with any specific ethnic or racial group but includes a wide range of cultural identities. Carr and Haynes reject this objection, however, on the grounds that the prejudice Muslims experience functions like conventional racism and has the same pernicious impact that acts of racism do on their victims. They deploy the concept of 'racialization' to capture the way in which Muslims are ascribed negative qualities, highlighting how 'the ascription of essentialized difference gives power to and informs racist ideologies and exclusionary practices' (2015: 24). The concept of racialization is central to this counter-argument because it highlights how markers of religion and markers of race can converge in constructions of 'otherness' that then form the basis of ongoing prejudice. It may also highlight cases of religious *misrecognition*, as outlined in Chapter 5. 'Racialization' captures the process of being reified into a racial category, even if that coincides with a religious identity. Indeed, as Leonie Jackson comments in her study of Islamophobia in Britain, claims that Islamophobia is nothing more than the legitimate criticism of a belief system are 'undermined by the fact that religious belonging has come to act as a symbol of racial difference' (Jackson 2018: 10).

This is evident in Carr and Haynes's study of Ireland, which found Muslims marked as different from an imagined cultural norm of 'Irishness': '[t]hey were not Catholic, most were racialized as non-white, and many were immigrants, lacking that most significant marker of belonging – an "authentic" Irish accent' (2015: 28). However, Carr and Haynes identify patterns of anti-Muslim prejudice that go beyond ethnic identity markers; speaking to Irish converts to Islam, they discover hostility is also levelled at those who are viewed as having betrayed their Irishness, as if being Muslim and being Irish were mutually exclusive. Lying behind this is the enduring assumption that to be Irish is to be Catholic, even if this is expressed in purely cultural terms.

Conclusion

Tracing the ways in which religious movements perpetuate or resist dominant patterns of prejudice, or sustain existing inequalities, calls attention to the capacity of our conceptual tools to identify such patterns. Maintaining a subtle conceptual approach to power is especially important when engaging with a neoliberal cultural framework. Much of the social scientific scholarship about the cultural impact of neoliberalism takes a thoroughly critical perspective, highlighting the complicity of neoliberal assumptions in a range of social problems, from racial injustice to the dismantling of the welfare state. These are fair accusations, but they are also often accompanied by a simplistic take on power, collapsing it into the imposition of the state or maintenance of elite class interests (Flew 2015). Power within neoliberal contexts is more complex than this, and religious frames of reference add to the complexity. As the examples addressed earlier illustrate, religious movements can be deeply complicit in the perpetuation of racism, misogyny and other forms of prejudice, and in the maintenance of social inequalities. But the emergent exercise of power is not simple nor inevitable and illustrates a capacity for resistance as well as compliance with prevailing religious or social norms. Most important for the sociology of religion is the task of tracing the connections between the religious and non-religious sources that enable expressions of power. Only then can claims of authority be examined critically and observations about power be useful within the context of moral debate. We return to this issue in Chapter 9.

Further reading

I claimed towards the beginning of this chapter that the best sociological studies of religion include close attention to how the concepts central to a movement's identity are formulated and lived out in empirical reality. The following examples also happen to address issues of power: its use and misuse.

Gerardo Marti's timely study *American Blindspot: Race, Class, Religion, and the Trump Presidency* (2020) is a superb examination of the complex factors which conspired to take Donald Trump to the White House in 2016. Carefully researched, it is a masterclass in an intersectional sociology which takes history seriously. Dana Malone's *From Single to Serious: Relationships, Gender, and Sexuality on American Evangelical Campuses* (2018) is an in-depth ethnographic study of how religious identities influence how romantic relationships are pursued and managed. It strikes an impressive balance between carefully evidenced observation and ethical comment. For an insightful and beautifully written study in visual anthropology, Emma Tarlo's *Visibly Muslim: Fashion, Politics, Faith* (2010) is excellent. Within other fields of sociology, studies by Beer (2016), Davies (2015) and Tyler (2020) illuminate various configurations of power distinctive to neoliberal conditions.

CHAPTER 8
THE SECULAR AND THE NON-RELIGIOUS IN NEOLIBERAL CONTEXTS

Introduction

In August 2016, a curious and alarming story made its way into the mainstream press. A woman had been approached by four policemen on a beach in the popular tourist resort of Nice, in southern France. She had been wearing a form of clothing that covered her head and body and had been instructed to remove some of her garments, which she did. This was to comply with the recently introduced ban on 'burkinis', a garment covering the entire body except the face, hands and feet, designed to reflect Islamic teaching on modest dress while also being lightweight and hence suitable for swimming. Nice was the latest in a series of French municipalities to ban the burkini that year, citing the inappropriateness of wearing clothing that 'manifests adherence to a religion at a time when France and places of worship are the target of terrorist attacks' (Quinn 2016). The previous month, on Nice's Promenade des Anglais, Tunisian French resident Mohamed Lahouaiej-Bouhlel had driven a cargo truck into crowds of people celebrating Bastille Day, killing 86 and injuring 458 others. The Islamic State terrorist group claimed responsibility for the attack. As a consequence, tensions were high, as were sensitivities surrounding terrorism committed in the name of Islam. But the evidence suggests this was not just about security. The same story made mention of a Muslim woman in Cannes, who had been fined on a beach after wearing leggings, a tunic and a headscarf. The ticket issued to her by the authorities apparently stated that she had not been wearing an outfit 'respecting good morals and secularism'.

This move to police secularism by issuing regulations about the kinds of religious dress not permissible in public is not restricted to France. Austria and Denmark banned face veiling in public in 2017 and partial bans have been passed into law in a range of other nations or federal regions across the globe. A ban on the public wearing of burqas – garments covering the entire body, head and face – has been in place in France since 2010 and is in keeping with its secularist tradition that views expressions of religious identity as improper within public spaces. The burkini bans marked a step change in this debate insofar as the letter and implementation of the new regulations extended well beyond full veiling garments. They also constituted new methods of disciplining gender identities not in the name of religious conformity but in the name of Western 'liberalism' – women were sanctioned for wearing *too much clothing* and thereby failing to uphold the secularity of the French Republic.

This set of cases is especially striking as it illustrates how forms of secularity are often shaped around *religious* identities. Upholding French secularism, in the examples cited, entails the repression of distinctively Muslim forms of self-expression. The women in Nice and Cannes were transgressing the rules of French secularism by dressing in a way that was read as inappropriately religious. But within the French context – with Muslims making up its largest religious minority, many of whom wear traditional Islamic dress, with some women veiled – 'inappropriately religious' may be read as Muslim.

James Beckford has argued that adopting a social scientific perspective on religion requires us to include 'examining critically the social processes whereby certain things are counted as religious' (Beckford 2003: 3). In other words, taking seriously the social character of religion involves taking seriously the routes we take in deciding what constitutes 'religion' and on what basis. The same logic applies to the secular. One of the 'blind spots' of much scholarship and popular understanding of the secular has been the assumption that it may be treated as an absence of religion, 'seen less as a concrete reality than a marker that flags where religion once stood' (Lee 2015: 7). Moreover, the absence of religion is taken to indicate a neutral space from which to view religion. Secularity has been treated as an intellectual vantage point, one untainted by ideology or bias in the way that religious identities are. As such, it has often been presented as especially well-suited to an academic perspective. Secularity has been accorded a status Ruth Sheldon associates with the contemporary 'Western' university: 'a transcendent site of neutral arbitration, passing judgement from an objective, ahistorical and deterritorialised location' (2016: 84). It maintains scholarly credibility by its presumed neutrality, sobriety and critical distance.

Recent scholarship on religion and the secular has problematized this understanding, drawing attention to how these two phenomena are mutually constitutive. As in contemporary France, the secular emerges in distinct forms that reflect both its cultural context and the forms of religion in relation to which it is being conceived. In this sense, religion and the secular exist in dialectical relationship, and a sociological approach demands we attend to the complex ways in which both are socially constructed. However, attending to these complexities also helps us clarify what we mean when we *use* these concepts. In other words, it has benefits in thinking through matters of theory and method. This is the central concern of the present chapter, which takes the 'secular' not as a discrete phenomenon but as a lens through which to examine how we conceive of religion, as well as related concepts, in the twenty-first century. As we do so, arriving at a more specific understanding of the 'secular' – rather than one that equates it with everything that is *not* religion – has distinct advantages (Lee 2015: 47).

The emergence of 'non-religion' as a category

Most analyses of secularization tend to present a wealth of data on eroding religious beliefs and practices but give scant attention to the identities of those who would eventually become known as the 'nones', those who, when asked questions on surveys about their religion, claim that they have none. One possible reason for this is the enduring assumption among social scientists that the 'irreligious' are characterized by rational, moderate thinking and so are less interesting than the religious (Campbell 1971). Over the past fifteen years or so, scholarly interest in the category of non-religion has grown considerably. Spurred on by the public visibility of 'new atheism' (Taira 2012), academic interest in forms of religion or spirituality not captured by conventional categories (Day 2013; Heelas and Woodhead 2005; Voas 2009) and the increasing proportions of survey respondents opting for 'non-religion' across the globe (Thiessen and Wilkins-Laflamme 2020), the non-religious became increasingly hard to ignore (Bullivant 2020).

In the ensuing scholarship, much interest has focused on developing a more finely grained understanding of those who fall outside of conventional religious categories of identity. This is the more empirical concern of the 'non-religion' field. How should we make sense of the variety of orientations that fall within this catch-all category? What does saying they have 'no religion' indicate about people's attitudes, values and perspectives on the world? And how does this relate to other human perspectives on religion, like atheism, agnosticism or secularism? How do these patterns vary across different cultures? How does an affirmation of 'non-religion' relate to religious practice or affiliation? The absence of membership and regular participation in a local place of worship will carry very different meanings for an evangelical Protestant, a Reform Jew and a Theravada Buddhist. We need to consider how we are measuring non-religion and whether this measure is suited to the traditions and circumstances we study (Ammerman 2021). We know there are contexts in which affiliation with a religious tradition is accompanied by a lack of religious belief, at least in the conventional sense of the term (Davies and Northam-Jones 2012). How should we handle cases where religious affiliation or self-ascription appears to function as a cultural, rather than religious, identity? Religious disaffiliation often carries different meanings for first- and second-generation immigrants, the latter coming to terms with their identities in light of their parents' heritage *and* their status as citizens of a different culture. In the UK, research has revealed how those who migrated from the Indian subcontinent in the 1960s and 1970s attach a different kind of significance to Islam from their children and grandchildren, who were born and raised in the UK context (Anwar 1979; Kashyap and Lewis 2013). As families transition to new environments, religion can, among other things, serve as a carrier of former cultural attachments, a source of moral wisdom passed across generations or a symbolic focus of difference in a new context viewed as uncomfortably 'secular'. In this sense, patterns of disaffiliation or rejection can illuminate the more complex ways in which religion and non-religion interrelate within different social settings.

But the debates about 'non-religion' also have a more conceptual dimension. The concern here is with the identities against which religion tends to be defined and practised. The interest is in non-religion *in relation to* religion, rather than as a complex category designating perspectives that are demonstrably not religious – or indeed *anti-religious*. Put another way, it is interested in the 'other' that is presupposed by different forms of religion. This conceptual angle is useful because it helps illuminate examples of non-religious phenomena which, while disavowing any link to religion, appear to mirror or imitate religious forms. One example would be humanist chaplaincy, which in the UK has developed into a well-resourced tradition of pastoral support in hospitals, prisons and universities, effectively adapting a pre-existing Christian tradition into a non-religious framework (Aune, Guest and Law 2019: 93–4). Another example would be the occurrence of identifiably religious concepts within non-religious perspectives. In their research into non-religious millennials across six European countries, Herbert and Bullock find young people invoking karma and the Christian 'golden rule' and interpret this as a belief in cosmic justice (2020: 166). Their interviewees' conviction that some non-material force was guiding the moral order of life suggested their worldview was not limited to rational-material assumptions.

The conceptual angle on non-religion is useful for a second reason. It aids us as we probe broader questions about power, the bases of social order and the constitution of knowledge, as phenomena that emerge from an interaction between religious and non-religious social forces. The late anthropologist Saba Mahmood's work was remarkable in this respect, repeatedly pushing back against concepts and arguments about religious phenomena that are framed around a 'Western' or 'Western Christian' perspective. Her intention was not simply to ensure greater inclusivity of hitherto excluded religious forms. Rather, it was to emphasize how religious developments always emerge in dialogue with or in reaction to notable 'others' – whether religious, non-religious or both – and that this relationship must inform our critical understanding. Mahmood published an incisive critique of Charles Taylor's *A Secular Age* (2007), in which she challenges his presentation of Christian history. Reviewing Taylor's account of Christian missionary work, Mahmood asks why he has not considered how these cultural encounters with potential Christian converts in turn shaped Christianity. He recounts how Christian missionaries encountered distant (and more proximate) cultures but does not examine how these asymmetrical power relationships were influential on how Christianity developed as a global force and carrier of 'Western' interests. As she puts it,

These encounters did not simply leave Christianity untouched but transformed it from within, a transformation that should be internal to any self-understanding of Christianity. Omission of this story is akin to the omission of the history of slavery and colonialism from accounts of post-Enlightenment modernity – an omission that enables both a progressivist notion of history and normative claims about who is qualified to be 'modern' or 'civilized'. (Mahmood 2010: 285–6)

To assess the social significance of religious movements and ideas and not consider their religious and non-religious contexts is to leave out half of the picture and to overlook how inequalities of power determine the terms of the debate. It is also inconsistent with a sociological approach attentive to how things emerge from social relationships.

It is in this sense that Lois Lee distinguishes 'non-religion' from the 'secular'. The 'non-religious', according to Lee, encompasses 'any phenomenon – position, perspective, or practice – that is primarily understood in relation to religion but which is not itself considered to be religious' (Lee 2015: 32). It is an approach that recognizes the relational way in which meaning emerges in social life. It includes, for example, human perspectives defined in contrast to traditional religious ones and the social forms of gathering or practice that follow templates inherited from religious phenomena, even as they may view themselves as diametrically opposed to those same religious phenomena. A striking example is the Sunday Assembly, established in London in 2013 as a non-religious version of a traditional church service, where hundreds regularly gather together to sing, hear poetry, listen to guest speakers and eat tea and cake (Bullock 2018). According to its website, there are now forty Sunday Assemblies across the world. The concept of 'non-religion' is in this sense structured around *difference*, in contrast with terms like 'irreligion', 'anti-religion' or 'post-religion', which assume a relationship of rejection. By emphasizing difference rather than rejection, 'non-religion' has an elasticity, an openness that is better suited to capture the complexities of those phenomena that emerge in relation to, even while being different from, religion. The conceptual space created by non-religion helps us make sense of the social significance of religion in a way that gets beyond the unhelpful binary of 'believers' and 'rejectors'. By admitting a variety of orientations to religion, it acknowledges the significance of those who are unsure, changeable or situationally selective, when it comes to their engagement with religious ideas and practices. It is also open enough to get beyond analyses of religion structured around the sovereign individual, as if the only thing 'religion' can be, if important, is the object of subjective personal assent. In other words, adopting this approach permits us to consider religion not only as a facet of identity but also as a political resource, an aesthetic indulgence, an aspect of family heritage or the target of acerbic humour, depending on the empirical evidence before us. In other words, it helps us imagine new ways of relating to religious phenomena.

In this respect, Lee's notion of the 'non-religious' is compatible with other approaches that have recently emerged in the sociology of religion that aim to retrieve the everyday complexity of social phenomena. For example, scholarship oriented around the idea of 'lived religion' or 'material religion' seeks traces of the religious in a broader range of social phenomena than has been traditionally the case in the social sciences. Rather than assessing conformity to established standards of religiosity (e.g. self-identification on surveys, regular worship, levels of belief), such approaches look first to the everyday experiences of people and to the significances they attach to them (McGuire 2008). Their theoretical insights have been transplanted into the study of 'non-religion', for example in research into 'lived humanism' (Engelke 2014). This is not to say that the 'non-religious', in this broad sense, may be collapsible into the 'religious', nor that it implies that 'non-religious' phenomena are *really* religious or *implicitly* religious. Rather, it is to acknowledge that the religious and non-religious interact in a variety of complex ways that defy simple categorization or easy binaries. The theory of 'non-religion' that Lee advocates is not intended to be an essentializing device, pointing to the fundamental nature of something as religious or non-religious. Rather, it is to sensitize sociological enquiry to empirical complexity. As she puts it, 'What is necessary is to recognize that empirical cases we take as our units of analysis are typically complicated, multifaceted, and, like all human cultural forms, perfectly capable of accommodating contradictions' (Lee 2015: 35).

By adopting this new approach to the 'non-religious', so Lee argues, we are also able to re-imagine the 'secular' as a much narrower, and therefore more useful, category. The 'secular', on this understanding, refers to the subordination of religious or spiritual concerns to other powers or interests. This understanding of the 'secular' echoes that explored in Talal Asad's influential book *Formations of the Secular* (2003). According to Asad, the concept of the 'secular', far from a neutral placeholder, emerges historically in a way that is attached to particular interests. It is in attending to how the secular is formed, argues Asad, that we arrive at a more nuanced grasp of why particular religious and non-religious narratives, practices and identities maintain a position of privilege, while others remain marginal or are objects of exclusion. A recurring theme in his book is the way in which the history of Europe has been framed around the exclusion of Islam as an uncivilized 'other'. Other scholars inspired by Asad's work have adopted a similarly critical approach in excavating the genealogy of the secular within post-colonial contexts, identifying the ways in which 'Western' formulations of religion and non-religion have framed our understandings of the global south (e.g. Egorova 2018; Engelke 2015; Mahmood 2016).

The UK through the lens of 'non-religion'

Following this conceptual discussion of non-religion in relation to other categories of analysis, it will be useful to observe how they may be applied. The contemporary UK provides us with an interesting case study. There have, for many years, been scholars who have argued that the UK is now, essentially, a non-religious country. The modern period has been characterized by a persistent decline in regular church attendance, a withdrawal of religious organizations from the governance of everyday life and a gradual erosion in traditional religious belief among the population at large (Guest, Olson and Wolffe 2012; Voas and Bruce 2019). While there are indications that labelling the UK as wholly and comprehensively unreligious would be simplistic and premature (the case of Northern Ireland is a clear exception to the overall rule), it is difficult to deny that the nation is not as religious in traditional terms as it used to be. The British Social Attitudes Survey (BSAS) has been collecting data on the opinions and lives of the British people (a cross-section of citizens resident in England, Wales and Scotland) since 1983. In its annual survey for 2018, the BSAS found that more than half (52 per cent) of the population now identified as not belonging to any religion. The longitudinal data (1983–2018) show a clear pattern of steady decline in the proportion self-identifying as Christian (from two-thirds to just over a third), a steady rise in the 'non-religious' (from just over 30 per cent to 52 per cent) and a more gradual increase in those identifying with a non-Christian religion (from around 2 per cent to just under 10 per cent). In its apparent majority non-religious status, the UK now mirrors a demographic pattern evident in at least seven other European nations (Herbert and Bullock 2018). But what characterizes this 52 per cent of the British public who identify as 'non-religious'? What kind of perspective on religion do they have? And do they share other perspectives or values, aside from distancing themselves from the category 'religion' when taking part in social surveys?

It is another symptom of Britain's secularized status that the British Social Attitudes Survey only asks a very limited set of questions about religion and belief, presumably on the understandable assumption that such things are of limited interest to most British people. So, it is especially helpful to have evidence from other sources, like the YouGov survey analysed by Linda Woodhead (2016) that tells us not only how many 'non-religious' people there are but what else distinguishes this group with respect to their perspective and attitudes. Are they all atheists, for example, or secularists? Do they have strongly anti-religious views, or are they just indifferent to matters of religion? And how do their social attitudes compare to those of religious people?

Woodhead (2016) found that to affirm a position of 'no religion' was more popular among younger rather than older people – 60 per cent of those under forty say they have 'no religion'; 40 per cent of those over forty affirm the same position. This is perhaps understandable; as religion fades from view, we can expect to find residual attachment among older generations, while younger generations are less interested as fewer have been raised in a religious tradition (Voas and Crockett 2005). In terms of ethnicity, the vast majority of the 'non-religious' identify as 'white British', perhaps highlighting stronger ties to religion among ethnic minorities. Whether the religion of those who trace their family origins to the Indian subcontinent, Africa or the West Indies represents a religious or cultural attachment is an interesting question and one that needs careful handling.

Woodhead's survey suggests the non-religious are more liberal in values than Christians and Muslims, that is more accepting of those who are different, more politically progressive, more permissive in their moral views. They are more internationalist, likely to see links with other countries as positive opportunities, rather than limitations on British sovereignty; unsurprisingly, therefore, they are also more pro-European than pro-Brexit. However, it is important to stress that the non-religious are not radically different from the general population in these respects. Also, the 'non-religious' are not a single, coherent group. They are united by a rejection of 'religious' as a label, rather than a positive affirmation of a particular non-religious perspective. They affirm a spectrum of orientations to the religious or spiritual and only a minority are convinced atheists. As Woodhead puts it, those who reject conventional religion by affirming they have 'no religion' 'do not necessarily become atheists, or abandon the belief that there are things beyond this life which give it meaning' (2016: 45).

This last point is important as it alerts us to the fact that the boundaries that distinguish the religious from the non-religious do not appear to be about belief in God, the divine or a 'higher power' as such. For example, when asked if they believe that 'There is definitely a God or some "higher power"', 39 per cent of those reporting a religion of some kind agree; the figure for the non-religious is 5.5 per cent. Faced with the statement 'No, there is definitely NOT a God or some "higher power"', 41.5 per cent of 'nones' agree, but so do 6 per cent of the religious (Woodhead 2016: 250). The differences are significant, but not definitive, and certainly rule out the notion that beliefs in the supernatural are the sole preserve of the religious or that the non-religious are distinguished by a rejection of such ideas. Several observations are worth highlighting. Those who hold a position of absolute confidence (either that there is a God or that there isn't one) are in the minority among both the religious and the non-religious. The majority among both groups affirm a level of uncertainty about this issue. Following on from this, a small but significant minority (16.5 per cent) of the non-religious nevertheless say they believe there is probably or definitely a God or 'some higher power'. So, to be non-religious is not necessarily to be a 'non-believer' as such. Conversely, among the religious, a similar proportion (17 per cent) say there is probably or definitely *not* a God or some 'higher power'. So, to affirm a religious identity is not the same as believing in God, and a significant number affirm one without affirming the other.

Other research on the UK has used empirical data to challenge conventional understandings of religious categories, illustrating, for example, the destabilization of Christianity as a category of identity (Guest et al. 2013). The label 'Christian' clearly encompasses a range of meanings, including some that have little or nothing to do with religious belief or practice. Other studies have explored its use to convey ethnic, national, moral or aspirational identities (Day 2013; Guest 2019; Storm 2013). Looking at things the other way around, we can see the benefits of examining non-religion in relation to religion. For example, Matthew Engelke's ethnographic study of a branch of the British Humanist Association in London demonstrates how its members define their humanism in relation to what they consider to be Christianity. Their humanism is defined in relation to a Christian 'other'. Members of the branch consider themselves to be rational, reasonable people who think freely and take evidence seriously, and they are definitely not religious. But their expressions of identity, value and practice as humanists are, as Engelke puts it, 'all acts, articulations, and assertions of what it means to be religious and not in contemporary Britain' (Engelke 2014: 299). For these humanists, to be religious – what they are *not* – is to have 'beliefs', which for them amount to irrational claims that 'believers' uphold without subjecting them to critical scrutiny. They are not explicable in 'scientific' terms and are bound to collapse should they be measured against good evidence.

In this sense, the humanists of Engelke's study mirror the post-Enlightenment argument that religion amounts to a set of (irrational) propositions. An abundance of scholarship over the past twenty-five years or so has demonstrated how purportedly universal definitions of 'religion' are heavily indebted to the liberal Protestantism of the nineteenth century, especially in the privileging of 'belief' (Lindquist and Coleman 2008). As Meyer and Houtman put it, '"belief" has been "universalized" through scientific, religious, and political practices, such as evolutionary schemes, Christian missionization, and colonial governance' (2012: 2). The naturalization of 'belief' has even been extended beyond religion, into constructs of non-religion, as with the UK's Equality Act (2010), which includes in its list of 'protected characteristics', alongside gender, disability and sexual orientation, 'religion *and belief*' (italics added). In one respect this has been a source of empowerment for religious *and* non-religious groups, as one party has appealed to the circumstances of others in their campaign for equal treatment. It has, for example, enabled Humanists UK (formerly the British Humanist Association) to establish a successful humanist pastoral care service in UK hospitals, in recognition that healthcare chaplaincy had long been dominated by Christian clergy and therefore failed to cater to the needs of non-religious patients. What McIvor calls the 'juridification' of religion – its regulation under anti-discrimination and equality legislation (McIvor 2020: 4) – also changes the way in which religious rights are established and enforced. Emerging legal disputes require religion – and 'belief' – to interact with other identity markers incorporated into those pieces of legislation, which often means religious controversies appear in the public realm alongside matters of gender and sexuality. It is important to note that such disputes do not always involve religious organizations defending a morally conservative position against a more 'liberal' state, despite high-profile evangelical organizations perhaps giving that impression. In Canada, for example, it was the actions of the Metropolitan Community Church in Toronto that precipitated the change in law – first at the provincial and then at the national level – to allow same-sex marriage. Its argument was based on the claim that its freedom to express its religious beliefs was impaired by this *not* being permitted in law.

In spite of this renewed presence in public disputes, an emphasis on 'belief' tends to imagine religion (and by extension, non-religion) as chiefly an interior matter: subjective, internal, private and whose place within the public sphere is contested. Insofar as this view is evident across 'Western' societies, it is unsurprising that expressions of religious identity within the public sphere can attract controversy. It also accords a particular vulnerability to those groups whose religious orientation is most visible. In European societies in which religion is viewed as a private matter, for example, the turban or hijab can attract suspicion as an affront to the secular public sphere. Newly built mosques or temples can provoke hostility for similar reasons. Campaigns to 'ban the burqa' or block the development of a new 'super mosque' are in this sense not simply about religious prejudice or racism but about cleansing the public realm of objects that disturb or unsettle. And yet to keep any symbolic expression of one's religious identity concealed in public is often a privilege of the white Christian or non-religious majority, both of whom benefit from the fact that their orientations to religion do not tend to be associated – rightly or wrongly – with particular styles of dress that stand out from the 'norm'. The 'norm' here is the key point of course; there is a privilege in being part of 'things as they normally are', which points to the close relationship between power and secularity. Despite the claims of some of its public advocates, secularism is not a neutral perspective facilitating equal treatment of religious groups. Rather, it emerges shaped by the social contexts in which it is found.

Political variants of secularism: The United States and France

If we follow Lois Lee in treating the 'secular' as a movement to subdue or subordinate religion, then 'secularism' is its ideological expression. Secularism represents an attempt to codify the subordination of religion in favour of other authorities within a moral-political programme. Secularism is not a simple or singular phenomenon, however, and it has taken a variety of forms within different cultural contexts. These have also changed over time, so that, for example, contemporary Russia is a very different context for religion than the explicitly atheistic Soviet Union, whose communist state viewed religion as incompatible with its vision for society. In extreme situations like these, secularism and atheism are merged in a totalitarian system; religion is illegitimate and therefore not permitted to be expressed. Such arrangements are much rarer nowadays, and while the fall of Soviet communism in the 1980s and 1990s has not removed elements of authoritarianism in certain former-communist countries (see Putin's Russia), hard-line secularism of the communist kind is a lot less common in the twenty-first century. What is more persistent and of international significance are the kinds of constitutional secularism we find in some liberal democracies, which tend to coexist with neoliberal economies. A couple of the most striking examples are worth examining in detail.

The United States is built on a secularist foundation insofar as its constitution affirms the separation of church and state. The constitution was formulated and ratified in the late 1700s and outlines a vision for a new kind of society for a modern age. It reflects how the founders of the United States sought to build their nation on a fresh set of principles that distinguish it from its British origins. The constitution has been subject to a number of amendments, the first ten of which, ratified in December 1791, are collectively referred to as the 'Bill of Rights'. The first amendment begins: 'Congress shall make no law respecting an establishment of religion, or prohibiting the free exercise thereof.' From its earliest days, therefore, the United States upheld as a core principle its rejection of the idea of an 'established' religion. Unlike the UK, with its established Church of England, the United States determined to privilege no single tradition and, instead, protect the rights of its citizens to practice the free exercise of religion. Indeed, this arrangement set the scene for a history of religious engagement in the United States markedly different from Western Europe.

It is important to warn against idealizing the US tradition. History teaches us that while rejecting the idea of an 'established' religion and becoming a context in which various forms of Christianity would thrive in a way difficult to imagine in Europe, the early US nation was hardly a 'level playing field' when it came to the 'free exercise' of religion. Indeed, 'religion' here really meant the denominations of Protestant Christianity, with some enjoying much more power than others. The experiences of marginal groups like Catholics, Quakers and Mormons were hardly of peaceful acceptance, and the persecution of the First Nations peoples is well documented (Marti 2020). However, the constitution did establish a separation of church and state that initiated a distinctively US version of secularism that survives – albeit with subtle cultural adjustments – to this day. It frames a number of religious controversies that remain contentious, such as the outlawing of prayer within public schools, or the use of Christian symbolism within or on public buildings such as law courts. Most intriguingly, the United States' secularism coexists with relatively high levels of religious participation for a liberal-democratic nation. While these levels are in decline and the proportion of the 'non-religious' has steadily grown, grassroots religious observance has consistently exceeded that found in many other economically prosperous nations. There is a juridical sense in which religion is kept out of elements of the country's governance and public services, but at the same time religion – especially conservative Protestantism – remains a vibrant and influential element of its national life (see Chapter 3). Moreover, survey research suggests atheists function as a principal symbolic 'other', attracting higher levels of distrust than most other groups. So, within the United States, a strong tradition of secularism coexists with high levels of stigma attached to atheism at the grassroots level, highlighting 'the historic place of religion in underpinning moral order in the United States' (Edgell, Gerteis and Hartmann 2006: 230).

The US situation can be contrasted with that of France, which was mentioned at the start of this chapter. Like the United States, France derives its secularist identity from a constitutional expression of values which emerged in the aftermath of a revolution in the late eighteenth century. But in the French case, secularism – or laïcité, as it is called – represents a much more thoroughgoing removal of religion from the French Republic. The Declaration of the Rights of Man and of the Citizen dates from 1789 and was written in consultation with Thomas Jefferson, one of the principal authors of the US Declaration of Independence and its third president (Smith 2006: 53–90). The document seeks to establish France on the basis of universal laws applicable to all of humanity and hence implies a kind of natural law that is secular insofar as it depends in no way on the teachings of the Church. Article 10 states that 'No one may be disquieted for his opinions, even religious ones, provided that their manifestation does not trouble the public order established by the law', reflecting the US constitution's affirmation of free exercise of religion and of speech. The Declaration is incorporated into the French Constitution, the most recent version being the Constitution of the Fifth Republic, introduced by President Charles de Gaulle in 1958. The Constitution upholds four key principles: free access to social welfare for those who need it, the democratic election of government, the French people indivisible by being united by a common language with all equal and laïcité, that is the separation of churches – and nowadays, all religion – from the state.

The French version of secularism is very different from the US one as it imagines equality and citizenship in secular terms. While it also rests on the separation of church and state, this separation is subject to a more maximalist reading. It is the removal of religion not simply from the formal machinery of the state but also from the public realm through which French national identity is constituted (Berger, Davie and Fokas 2008: 17). To affirm equality for all is to affirm that all have in common their membership of the French Republic, which is secular. Religion, if it is to have a place in life, should be confined to the private realm, a matter for families and individuals to pursue in ways that do not compromise their public expression of French identity. This means that religion is not just removed from systems and contexts of government; it also means its open and visible expression in public is viewed as problematic, perhaps even disloyal. It is important not to allow this description to slip into a caricature, though. Despite its rather uncompromising secularism, the division between religion and the state in France is not absolute. Around a fifth of French schoolchildren are taught in religious (mainly Catholic) schools that are state-subsidized. And since 2003, France has had a national Muslim council (the Conseil Français du Culte Musulman), which serves as an official body representing Muslims in dialogue with the French state (Modood 2019: 125; 168). So the French state maintains institutional linkages to religious bodies, even while affirming a strong commitment to laïcité.

The vignette that opened this chapter provides a powerful example of how the French tradition of laïcité has had a particularly constrictive impact on Muslims in recent years. Since 2004, it has been illegal in France for Muslims to wear headscarves in public schools. This was justified with reference to an earlier law passed in the spirit of laïcité, which states that no visible religious symbols should be worn by students or staff within French public schools. However, politicians' justifications for this and other rulings have cited other factors, such as the presumption that the burqa represents the oppression or isolation of women and that face veiling is a security threat. It would appear that the formal expression of laïcité is sometimes less intolerant than its cultural elaboration among politicians and officials.

Within contexts where acts of terrorism have recently occurred in the name of Islam, its public visibility is a sensitive issue. And yet there are no moves at all within the UK context to impose regulation of the kind found in France as well as various other European nations, despite similar terrorist incidents occurring on British soil. Chapter 5 described how Islam in the UK has been subjected to a state-driven process of securitization in recent years, and hostility to traditional Islamic dress is a well-documented phenomenon among the public and some politicians (Jackson 2018). That this has not been translated into legislation against religious clothing reflects the very different traditions of secularity within the two countries. The French case also highlights the close relationship between the regulation of religion by the state and patterns of religious tolerance and intolerance. According to Luca Mavelli, the situation in France assumes 'an interventionist idea of the state, whose role is to "liberate" the individual – primarily women – by disciplining them in a secular understanding of the self characterised by the privatisation of religion' (Mavelli 2013: 177).

The French case is distinguished by an especially strident tendency on the part of the state to intervene in cases of religious – especially Islamic – public expression. Quite aside from what this says about Islam as Europe's religious 'other' (see Chapter 3), it is also part of a pattern of tensions that have, in recent years, seen forms of Islamic and secular militancy go head-to-head in public disputes (Nielsen 2010). Sadly, this has involved acts of terrorism and angry counter-reactions in several European countries, which have heightened religious intolerance at a time of already strained relationships. These expressions of secular militancy have coalesced around issues of free speech, provoked especially by two related incidents.

In September 2005, the Danish national newspaper *Jyllands-Posten* published a set of twelve cartoons depicting the Prophet Muhammad. Given the Islamic tradition of aniconism (opposing the depiction of revered figures, including the Prophet) and the nature of the images (which exploited caricatures of Muslims, including as terrorists), the publication triggered a hostile response from across the Muslim community in

Denmark, across Europe and beyond. Some Muslim nations boycotted Danish goods. There were mass protests in Muslim countries, and the consequent hostilities led to around 200 deaths. While Muslim critics called attention to the offensive nature of the images, others defended their publication on the basis of freedom of expression. The cultural editor of *Jyllands-Posten* justified the publication of the images as a means of assisting 'Muslims to be acculturated into Danish public culture' (Modood 2019: 170). This same editor expressed the view that in expecting their religious sensitivities to be observed, some Muslims were demanding special treatment which 'is incompatible with secular democracy and freedom of expression, in which one must be prepared to tolerate derision, mockery and ridicule' (quoted in Nielsen 2010: 223). The incident triggered an international debate about the proper limits to religious tolerance within so-called secular cultures. The Danish prime minister, Anders Fogh Rasmussen, referred to the cartoon controversy as the country's biggest foreign policy crisis since the Second World War (Kühle 2018: 219).

Ten years later, in January 2015, two brothers broke into the offices of the French satirical magazine *Charlie Hebdo*; they were armed and killed twelve people, injuring eleven others. The attackers claimed allegiance to the Yemeni branch of Al-Qaeda, and their attack marked a culmination of a series of plots that targeted the magazine for its irreverent depiction of Islam, including the reproduction of the cartoons from *Jyllands-Posten*. The incident led to a mass demonstration of solidarity in Paris – 'Je suis Charlie' – as well as a renewed defence of freedom of speech as a quintessentially French – and Western – value (Figure 11).

The two incidents were united in provoking a public clash between secularity and religion, specifically Islam. In so doing, they highlight a fervent secularism commonly

Figure 11 A 2015 rally in Brussels in support of the victims of the *Charlie Hebdo* shootings. *Source*: Miguel Discart via Wikimedia Commons.

associated with Western Europe that has made Islam its primary 'other' (Miera and Pala 2009). The cartoons published by *Jyllands-Posten* and *Charlie Hebdo* raise questions about what constitutes religious or cultural offence and what counts as a reasonable response, including the question of regulation and legal protections. The incidents also illustrate the power of a secularist campaign that hinges on freedom of expression as a moral value. The othering of Islam as a special case and its construction as a religion incompatible with European identity were reinforced by the invocation of a moral principle that could be claimed to be quintessentially of 'the West'. As many Muslim and non-Muslim commentators have since affirmed, this opposition between freedom of expression and Islam is a gross contrivance (Asad et al. 2013). However, the rhetoric is powerful and reinforces the dualistic Islam versus the West logic that has been worryingly prevalent in recent years.

Secularism and the neoliberal subject

While often framed by national identity, ideological traditions of secularism are not always contained by national borders. French laïcité was a key inspiration for the former Ottoman Empire as well as the foundation of the Turkish Republic in the early twentieth century (Gökariksel and Mitchell 2005: 148). International regulatory bodies like the European Court of Human Rights have played an important role adjudicating over legal disputes involving religious expression, effectively contributing to the definition of secularity within nation states. But is there also a sense in which secularity proceeds in alignment with neoliberal economics as a cross-national movement? Is there a relationship between the two that suggests the cultural expressions of neoliberalism favour a form of secularism?

Acknowledging that secularism relates to forms of power, Gökariksel and Mitchell, in a comparative study of France and Turkey, connect it to strategies of control, particularly in the hands of the state: 'As part of a narrative of modernity and progress, secularism is one of the many technologies of control that state actors wield to discipline the wayward bodies of those defined as existing outside the cultural boundaries of the nation, particularly women and migrants' (Gökariksel and Mitchell 2005: 150).

Gökariksel and Mitchell go on to argue that secularism is used as a means of constituting and policing the neoliberal subject. Here they echo other thinkers who identify a tendency among politicians to approach visible signs of religious commitment as impediments to the neoliberal individual (e.g. Mavelli 2013). Ties to cultural or religious identities are read as getting in the way of individuals being free, unattached consumers, capable of engaging freely in the global economic marketplace. Identity difference based on religion is viewed as indicative of bias and constraint, whereas the neoliberal subject is imagined to be 'neutral, rational, equal and competent in neoliberal terms' (Gökariksel and Mitchell 2005: 150). Thinking along these lines, the policing of the burkini in France may be viewed not just as a means of cultural exclusion but of economic discipline. The ideal neoliberal consumer is not weighed down by the loyalties and attachments of religion, so that to be 'secular' is also to be a more functional contributor to neoliberal society. Similar arguments have been used to reinforce the claim that neoliberalism is a driver of secularization, although the national-level evidence paints a variable picture (Hirschle 2010).

Debates about secularism are always bound up in debates about multiculturalism and religious difference. When the secular is invoked as a means of 'othering' Islam, effectively demonizing Muslims as misogynistic, uncivilized or violently fanatical, then there is a need for secularism to be reconfigured along different lines. In a recent collection of essays, Tariq Modood calls for secularism as an orientation of the state to be revised to better accommodate religious diversity. The proposed model would jettison the conceptualization of secularism in terms of neutrality and a strict public-private divide, reconceive equality from sameness to a respect for difference and take a pragmatic approach to dealing with conflict, rather than an ideological, uncompromising one (Modood 2019: 128). Modood describes these aspirations in terms of 'moderate secularism', which he sees as a historical movement in Western Europe, a partially realized social reality from which lessons may be learned. One key characteristic of moderate secularism is its acknowledgement of religion as not just of potential private benefit but also of potential public good (2019: 180). Moreover, this is a case of recognizing not just the contribution religious groups make to society but also the wider damage inflicted by an anti-religious secularism. When intolerance is a persistent reality, the public expression of religious identity can be opposed even among those who have a benign perspective, for they may fear antisocial counter-reactions within their community. This is demonstrated in Sophie Watson's study of opposition to the erection of Orthodox Jewish boundaries (*eruvim*) within neighbourhoods in London and New Jersey (Watson 2005). *Eruvim* are symbolic boundaries that recodify public space as semi-private, thereby making observance of sabbath laws practical without causing avoidable distress or risking harm to vulnerable residents. They typically follow already existing material boundaries – walls or fences, for example – with gaps marked with lengths of cord erected high above the street level, often attached to telegraph poles. To non-Jews they are likely to be invisible, and yet communities become aware of them as their establishment requires local authority permission. Watson found there was significant opposition to *eruvim* within both UK and US case-study locations. Opposition included concerns from Jewish and non-Jewish residents who feared reprisals from racists and the provocation of anti-Jewish sentiments. Public visibility of a Jewish presence was expected to provoke antisocial behaviour that would harm the quality of community life. Put another way, fear of intolerance risked perpetuating the exclusion of religious minorities from public spaces.

As we can see with the example of the burkini ban discussed earlier, the claim that secularism is neutral and benign is often difficult to sustain. In truth, though, some models of secularism never claim to be. Tariq Modood describes the more proactive state secularism found in the cases of France and the Netherlands as a form of 'liberal perfectionism . . . the view . . . that it is the business of a liberal state to produce liberal individuals and promote a liberal way of life' (2019: 171). In other words, the relationship of the state to its citizens is not about upholding diversity but ensuring liberal ideals are embodied in their lives. In practice, this approach can only be sustained if 'liberal' is conceived in fairly broad terms. However, a more common strategy focuses on conspicuous minorities understood to be dissenting from this ideal. There is much political capital to be made from repeating this narrative, especially among populist parties promoting a right-wing, anti-immigration message. In such cases, liberalism develops into illiberalism, as a tradition of freedom is used to foster intolerance.

By contrast, Modood's case for a moderate secularism is based around mutual respect of religious difference, rather than an expectation of sameness or religious privatization. It is also one that demands a maintenance of arrangements at the state level and so is capable of generating policy recommendations. In this sense, it is able to push against the more thoroughgoingly individualistic tendencies of neoliberalism and imagine the secular in socially positive terms. In so doing, it bridges sociological description and social ethics, illustrating how a sociological engagement with religion and non-religion may speak to issues of moral import. In the final chapter, I will discuss why this dual purpose might be an especially important challenge for the sociology of religion and why it is worth retrieving an ethical role for the sub-discipline.

Further reading

Literature that starts with the lens of the 'non-religious' is now much more abundant than it was a few years ago. The non-religion and secularity research network, established by Lois Lee and Stephen Bullivant, has been instrumental in this respect. It also launched an open access online journal – *Secularism and Non-Religion* – which continues to be a valuable resource for current research (see https://secularismandnonreligion.org/).

For a complex, subtle and wide-ranging discussion of these conceptual issues, Lois Lee's *Recognizing the Non-Religious: Reimagining the Secular* (2015) is an excellent guide. A conceptually rich account, focusing on Egypt but with far-reaching implications, is Saba Mahmood's *Religious Difference in a Secular Age* (2016). Illuminating article-length studies of various cultural contexts can be found in Ammerman (2021), Engelke (2014, 2015) and Thiessen and Wilkins-Laflamme (2020). Modood's *Essays on Secularism and Multiculturalism* (2019) connects the debate to issues of ethics and public policy with characteristic insight.

CHAPTER 9
RETRIEVING ETHICS FOR THE SOCIOLOGY
OF RELIGION

Introduction

British sociologist of religion Grace Davie has highlighted the paradox that just when there is an urgent need for clear and well-informed conversations about religion, we appear to be losing 'the vocabulary, tools and concepts' required for this to happen (2015: xii). She is talking about Britain, but the observation could be equally applied to a range of societies in the global north. Secularization has eroded religious literacy as religious authorities have retreated – or been excluded – from the governing institutions of society. At the same time religious matters have resurfaced at the level of culture and demand our attention. Lois Lee has made a similar point about the 'secular' (Lee 2015: 49). Our times are characterized by a mismatch between the social realities of religion and the academic concepts we use to understand it.

This book has attempted to offer a response to this problem by exploring how religious phenomena might be understood sociologically, given the social circumstances of the twenty-first century. It has been concerned with the ways in which neoliberal economics shapes cultural life in ways that have significant implications for religion. In this respect it has not pretended to be global in its coverage nor comprehensive in its treatment of religious movements. Rather, its starting point has been a particular set of economic-social patterns and their cultural consequences. These extend across many corners of the globe but are by no means universal; they also influence religious phenomena to varying degrees and in varying ways, even within the social contexts in which neoliberalism has become normative. This partial approach is deliberate. It reflects my conviction that it makes more sense to consider the sociological tools best suited to religious phenomena emerging from a common set of social conditions than to pretend that the same set of conceptual tools will equip us to study all kinds of religion wherever we might find them. Others have made the same point but in different ways. For example, in his fascinating book *Alternative Sociologies of Religion: Through Non-Western Eyes*, Jim Spickard considers how the sociology of religion might look had it not been formulated within a context of Euro-American Christianity and not been structured around assumptions like religion is essentially about organizations and beliefs. His is a thought experiment structured around the case studies of Confucianist China, Muslim North Africa and Native American religion, each furnishing indigenous concepts capable of challenging how the sociology of religion should be done (Spickard 2017). By contrast, I have not strayed far from Euro-American contexts, although they too, I argue, present a set of challenges that demand religion be addressed in new ways as a consequence of recent social change. In keeping with the observation that religion is socially constructed, our methods of study need to attend to the forces that contribute to this construction.

In applying this approach, this book has identified five cultural forces that are especially important as sites of neoliberal influence (each addressed in Chapters 2–6). Marketization draws religious movements into the logic of commercial markets, populism reshapes opportunities for political engagement, a destabilization of knowledge exposes new ways in which religious innovations become plausible and visible in the public realm, patterns of securitization reveal how religion becomes a target of state regulation and a heightened individualism converges with marketization to produce entrepreneurial orientations to religious selfhood. The consequences of these social forces for religion are not straightforward, simple, nor inevitable, but dominant patterns are identifiable nonetheless. None of these forces is entirely confined to the twenty-first century, but their social significance has been amplified to new levels and in new ways in recent years. Building on the emerging analysis, Chapters 7 and 8 turned to specific themes that are especially important to the sociology of religion as it addresses our changing times: the relationship between power and religious difference, and the study of non-religion and the secular.

The preceding chapters have had much more to say about certain traditions and geographical regions than others. Evangelical Christianity constitutes an obvious case of neoliberal engagement because of its long history of 'elective affinity' with capitalism. As a paradigmatic case notable for its portability, it has also served as an effective vehicle for the spread of pro-capitalist developments across the world. This is especially the case for Pentecostalism, the democratization of the Spirit carrying with it an incentive to take control of one's circumstances in overcoming the limitations of the past, so that 'the global spread of Pentecostalism from Africa to Oceania illuminates the profound synergy of this strand of Christianity with market morality, a resonance due to its focus on individual responsibility for salvation' (Osella and Rudnyckyj 2017: 4). The overall picture is uneven, with neoliberal affinities more visible and more numerous among conservative Protestants. However, the spread of neoliberal economic influence extends into less obvious cultural contexts, and nations in the global south which show evidence of neoliberal norms shaping religious life include many diverse examples (Tuğal 2012: 46). Some of these have featured in the preceding chapters. There are plenty more, from Indian self-help gurus who integrate Hindu folklore into corporate human resource management (Gooptu 2017) and the popularization of Islam via commercial TV in Indonesia (Barkin 2014) to the emergence of an entrepreneurial class of 'boss Christians' in the Chinese city of Wenzhou, who apply business skills in projects of church development as a means of gaining respectability in the broader community (Cao 2008). All reflect an interrelated pattern of neoliberal economic change that stretches across the globe while also demonstrating the capacity of local religious movements to harness opportunities presented by these new circumstances. These are not simply channels for 'Western' influence, and an approach that recognizes hybrid forms of socio-religious innovation would be more appropriate. But the looming presence of economic forces is always there, often traceable to powers and monetary interests originating elsewhere on the global map.

This recognition of how religious change is caught up in processes of economic exploitation raises obvious ethical concerns. The thematic discussions I have pursued in this book have raised these – and other moral questions – at various points. Chapter 3 explored the relationship between movements of religion and movements of racial prejudice, Chapter 5 discussed the relationship between state regulation and the stigmatization of Muslim communities and Chapter 7 addressed issues of power and inequality. This has been deliberate and rests on our conviction that it is impossible to do the sociology of religion within the twenty-first century without confronting ethical questions. But how should the sociology of religion respond to ethical concerns and on what basis? What might the sociology of religion have to say about ethically important issues that are illuminated by a neoliberal lens, issues such as racial prejudice and Islamophobia, the deliberate distortion of public discourse, or dishonest or incorrect accounts of how religious groups live? How can sociologists of religion exercise their academic power responsibly? What are the possibilities of social critique for the sociologist of religion? These questions are the concern of the present chapter. An argument is proposed in favour of addressing these questions explicitly if we are to address adequately the challenges of our time.

The inescapable ethical concerns of the neoliberal age

Most contemporary discussions of neoliberalism have a critical edge. For example, in his excoriating analysis, sociologist David Harvey argues that neoliberal economics is little more than a cover for elite class interests, configured to serve those with wealth and power and help them keep it (Harvey 2007). Wendy Brown focuses on the migration of neoliberal norms into non-economic spheres of life, concluding that a privileging of market reasoning effectively strips citizens of the means to be empowered and informed contributors to a functioning democracy (Brown 2015). Some studies have focused on the capacity of neoliberalism to frame human thought (Peck 2010). Indeed, according to Carrette and King, this is one of the reasons why it is so dangerous. Drawing on the insights of Noam Chomsky, they argue that neoliberal assumptions have been rendered normative and self-evident and, that being the case, neoliberalism is not simply a dimension of contemporary life but an ideology that shapes the way in which people think. Indeed, it sets 'limits on the very possibility of thinking' (Carrette and King 2005: 11). If this thinking is governed by the same logic as markets, so philosopher Michael Sandel argues, it is also ill-suited to ethical decision-making (Sandel 2012). One reason for this is that neoliberal and 'market-based' thinking tends to reduce things to matters of abstract calculation, a cost-benefit analysis without moral content. And yet neoliberal thinking embodies very particular values and assumptions; as one influential volume on the topic reminds us, 'Markets and morals are not mutually exclusive' (Gauthier,

Woodhead and Martikainen 2013: 12). But in denying their existence, neoliberalism naturalizes these values, insulating them from critical examination. Exposing the mechanisms of neoliberalism and their implications for human life is an essential precondition for responsible ethical debate within contemporary social science.

Cynicism about the motivations of state representatives has been heightened following the 2008 economic crash and the fact that it *didn't* halt neoliberalization. The excesses of the financial industries were rewarded with state bailouts, leading to the headline that they were 'too big to fail'. Meanwhile, governments introduced policies of austerity as a means of balancing the books, the resulting cuts chiefly impacting the poorest in society. Following the crash, the UK government introduced multiple cuts to public funding, including to social benefits on which the less privileged depend. Under the new regime, those in receipt of state support not only received less (or nothing); they were also subject to processes of review, accountability and sanction that generated an experience that was highly unpredictable for those dependent on support because of lack of employment, disability or health-related problems. The development of state support under the UK's austerity programme produced a system governed by bureaucratic rules that fostered precarity, rather than security, among those most in need. As with zero-hours contracts, state benefits under neoliberal conditions reflect a move towards maintaining flexibility of opportunity but favouring those with pre-existing power and wealth (Tylor 2020).

Much has been written on how the imposition of neoliberal economics by prosperous capitalist powers on poorer parts of the globe has been instrumental in exacerbating levels of inequality and deprivation. Nicaragua's continuing poverty owes much to the United States' forced deposition of the Sandinista regime in the 1980s, which also involved the imposition of neoliberal austerity (Spickard 2017: 248–9). The introduction of neoliberal reforms in Mali – including deregulation and privatization of state-owned enterprises – has been a condition of its receipt of relief funds from the International Monetary Fund. These changes have become associated with a rise in unemployment and economic decline for many, and a concentration of extreme wealth in the hands of a small elite (Soares 2017: 146–7). Such cases from the global south raise the question of the ethics of cultural appropriation and how neoliberal forces might be complicit in this. Cultural appropriation has become the subject of a vibrant global debate, informed by post-colonial scholarship that seeks to retrieve voices previously subordinated to dominant Western powers. It is not simply cultural borrowing, which is almost ubiquitous, at least in contexts influenced by globalization. Rather, it is an appropriation marked by an asymmetrical power relationship. It consists in, as Spickard puts it, 'a powerful minority appropriating for its own benefit a less powerful group's cultural property' (2017: 232). Intellectual appropriation of ideas plays an important role in this. Edward Said's influential book *Orientalism* showed how 'Western' constructions of the Orient re-inscribed inequalities of power in a way that portrayed 'the West' as dynamic and skilled in harnessing knowledge for universal good, while 'Eastern' cultures were static, undeveloped and restricted by their weddedness to tradition (Said 1978). This recurring logic was used to justify colonial impositions of power. It also reinforced and authorized the West's own attempts to understand colonized peoples, privileging

Western over non-Western thought. The twenty-first century has seen Euro-American global dominance gradually disrupted, with new centres of economic power emerging in Russia, China and the Middle East. The future will reveal whether these new global superpowers will simply adopt neoliberal frames of reference or adapt them to their own cultural circumstances before exporting their influence abroad. Implications for religious development may prove especially unpredictable. Whatever the case, there are few signs that an ethically responsible neoliberalism is any more likely to emerge than it has in the recent past.

The social consequences of neoliberal economics present a range of ethical concerns. But there is also an in-built quality to neoliberal thinking that makes an ethical perspective especially important. According to William Davies, when it comes to the evaluation of modern bureaucracy, Max Weber and Friedrich von Hayek – the intellectual father of neoliberalism – point in opposing directions. Weber criticized modern bureaucracy for its cold anonymity and lack of any public sense of its value for humanity. Hayek, on the other hand, celebrated markets because they promoted the same qualities. To be detached from a substantive ethical or political perspective was, for Hayek, a positive feature of economics, because its 'technical forms of quantitative evaluation' were a more effective means of securing liberal values more generally (Davies 2017: 9). In other words, according to Hayek, the best outcome – in terms of economic efficiency and human values – emerges when we leave markets to function with minimal interference. Markets left well alone are good for all of us. It's difficult to sustain that view given the evidence discussed earlier, and yet there is strong evidence that the principles of neoliberalism advocated by Hayek remain embedded in dominant forces of economic and social change across the globe (Peck 2010). Furthermore, the tendency to treat market forces as best unhindered by moral discourse means there is a logic within neoliberalism that resists moral conversation. This is why that conversation is especially important.

Neoliberalism and ethics in the sociology of religion

On one level, ethical questions can be claimed as central to the sociology of religion because ethical concerns have emerged as central to debates about religious movements in the twenty-first century. Media stories about religion are often focused on abuse, terrorism, bigotry or sexual misconduct because sensational, prurient exposés are assumed to have public appeal. Bad religion sells better than good religion. But it's also true that a combination of factors has led to undeniable cases of immoral practice coming to light that had previously been hidden from view.

Neoliberal cultural conditions privilege individual subjectivity in a way that generates ethical controversies out of religious contexts characterized by hierarchy or strict codes of behaviour. Conformity to group norms appears anomalous – even suspect – in a context in which individual freedoms are paramount. The recent history of New Religious Movements and their social reception is instructive here. In the 1970s and 1980s, it was arguably the strangeness and exoticism of NRMs that attracted suspicion. They struck many people as odd and their beliefs and practices were viewed as eccentric. There was also at that time a predictable tendency to place the most well-known, 'mainstream' religious groups on the 'more or less benign and trustworthy' end of the spectrum, with suspicion heightening relative to how strange, unfamiliar or alien religious movements seemed. So, a non-religious observer might view a Roman Catholic priest as peculiar but harmless, a Jehovah's Witness as eccentric, but a Scientologist as sinister. The strictness with which a tradition maintained its beliefs was less important than its cultural abnormality. Things have changed a lot since the heyday of the NRMs, however. In the most neoliberalized contexts, the cultural distance between all forms of religion and the non-religious has, in many respects, widened (Dinham and Francis 2015). Strict religion is quite likely to be viewed not as just odd but as potentially manipulative or abusive. 'Religion' as a generic category has, for many sceptics, become a pathological phenomenon, a catch-all word for strange, nonsensical and liable to abuses of power. And while contentious or unjust in many cases, sociologically speaking, these judgements are understandable. They are understandable because of the assumptions about identity that have been internalized within societies shaped by neoliberal conditions, most importantly a heightened individualism that privileges opportunities to consume over shared responsibility.

This accounts for the intermingling of religious and ethical concerns at the level of social reality. The social status of religious phenomena is often bound up in concerns about the proper use of authority, deception and trust or the causes of violence. It is quite another thing to argue that attending to such relationships falls within the proper remit of the sociology of religion. Sociologists of religion have attended to such matters in the past but usually as dimensions of the social reception of religious movements. Examining patterns of social outrage directed at religious controversies can tell us a great deal about how religion – and particular religious groups – are viewed by society and about the assumptions that underpin religion, secularity and social values (Beckford 1985). But is there an argument for the sociology of religion to adopt a more active role within ethical debate, not just as an observer of ethical dispute but as a contributor to its resolution?

One potential impediment here is the principle of value neutrality, which has been maintained – either explicitly or implicitly – within much of social science, including the sociology of religion, for much of its history (Wilkinson and Kleinman 2016). The idea of value neutrality was formulated most explicitly by Max Weber, who emphasized the distinction between the realm of facts and the realm of values. The former are subject to empirical verification and hence are properly within the remit of social science; the latter are subjective and emerge from human will, and hence are outside of the remit of social science, even if they may be the concern of theology (Weber 1949; Seubert 1991). There are values that, one would assume, are necessary for the practice of good social science, values like rigour, consistency, faithfulness to evidence, even-handedness in analysis and so on. Weber also acknowledges that values may inform social science as a guide to what is perceived to be a worthwhile focus of study – societies going through a period of economic recession, for example, may lead to research into why this has occurred but may also be motivated by a concern for the poor or a perception of economic mismanagement by the state. However, according to Weber, this does not undermine the possibility of maintaining value neutrality. Indeed, this is essential as a guard against bias and to preserve the standing of the scholar as an authority within a society distinguished by a plurality of perspectives.

Weber's notion of 'value neutrality' is not without its problems; indeed, it can be argued that his own work includes numerous examples of its impossibility (Barbalet 2020: 908). It is also fair to say that Weber's point of view would, in the present day, be subjected to robust critique. Its presumption of a neutral position from which knowledge claims may be adjudicated arguably depends on a 'view from nowhere', detached from the values of the researcher. Weber does acknowledge that sustaining an avoidance of bias constitutes effort, but he does not question 'bias free' scholarship as a possibility. There is also the problem of values being intrinsic to certain kinds of research. It can be argued that academic disciplines embody particular ethical values, which are sometimes normalized to the point where their presence goes unquestioned. Sociology has arguably been framed by the values of humanitarianism (Seubert 1991) and may be justified as a defence of civil society (Burawoy 2005), although post-colonial scholarship may question this utopian characterization. David Martin, in an early essay, famously criticized the formulation of secularization theory as an ideological project driven by secular rationalism and existentialism (Martin 1965). If theories, as well as disciplines, can be conveyors of values, then the quest for value neutrality appears a lost cause from the outset. How do we detach ourselves from ideas while also contributing to a meaningful intellectual conversation? There is also a serious concern about the way in which 'Western' academia is built on an unequal scaffolding of power relations that means its very existence raises ethical questions that need to be addressed. To pretend otherwise is to grant an unproblematic authority to a production of knowledge that rests on a history of exploitation (Bhambra, Gebrial and Nişancıoğlu 2018).

These concerns have been debated within sociology and anthropology – among other disciplines – for several decades now. Emerging insights have enabled scholarship to navigate issues of ethical responsibility in a way that acknowledges the imbalances of power upon which our work rests. Post-colonial scholarship has unsettled presumptions of epistemological and moral pre-eminence and encourages a healthy critical reflexivity about how one's own assumptions and positionality frame the research process (e.g. Clifford and Marcus 1986; Smith 2012). At the same time, according to some commentators, critical social science has lost the radical edge it had in the 1970s, when emancipation from oppression was an openly declared and passionately embraced agenda. While now a more widespread orthodoxy, criticality in this sense has become diluted, while its advocates appear less comfortable making normative statements. Andrew Sayer argues that this can be explained with reference to an enduring legacy of modernism that sustains a strict separation of reason from value. This has produced a tendency to 'treat values and ethics as beyond the scope of reason and hence induce a reluctance to discuss conceptions of the good, or of well-being or human flourishing in social science' (Sayer 2009: 768).

That being so, debate about the place of ethical responsibility in the social sciences is long overdue. There is an abundance of ethical conviction but little discussion about its proper status. In this wider context, the sociology of religion is particularly disadvantaged by its lack of a systematic debate about the distinctive forms of moral responsibility that emerge from its own subject matter. In one sense, this is a by-product of the wider politics of the discipline. Between the 1940s and the Jonestown massacre in 1978 (see Chapter 5), for example, religion had rarely been associated with public controversy in the United Kingdom or the United States, so there was little pressure on the academy to confront ethical questions about the propriety of religious beliefs and behaviour (Catto 2012: 273–4). More broadly, academic thinking about religion after the Second World War was largely framed by the secularization debate. As a focus of scholarship, religion, unlike politics or literature, for example, is inclusive of truth claims commonly assumed to be radically at odds with those governing mainstream society. The secular rationalism Martin identified in the 1960s had a major impact on how religion was perceived within the academy. As a consequence, scholars often made a concerted effort to distance themselves from the religious claims made by the movements they studied and affirmed the value of neutrality as a means of securing intellectual credibility. While intellectual secularism is not so normative as it was in the 1960s and 1970s, its legacy remains, especially within the social sciences. This is evident in the reluctance to treat religion as anything but a weaponized form of power within some sociological circles (Scott-Baumann et al. 2020: 26).

An influential formulation of critical distance distinctive to the sociology of religion is Peter Berger's concept of methodological atheism. This is an idea Berger developed in *The Sacred Canopy*, as an extension of his phenomenological argument that religion emerges as projections: 'products of human activity and human consciousness' (Berger 1969: 100). It is these projections, Berger argues, that are subject to empirical investigation; their possible reality as *anything beyond* human projection is something about which the sociology of religion cannot speak. Berger describes the process of maintaining this methodological atheism in terms of *placing brackets* around this question. In other words, one's own view on whether what one is observing constitutes merely a human activity *or* a human activity that points to a more ultimate truth can – and *should* – be set aside for the purposes of sociological study.

Berger apparently maintained this position until his death in 2017. A comment made in a blog post marking the 500th anniversary of the Protestant Reformation, published in 2015, recounts his perspective with typical clarity:

I have never understood why it should be so difficult to have a strong faith commitment and to bracket it while one does objective social science (any more difficult than playing Mozart today and Country [and] Western tomorrow). In any case, what I have to say about the empirical impact of the Lutheran Reformation and its enormously variegated Protestant progeny (Calvinist, Anabaptist, Anglican) would be no different if I were a Buddhist or an atheist. (Berger 2015)

Berger's view that his arguments as a sociologist could be formulated entirely independently – indeed, regardless – of his personal faith commitment is not one that many scholars would so uncritically hold today. To suppose one could imagine oneself as a follower of an entirely different religion and suppose this would make no difference to one's academic work seems an imaginative leap too far. A more substantive critical response, at least as I see it, proceeds in two steps. First, it is impossible to deny that our personal values and convictions have an impact on the way in which we attempt to make sense of the world sociologically. This is not to suggest this influence is predictable, simple or impossible to mitigate to some degree, but it is always there. Second, if this is true, then what grounds are there for treating orientations to religion as a special case, as if this were an especially privileged portion of our identity to which all other aspects are subordinate? This may be the case for some but to assume this in all cases where people self-identify as religious is to put the proverbial cart before the horse. It is a case of what has been described as the 'oversocialized conception of religious man [sic]' (Beckford 1983: 14). It is the character of religious identity – including its relative salience in people's lives, its patterns of practice, its relationship to official traditions – that should be the *subject* of sociological enquiry. We cannot make sweeping assumptions about such things when speaking of religious people we are studying, so why would we apply a different principle to understanding the religious identities of scholars? In theory, there is an understandable relationship between my conduct as a researcher and my religious commitment as a Quaker. But I would not assume the latter to be a homogenous category, despite the common patterns of speech, professed values and dress sense evident when I gather with other Friends. Furthermore, my conduct is also shaped – often more so – by other factors: the values of my upbringing, my taste in music, my institutional context as a university employee, my involvement in activism and community organizing, and my experience living in the north of England as a white, heterosexual man in my forties. I can focus my energies so that I apply different sets of skills when I'm researching or writing, but I cannot 'bracket off' my identity any more than I can pack it away in a suitcase and store it in the loft.

It is the legacy of 'methodological atheism', I would suggest, that has ensured such a determination among sociologists of religion to maintain a separation of 'sociological' from 'value-based' discussion, the latter incorporating moral as well as religious convictions.

Let us take another example. In an insightful article based on his ethnographic fieldwork in the Philippines, Paul-François Tremlett argues against the practice – enduringly advocated in the discipline of religious studies – of 'epoché' (or 'bracketing'): 'a commitment to study religion without prejudice and to privilege the believer's point of view' (Tremlett 2007). This amounts to a development of Berger's position insofar as the researcher is expected not simply to put their own identity aside but also to privilege the perspective of the people who are the subject of the research. Tremlett observes how belief in local folklore and witchcraft leads Filipinos to misattribute causes of ill-health and disease. In light of these circumstances, so Tremlett argues, 'for analysis to cease at the believer's point of view . . . emerges not as ethical, sympathetic or empathic, but as the abdication of responsibility towards those whom one is engaged in representing' (2007). This is a strong ethical argument in favour of privileging 'Western' medical science over religious claims that undermine it, at least in cases of human health. This is not a case whose relevance is restricted to the developing world either. The same principle could be applied within research among evangelical Christians who deny the reality of the coronavirus, refuse to engage in social distancing and resist vaccination programmes (Whitehead and Perry 2020b). But should we only make an epistemological stand for matters of public health? What about when research speaks to issues of domestic violence, racial prejudice or religious discrimination?

Perhaps it would help to draw a distinction here. I cannot see a strong argument for making it the business of the sociology of religion to tell religious people that their beliefs are false. In this respect I would advocate a kind of methodological agnosticism. I say 'kind of', because I have some reservations about this idea, understood in a strict sense. On the one hand, suspending judgement about whether someone's religious convictions are based on some kind of ultimate reality seems a wise and polite strategy when engaging in conversation. In my own research among evangelical Christians, I was once told that God had sent me to the church so that I could tell their amazing story to the world. I have no idea whether that's true, obviously, but I also didn't dismiss the claim as nonsense. It was important to build rapport with the congregants and also to be respectful of their convictions, whatever my personal feelings about them. But if methodological agnosticism is interpreted as an avoidance of the topic of ultimate beliefs or a reluctance to venture any view on the topic, then that would seem to be poor research practice. We learn through conversation, and once we are familiar and comfortable with those we seek to understand, we should try and ask about such matters and to pay them the courtesy of a robust discussion, at least if they appear comfortable with this. Moreover, if they are sharing their lives with us, haven't they a right to hear our own perspective? The conversation would seem a little one-sided, possibly exploitative, otherwise.

In practice, most sociologists of religion do not venture crass judgements about the validity of religious beliefs. However, at a more subtle level we might detect a greater tendency to direct scepticism towards some traditions over others. Here I am thinking of conversations in which 'Christianity' and 'Buddhism' (as if they were singular phenomena) are treated as inherently more 'reasonable' than Mormonism or the Jehovah's Witnesses. In the context of such discussions, it is difficult to see whether the criteria of 'reasonableness' have to do with the age of the tradition, its apparent coherence with dominant cultural norms, or the stigma attached to traditions deemed suspect in the popular imagination. Whatever the reason, it is one that would be difficult to defend in sociological terms. While the sociologist must acknowledge the social construction of religious phenomena, they must also – if they are to be consistent – acknowledge the socially constructed status of their own perspective and reasoning (Spickard 2017). This is not to collapse all into hopeless relativism but simply to recognize how difficult it is to assume a position of unassailable epistemological supremacy.

Another way into this issue is via the process of relativizing religious activity. None of us are immune from projecting the assumptions of our own experience onto the phenomena we are trying to understand. But an appropriately reflexive sociology seeks ways in which we can be self-critical about the categories we use and the assumptions we bring to the table (Davies 1999). As such, we should always ask why certain religious groups strike us as especially dubious or benign. A studied neutrality is counterproductive in these circumstances; we need to be honest with ourselves and acknowledge the prior assumptions with which we begin the process of understanding. This is not to suggest that all religious groups deserve to be treated the same, but if our inclination is to treat them differently, we ought to reflect on why that is so (Flanagan 2001).

There is also a strong *ethical* argument against passing judgements on the veracity of religious claims. In studying religion using social scientific method, we must gather empirical evidence about religious phenomena. This requires a degree of cooperation with religious groups and individuals, a cooperation subject to ethical principles – informed consent, transparency and so on – some of which are encoded into law, others into university ethical approval processes. But cooperation also places upon us an ethical obligation to treat the religious people we study with respect. If they willingly open their lives to us, we enter into a relationship of trust; in exchange for their cooperation and openness we ought to represent their lives in a way that is respectful of their complexity, and this includes exercising restraint against making simplistic, crass or tendentious claims. This is partly also a matter of method and relates to our obligation to be rigorous and careful in marshalling appropriate evidence for our arguments. But it also involves an ethical obligation that should inform how we write and speak about religious groups. I have no interest in advocating for any regulatory regime, but I would strongly support adhering to principles of respect, fairness and civility, as well as developing the skills of active listening. I am reminded of sociologist Les Back's endorsement of an approach that 'prizes patience, commitment to dialogue and careful and reflective claims to truth' (Back 2007: 20). We can adhere to all these principles while also conducting rigorous, evidence-driven social science.

Nevertheless, as researchers we are also obliged to speak from the evidence available, even if our arguments conflict with explanations favoured by the religious people we are studying. When Roy Wallis researched the Church of Scientology in the 1970s, his draft account was received with scepticism by the Scientologists who read it. Wallis still published his book, *The Road to Total Freedom* (1976), retaining the interpretation he favoured, but he published a critical response from one Scientologist, in the form of a letter, as an appendix to the book. The disagreement was open and transparent. This is of course easier to do if you have no aspirations to continue researching the community in question and are not a member of it yourself. Managing one's relationship to religious communities we study always carries risks of awkwardness, misunderstanding and split loyalties, sometimes even hostility. This is rarely easy, but an open and honest engagement makes any emerging problems more straightforward to tackle. It also makes it easier to build relationships of trust, and these have the double benefit of generating richer data and enabling ethical responsibilities to be visibly maintained.

I've mentioned several ethical principles that I think are important: honesty, transparency, civility, respect and fairness. These relate to the conduct of research in the sociology of religion; are there also ethical obligations that demand a calling out of ethical wrongdoing, of injustice or suffering? I would argue that the sociology of religion has an ethical responsibility to speak honestly and openly about power and its consequences. This includes the application – and misapplication – of power within religious groups and by religious groups upon others. It also includes exercising critical reflexivity about the power we have as individual scholars, students or observers of human life. As Spickard puts it, 'As scholars dedicated to expanding human knowledge, we cannot ignore the context in which that knowledge is generated. Nor can we ignore how it is put to use' (Spickard 2017: 225–6). These are properly sociological matters, as they relate directly to the properties of relationships among individuals and groups. They also happen to be relevant to some of the most pressing moral issues concerning religion that we face in the twenty-first century. Therefore, I see no reason why sociologists should not make important contributions to ethical debate, not necessarily in issuing ethical judgements but in resourcing debate with observations about how power has been exercised.

Power as an ethical focus

This focus on power is compatible with Titus Hjelm's call for a 'critical sociology of religion', distinguished by a recognition of the role that religious groups play in sustaining inequalities and a related interest in the social legitimation (and de-legitimation) of religious groups (Hjelm and Zuckerman 2013: 8; Hjelm 2014). This approach may take inspiration from the Frankfurt School of Sociology which – associated with Walter Benjamin, Max Horkheimer and later, Jürgen Habermas – made an important contribution to social science in calling attention to relationships of power integral to academic labour itself, thereby advocating for a more reflexively critical orientation to the concepts we use and the intellectual traditions we inhabit (Goldstein 2006).

Within the sociology of religion, this kind of analysis demands attention to multiple institutional contexts, as well as a critical reflexivity. It also demands an especially careful assessment of available evidence if responsible claims about power and its distribution are to be made. Consider an example. Between 2014 and 2020 I was part of a national team researching how Islam and Muslims are perceived within contexts of higher education in the UK (Guest et al. 2020; Scott-Baumann et al. 2020). The whole project was overshadowed by the roll-out of the government's counterterrorism Prevent Strategy in universities following the Counter-Terrorism and Security Act, 2015 (see Chapter 5). Prevent was viewed as intrusive and Islamophobic by many within the HE sector. The research team all had their concerns about this state-run programme of surveillance that appeared to have alienated many British Muslims who felt targeted and stigmatized as a security risk. Within this context, it was clear that there were several dominant narratives. There was the government narrative, in which Prevent was a necessary, impartial measure designed to protect British citizens and deter those who might be tempted into terrorist activity. And there was a dissenting narrative, held among many university academics and some students, in which Prevent was an unqualified imposition that was effective only at demonizing Muslims, chilling freedom of speech and compromising academic freedom. As social scientists studying the emergence and legitimation of ideas associated with Muslims, we were obliged to subject *both* narratives to critical scrutiny and examine the claims of each against the available evidence. We could not, and should not, simply attack Prevent as a bad idea just because we dislike it on principle. As it happens, there are plenty of evidence-based reasons to critique the programme, as we found out. And this is perhaps the most important point: we found out. We did not simply seek out evidence that supported the opinions we already held. We held opinions, of course, and we were open about them, but working sociologically must include an acknowledgement of the possibility of being wrong. Put bluntly, if we conduct research without being willing to have our minds changed, then we are not doing research.

Addressing the complicity of the state in perpetuating religious prejudice is an important focus of research in the neoliberal age, especially as a corrective to the assumption that marketized societies constitute greater freedom of expression (Holmwood and O'Toole 2018). Chapter 5 demonstrated how this is not the case, and that the relationship between state authorities and Muslim communities is often a fraught one that demands careful examination. Just as the power of the state and of Muslims is often underestimated or misjudged, so our understanding of the distribution of power among religious and non-religious parties is sometimes flawed (Jones 2020). But there is also a need to recognize how religious groups are sometimes complicit in the perpetuation of injustice. Some of the cases of physical, sexual and emotional abuse that have come to light in recent years were mentioned in the previous chapter. They underline the value of social scientific input into discussions about culpability and the necessity for institutional change. The sociology of religion can make a valuable contribution here, both in clarifying distributions of power and their institutional scaffolding, and in explaining religious cultures of practice for the benefit of external observers. There is a high risk of misunderstanding and hasty judgement in these cases, for understandable reasons. In contexts distinguished by low levels of religious literacy and/or religious diversity, including a sociological account of religious institutions complicit in enabling or covering up abuse may facilitate realistic conversations about the causes of and possible responses to painful situations.

Part of this issue is about shared responsibility, a challenge especially difficult within religious traditions that emphasize individual agency. It's not enough for Christian theologians and leaders, for example, to see how Donald Trump's power was upheld by Christian voters and respond by saying that these Trump voters are not proper Christians. They claim this identity and so we have to contend with their consequent political influence as an identifiable social group. This evokes concerns raised in Chapter 7 in relation to 'anti-structuralism', the reluctance to recognize human problems as shaped by social forces. This tendency, common among some conservative religious movements, constitutes a barrier to sociological engagement and to an acknowledgement of the social dimensions of ethical responsibility. If we function as social scientists, we are bound to attend to the social contexts of moral concern, and this means recognizing that individuals never act in a vacuum. The decisions they make are framed by opportunities shaped, at least in large part, by the social circumstances in which they find themselves and hence moral accountability has to be understood with this in mind. This as well can be addressed via questions of power. In her book *Everybody Knows: Corruption in America*, Sarah Chayes (2020) conceives of corruption not as an individual vice but as endemic within the culture of powerful institutions. Taking this approach, a sociological treatment of alleged abuse might focus on offering not a moral judgement but a sociological explanation of how configurations of power and misuses of power come about, and how they come to be established as normative.

We must also attend to the *relative power* of social-religious circumstances to frame and limit the opportunities of different kinds of people. It is no good acknowledging the importance of social circumstances if we simply expect individuals to transcend these limitations whenever faced with a pressing moral dilemma. The case of Mars Hill Church in Seattle, discussed in Chapter 7, is a striking example of how intersectional factors were overlooked to the detriment of congregants and their families. Mark Driscoll's preaching constructed men according to a hypermasculine image that demanded gainful employment, a heteronormative family structure, male headship, female submission, successful procreation and an attitude characterized by bullish confidence and unapologetic male supremacy. At the same time, a global recession meant many were struggling financially, with jobs scarce. Maintaining a strict 'male breadwinner/ stay at home mom' arrangement was, for many, economically impossible. Moreover, Seattle is known for its liberal, progressive culture, so those attending Mars Hill's mother church are likely to have faced alienating friends and family members by adhering to the church's fervent gender conservatism. Of course, this tension might be justified – even welcomed – by conservative evangelicals keen to see the Christian life in terms of an ongoing struggle against 'the world'. But this is unlikely to make things easier for unemployed men struggling with depression.

Numerous examples considered in this book enable us to see how cultures of religious practice might contribute to the generation of ethical problems. It is not our job to resolve these issues but avoiding them altogether is arguably an abdication of academic responsibility. Laying bare such configurations of empowerment and disempowerment is entirely consistent with traditions of social science that can be traced back to the 1970s. Marxist and feminist sociology made it their business not only to understand the situations of women and the poor in society but also to make plain the social forces that conspire to keep them in a position of marginality (e.g. Skeggs 1997; Willis 1977). Religious movements are not exempt from these distributions of power, whatever their representatives might say to the contrary. Indeed, a number of authors have drawn inspiration from feminist and Marxist traditions within more critical analyses of religious phenomena (e.g. Johnson 2018; Maddox 2013; Mahmood 2005; Malone 2018). Others draw lessons from debates about intersectionality or critical race theory in highlighting how religious movements contribute to the perpetuation of social hierarchies and patterns of exclusion (e.g. Bjork-James 2021; Bracey and Moore 2017; Carr and Haynes

2015; Marti 2020). Queer theory has informed further studies that have addressed the experiences of LGBT+ people, including their accommodation and exclusion within religious communities (Page and Shipley 2020; Page and Yip 2020). There is much to be learned from these studies. I hope, in the future, that more coordinated conversations will occur among scholars engaging with questions of power and ethical responsibility within religious groups, and between them and representatives of religious and state powers. We only achieve so much by talking among ourselves.

Religion, accountability and the twenty-first-century university

Having expressed reservations about the myopia of academics, I am naturally moved to conclude with a section on the twenty-first-century university. In addition to matters of institutional religious practice, we need also to consider the institutional contexts of the sociology of religion, charged with the stewardship of teaching and research in this field. The ethical responsibilities that emerge from the sociology of religion cannot be realistically considered without also taking account of how it is formulated to those who learn about it and how its practice is modelled within university environments (Spickard 2017: 225–6). It is tempting to treat academic work as individualistic, driven by inspired personalities, rather than something that is always embedded in collective, shared contexts of research teams, cohorts, networks and social media. It is a highly codependent endeavour and that should be cause for some humility once in a while. Those of us employed by universities are also accountable to those universities and to their standards of practice and ethical guidelines. We are also, of course, accountable to the society in which we live and to the laws of the land, whatever our views of the current government. I say this as a corrective to those who would characterize scholarship as an indulgence and those who indulge in it.

I once attended a panel debate about de-colonizing the curriculum at a university in the UK (not my own). It was lively and featured speakers who felt passionately about retrieving a sense of cultural authenticity from a higher education system that was marketized and, in their view, repressive. It had become a conveyor belt of modularized assessment, rather than a means of personal empowerment. Universities were complicit in racial exclusion and religious prejudice, and they were driven by profit rather than the emancipatory power of learning. Then one panellist commented that she didn't write essays for the university, she didn't care about the university; she wrote them for herself. This struck me as an odd thing to say, and another audience member apparently felt the same. He said he was the first person in his family to go to university. This mattered to him, and he was there to get a degree so that he could earn a good living. He didn't want to dismiss the university; for him it was a genuine source of empowerment. Amid an abundance of voices calling for an uprising against the university – a symbol of marketization, exploitation, white privilege and established power – there was a sole, clear voice offering a different point of view. There was a lot going on in that exchange, and it was a fascinating insight into student culture at that institution. I recount the incident here for several reasons. First, it underlines the value in having multiple, divergent voices within university life. Mutual accountability and robust debate depend on it. Second, it illustrates how multiple power agendas can coexist within the same institution. The tensions in the room had to do with management versus the students, white power versus BAME power, and social class inequalities, and these intersected in complex ways. Third, it shows, I hope, how claims of independence and individual freedom are always to be understood in relation to more collective movements and allegiances. Universities include multiple forms of accountability and negotiating ethical responsibility in light of them is never a straightforward process.

This pattern of responsibilities extends to contexts of teaching and learning, the production of knowledge and the construction of religious identities within university settings. For example, writing about appropriations of 'Islam' in European systems of education, Shiraz Thobani comments that 'Islam' and 'Muslims' are frequently associated with an orientation to life that is authoritarian, anti-rational, dogmatic and intolerant (2014: 70). Thobani traces this pattern to liberal humanist models of education inherited from the Enlightenment, which were universalist in principle but ill-equipped to account for cultural differences encountered throughout the colonial period. The research for the 'Representing Islam on Campus' project, to which I contributed between 2014 and 2020, revealed multiple ways in which the culture of academic debate and learning contributed to the exclusion of Muslims. If the sociology of religion is to take seriously matters of power, it needs to direct its attention to its own institutions of learning as well as broader contexts of practice.

An important principle here is reflexivity and being mindful of the positions from which we see, speak and write. Within the sociology of religion, we must contend not only with the disproportionate influence of particular institutions of higher education within Europe and the United States, but also with the fact that the vast majority of the most influential academics in the field for the last 100 years have been white, male and have either identified with some form of Christianity or been non-religious. This is not to suggest that their work has nothing to say beyond their own social milieu, but it would be naïve to suggest their distinctive demographic profile has not been a significant factor in shaping the conceptual contours of the sub-discipline.

Beyond the power dynamics implicit in the construction of curricula, universities also frame the way religious difference is presented in cultural terms. Research has mapped the ways in which universities can reproduce social inequalities and prejudices, including against religious groups (Bathmaker, Ingram and Waller 2013; Dinham, Francis and Shaw 2017; Valentine, Holloway and Jayne 2010). Mechanisms of exclusion are often invisible, not least because universities are typically highly eloquent about their embrace of 'diversity' at the policy level. They are also governed by narratives cast by a very narrow demographic – disproportionately white, middle class and male – whose academic capital lends their words the authority that comes with historical privilege. In recent times, academic freedom has been invoked as a further justification for the publication of views offensive and exclusionary to minority groups, highlighting an 'intellectual complicity in racism' (Back 2004: 3) that is sometimes extended into Islamophobia.

Such an emphasis on cultural dynamics also calls attention to individual agency in the form of resistance or counter-hegemonic discourses. Acknowledging inequalities of power should not be allowed to paper over significant attempts by minorities – including Muslims and other religious actors – to forge spaces for themselves that resist or defy institutional cultures that might otherwise marginalize them. Williams (2015) points to how ethical social outreach by the Salvation Army in the UK has formed effective counter-spaces to neoliberalism. There are also a variety of such examples among Muslim students in UK universities, some affirming activism and citizenship in ways that transcend the radical/moderate binary by which they are often defined (Brown and Saeed 2014: 1962). There are important variations among universities within the UK HE sector, driven by diverse histories, understandings of institutional ethos, demographics of the student intake, academic specialisms and their associated cultures of practice, the topography of the 'campus' and the variety of pressures that emerge from the distinctive socio-economic constituency of the local area. All of these factors play a part in framing the ways in which religion is permitted to occupy the university environment. But it is the behavioural patterns that they foster – emerging as social norms that, while unstable, nevertheless take on distinctive, durable forms – that have the most profound influence over the place of religious identities within the lives of staff and students. One of the aims underpinning the Representing Islam on Campus research was to trace the ways in which 'campus cultures' emerge in a variety of university contexts, and in so doing enable perceptions of Islam and Muslims to emerge, take hold, become reinforced but also be challenged. The politics of the sociology of religion is about not just its relationships with religious movements but also its configuration of religious identities within the institutional contexts in which it is practised.

By way of conclusion, let us return to a quintessentially neoliberal topic: choice – not to assess what might be right or wrong choices, or even the ethics of decision-making itself, although these are important. I mention it to highlight the issue of discerning when choices are available and acknowledging their status as choices. There remains much to be learnt from Peter Berger's early work on how socialization leads to what he calls 'bad faith'. People acquire a sense of what is socially normative through their upbringing, education and experience, but these processes of socialization can be so effective that some matters that are subject to choice acquire the status of necessity. The presence of these 'fictitious necessities' (Feltmate 2018: 72) is ethically significant because they permit individuals to avoid responsibility for their speech and actions, citing them as 'natural' or 'plainly true' rather than subject to decisions they have made. The same phenomena also obscure the contingency behind the claims of others, insulating them from critical scrutiny, especially when such claims emerge from sources granted special theological legitimacy. Berger's discussion takes us so far in drawing ethical questions from sociological argument. In our age of 'post-truth' and 'fake news', our analysis needs to go a little further. 'Bad faith' may not be as innocent as it once was, and the manipulation of public discourse we have noted in earlier chapters suggests there is a degree of strategy behind some claims that seek to close off debate or proclaim unequivocal truth. This has long been acknowledged in political science, and our increasing willingness to recognize such phenomena among religious agents – both fringe and mainstream – perhaps reflects how the boundaries between religion and politics have become increasingly blurred in recent years. If this is true and constitutes a movement that has momentum, then ethical questions are likely to be even more unavoidable for the sociology of religion in the future.

Further reading

There is very little written about ethical responsibility in the sociology of religion; one hope is that this book will reinvigorate some debate. Until that happens, the ethical implications of neoliberal culture have been mapped in a range of critical studies, including Bradley (2017), Brown (2015) and Carrette and King (2005). The collection edited by Rudnyckyj and Osella, *Religion and the Morality of the Market* (2017), includes some insightful essays from an anthropological perspective. Wilkinson and Keinman's *A Passion for Society* (2016) offers a thoughtful, nuanced call for social science to engage with human suffering. Models for the use of sociology in exposing injustice and highlighting ethical responsibility can be found in Holmwood and O'Toole (2018) and Tylor (2020).

On ethical issues in neoliberal institutions, Brown (2015) and Davies (2017) offer sharp, critical discussions. All those who work or study in universities ought to read Stefan Collini's work, especially *What Are Universities For?* (2012).

REFERENCES

Ádám, Z. and A. Bozóki (2016), 'State and Faith: Right-wing Populism and Nationalized Religion in Hungary', *Intersections: East European Journal of Society and Politics*, 2 (1): 98–122.

Al Atom, B. (2014), 'Examining the Trends of Islamophobia: Western Public Attitudes since 9/11', *Studies in Sociology of Science*, 5 (3): 83–8.

Aldridge, A. (1999), *Religion in the Contemporary World: A Sociological Introduction*, Cambridge and Malden, MA: Polity Press.

Allen, K. (2014), '"Blair's Children": Young Women as "Aspirational Subjects" in the Psychic Landscape of Class', *Sociological Review*, 62: 760–79.

Altglas, V. (2014), *From Yoga to Kabbalah: Religious Exoticism and the Logics of Bricolage*, Oxford: Oxford University Press.

Ambrose, L. M. (2017), 'Aimee Semple McPherson: Gender Theory, Worship, and the Arts', *Pneuma*, 39 (1–2): 105–22.

Ammerman, N. T. (2021), 'The Many Meanings of Non-Affiliation', in J. L. Heft and J. E. Stets (eds), *Empty Churches: Non-Affiliation in America*, 27–55, New York: Oxford University Press.

Ansari, H. (2004), *The Infidel Within: Muslims in Britain since 1800*, London: Hurst & Company.

Anwar, M. (1979), *The Myth of Return: Pakistanis in Britain*, London: Heinemann.

APPG on British Muslims (2018), *Islamophobia Defined: The Inquiry into a Working Definition of Islamophobia*. Report available at: https://static1.squarespace.com/static/599c3d2febb d1a90cffdd8a9/t/5bfd1ea3352f531a6170ceee/1543315109493/Islamophobia+Defined.pdf (accessed 28 February 2022).

Asad, T. (2003), *Formations of the Secular: Christianity, Islam, Modernity*, Stanford, CA: Stanford University Press.

Asad, T., W. Brown, J. P. Butler and S. Mahmood (2013), *Is Critique Secular? Blasphemy, Injury, and Free Speech*, New York: Fordham University Press.

Aune, K. (2006), 'Marriage in a British Evangelical Congregation: Practising Postfeminist Partnership?', *The Sociological Review*, 54 (4): 638–57.

Aune, K., M. Guest and J. Law (2019), *Chaplains on Campus: Understanding Chaplaincy in UK Universities*. Coventry, Durham and Canterbury: Coventry University, Durham University and Canterbury Christ Church University.

Awan, I. and S. Guru (2017), 'Parents of Foreign "Terrorist" Fighters in Syria: Will They Report Their Young?', *Ethnic and Racial Studies*, 40 (1): 1–19.

Back, L. (2004), 'Ivory Towers? The Academy and Racism', in I. Law, D. Phillips and L. Turney (eds), *Institutional Racism in Higher Education*, 1–6, Stoke on Trent: Trentham Books.

Back, L. (2007), *The Art of Listening*, London: Bloomsbury.

Bailey, H. (2021), 'Trump's Twitter Ban Obscures the Real Problem: State-Backed Manipulation Is Rampant on Social Media', *The Conversation*, 13 January. Available at: https://theconversation.com/trumps-twitter-ban-obscures-the-real-problem-state-backed -manipulation-is-rampant-on-social-media-153136 (accessed 4 November 2021).

Balch, R. (2006), 'The Rise and Fall of Aryan Nations: A Resource Mobilization Perspective', *Journal of Political and Military Sociology*, 34 (1): 81–113.

Barbalet, J. M. (2020), 'Weber, Max', in A. Possamai and A. J. Blasi (eds), *The Sage Encyclopedia of the Sociology of Religion*, 906–11, London: Sage.

Barker, E. (1984), *The Making of a Moonie: Choice or Brainwashing?* Oxford: Blackwell.

References

Barkin, G. (2014), 'Commercial Islam in Indonesia: How Television Producers Mediate Religiosity among National Audiences', *International Journal of Asian Studies*, 11 (1): 1–24.

Barkun, M. (2013), *A Culture of Conspiracy: Apocalyptic Visions in Contemporary America*, 2nd edition, Berkeley, CA: University of California Press.

Barrett-Fox, R. (2018), 'A King Cyrus President: How Donald Trump's Presidency Reasserts Conservative Christians' Right to Hegemony', *Humanity and Society*, 42 (4): 503–22.

Barrett-Fox, R. and A. K. T. Yip (2020), 'Crosses and Crossroads: American Conservative Christianity's Anti-Intersectionality Discourse and the Erasure of LGBTQ+ Believers', in S-J. Page and A. K. T. Yip (eds), *Intersecting Religion and Sexuality: Sociological Perspectives*, 212–27, Leiden: Brill.

Bathmaker, A., N. Ingram and R. Waller (2013), 'Higher Education, Social Class and the Mobilisation of Capitals: Recognising and Playing the Game', *British Journal of Sociology of Education*, 34 (5–6): 723–43.

Beaman, L. (2013), 'Religious Freedom and Neoliberalism: From Harm to Cost-Benefit', in T. Martikainen and F. Gauthier (eds), *Religion in the Neoliberal Age: Political Economy and Modes of Governance*, 193–209, Aldershot: Ashgate.

Beckford, J. A. (1983), 'The Restoration of "Power" to the Sociology of Religion', *Sociological Analysis*, 44 (1): 11–31.

Beckford, J. A. (1985), *Cult Controversies: The Societal Response to the New Religious Movements*, London: Tavistock.

Beckford, James A. (1989) *Religion and Advanced Industrial Society*, London: Unwin Hyman.

Beckford, J. A. (2003), *Social Theory and Religion*, Cambridge: Cambridge University Press.

Beer, D. (2016), *Metric Power*, London: Palgrave Macmillan.

Bellah, R. (1967), 'Civil Religion in America', *Daedalus*, 96 (1): 1–21.

Bellah, R. et al. (1985), *Habits of the Heart. Individualism and Commitment in American Life*, Berkeley, Los Angeles and London: University of California Press.

Berger, P. L. (1969), *The Sacred Canopy: Elements of a Sociological Theory of Religion*, Garden City, NY: Anchor Books.

Berger, P. L. (1992), *A Far Glory. The Quest for Faith in an Age of Credulity*, New York: The Free Press.

Berger, P. L. (1999), 'The Desecularization of the World: A Global Overview', in P. L. Berger (ed.), *The Desecularization of the World: Essays on the Resurgence of Religion in World Politics*, 1–18, Washington: Ethics and Public Policy Center & Grand Rapids: Eerdmans.

Berger, P. L. (2010), 'Max Weber Is Alive and Well, and Living in Guatemala: The Protestant Ethic Today', *The Review of Faith and International Affairs*, 8 (4): 3–9.

Berger, P. L. (2015), '500 Years of Protestantism', *American Interest*. Available at: https://www.the-american-interest.com/2015/07/15/500-years-of-protestantism/ (accessed 9 October 2021).

Berger, P. and T. Luckmann (1966), *The Social Construction of Reality. A Treatise in the Sociology of Knowledge*, London, Fakenham and Reading: Penguin.

Berger, P., G. Davie and E. Fokas (2008), *Religious America, Secular Europe? A Theme and Variations*, Aldershot: Ashgate.

Bhambra, G. K., D. Gebrial and K. Nişancıoğlu, eds (2018), *Decolonising the University*, London: Pluto Press.

Bielo, J. S. (2018), *Ark Encounter: The Making of a Creationist Theme Park*, New York: New York University Press.

Bielo, J. S. (2019), 'The Materiality of Myth: Authorizing Fundamentalism at Ark Encounter', in E. Roberts and J. Eyl (eds), *Christian Tourist Attractions, Mythmaking and Identity Formation*, 43–57, London: Bloomsbury.

Birt, J. (2006), 'Good Imam, Bad Imam: Civic Religion and National Integration in Britain Post-9/11', *The Muslim World*, 96: 687–705.

Bjork-James, S. (2021), *The Divine Institution: White Evangelicalism's Politics of the Family*, New Brunswick, NJ: Rutgers University Press.

Block, F. and M. R. Somers (2014), *The Power of Market Fundamentalism: Karl Polanyi's Critique*, Cambridge, MA: Harvard University Press.

Bourdieu, P. (1984), *Distinction: A Social Critique of the Judgement of Taste*, New York and London: Routledge.

Bourdieu, P. (1985), 'The Forms of Capital', in J. G. Richardson (ed.), *Handbook of Theory and Research for the Sociology of Education*, 241–58, New York: Greenwood.

Bourdieu, P. (1987), 'Legitimation and Structured Interests in Weber's Sociology of Religion', in S. Lash and S. Whimster (eds), *Max Weber, Rationality and Modernity*, 119–36, London: Allen & Unwin.

Bourbeau, P. (2014), 'Moving Forward Together: Logics of the Securitization Process', *Millennium: Journal of International Studies*, 43 (1): 187–206.

Bowler, K. (2013), *Blessed: A History of the American Prosperity Gospel*, New York: Oxford University Press.

Bozkurt-Güngen, S. (2018), 'Labour and Authoritarian Neoliberalism: Changes and Continuities under the AKP Governments in Turkey', *South European Society and Politics*, 23 (2): 219–38.

Bracey, G. E. and W. L. Moore (2017), '"Race Tests": Racial Boundary Maintenance in White Evangelical Churches', *Sociological Inquiry*, 87 (2): 282–302.

Bradley, T. (2017), *Women and Violence in India: Gender, Oppression and the Politics of Neoliberalism*, London: I.B. Tauris.

Brady, N. (2012), 'From "Moral Loss" to "Moral Reconstruction"? A Critique of Ethical Perspectives on Challenging the Neoliberal Hegemony in UK Universities in the Twenty-First Century', *Oxford Review of Education*, 38 (3): 343–55.

Brasher, B. (2001), *Give Me That Online Religion*, San Francisco: Jossey-Bass.

Braunstein, R. (2017), *Prophets and Patriots: Faith across the Political Divide*, Oakland, CA: University of California Press.

Braunstein, R. (2018), 'A (More) Perfect Union? Religion, Politics, and Competing Stories of America', *Sociology of Religion*, 79 (2): 172–95.

Brown, K. (2008), 'The Promise and Perils of Women's Participation in UK Mosques: The Impact of Securitization Agendas on Identity, Gender and Community', *British Journal of Politics and International Relations*, 10: 472–91.

Brown, K. E. and T. Saeed (2014), 'Radicalization and Counter-Radicalization at British Universities: Muslim Encounters and Alternatives', *Ethnic and Racial Studies*, 38 (11): 1952–68.

Brown, W. (2015), *Undoing the Demos: Neoliberalism's Stealth Revolution*, Brooklyn, NY: Zone Books.

Brubaker, R. (2017), 'Between Nationalism and Civilizationism: The European Populist Movement in Comparative Perspective', *Ethnic and Racial Studies*, 40 (8): 1191–226.

Bruce, S. (2002), *God Is Dead: Secularization in the West*, Oxford: Blackwell.

Bullivant, S. (2020), 'Explaining the Rise of "Non-Religion Studies": Subfield Formation and Institutionalization within the Sociology of Religion', *Social Compass*, 67 (1): 86–102.

Bullock, J. (2018), 'The Sociology of the Sunday Assembly: "Belonging without Believing" in a Post-Christian Context', PhD thesis, University of Kingston.

Burawoy, M. (2005), '2004 American Sociological Association Presidential Address: For Public Sociology', *British Journal of Sociology*, 56 (2): 259–94.

Busher, J. (2016), *The Making of Anti-Muslim Protest : Grassroots Activism in the English Defence League*. London: Routledge.

Busher, Joel, Tufyal Choudhury, Paul Thomas and Gareth Harris (2017), *What the Prevent Duty Means for Schools and Colleges in England: An Analysis of Educationalists' Experiences*. Project Report. Aziz Foundation, London.

References

Butler, J. (1993), *Bodies That Matter: On the Discursive Limits of Sex*, London: Routledge.

Cadge, W. and M. E. Konieczny (2014), '"Hidden in Plain Sight": The Significance of Religion and Spirituality in Secular Organizations', *Sociology of Religion*, 75 (4): 551–63.

Campbell, B. and J. Manning (2018), *The Rise of Victimhood Culture: Microaggressions, Safe Spaces, and the New Culture Wars*, Cham, Switzerland: Palgrave Macmillan.

Campbell, C. (1971), *Toward a Sociology of Irreligion*, London: Macmillan.

Campbell, H., ed. (2013), *Digital Religion: Understanding Religious Practice in New Media Worlds*, London: Routledge.

Cao, N. (2008), 'Boss Christians: The Business of Religion in the "Wenzhou Model" of Christian Revival', *The China Journal*, 59: 63–87.

Carr, J. and A. Haynes (2015), 'A Clash of Racializations: The Policing of "Race" and of Anti-Muslim Racism in Ireland', *Critical Sociology*, 41 (1): 21–40.

Carrette, J. and R. King (2005), *Selling Spirituality: The Silent Takeover of Religion*, Abingdon: Routledge.

Casanova, J. (1994), *Public Religions in the Modern World*, Chicago and London: University of Chicago Press.

Casanova, J. (2007), 'Rethinking Secularization: A Global Comparative Perspective', in L. Beaman and P. Beyer (eds), *Religion, Globalization, and Culture*, 101–20, Leiden: Brill.

Castelli, E. A. (2007), 'Persecution Complexes: Identity Politics and the 'War on Christians'', *Differences: A Journal of Feminist Cultural Studies*, 18 (3): 152–18.

Catto, R. (2012), 'Bracketing Out the Truth: Managing Bias in the Study of New Religious Movements', in M. Guest and E. Arweck (eds), *Religion and Knowledge: Sociological Perspectives*, 269–85, Aldershot: Ashgate.

Central Statistics Office (2017), *Census 2016 Summary Results – Part 1*. Central Statistics Office, Ireland. Available at: https://www.rte.ie/documents/news/census-2016-summary-results-part-1-full.pdf (accessed 4 June 2021).

Chaves, M. (1994), 'Secularization as Declining Religious Authority', *Social Forces*, 72 (3): 749–74.

Chayes, S. (2020), *Everybody Knows: Corruption in America*, London: C. Hurst & Co.

Chong, A. (2013), 'Neoliberalism and Counterterrorism Laws: Impact on Australian Muslim Community Organizations', in T. Martikainen and F. Gauthier (eds), *Religion in the Neoliberal Age: Political Economy and Modes of Governance*, 161–76, Aldershot: Ashgate.

Choudhury, T. (2017), 'Campaigning on Campus: Student Islamic Societies and Counterterrorism', *Studies in Conflict & Terrorism*, 40 (12): 1004–22.

Clark, E. S. and B. Stoddard, eds (2019), *Race and New Religious Movements in the USA: A Documentary Reader*, London: Bloomsbury.

Clifford, J. and G. E. Marcus, eds (1986), *Writing Culture: The Poetics and Politics of Ethnography*, Berkeley, Los Angeles and London: University of California Press.

Coleman, S. (1996), 'Words as Things – Language, Aesthetics and the Objectification of Protestant Evangelicalism', *Journal of Material Culture*, 1 (1): 107–28.

Coleman, S. (2000), *The Globalisation of Charismatic Christianity: Spreading the Gospel of Prosperity*, Cambridge: Cambridge University Press.

Colgan, E. (2018), 'Let Him Romance You: Rape Culture and Gender Violence in Evangelical Christian Self-Help Literature', in C. Blyth, E. Colgan and K. Edwards (eds), *Rape Culture, Gender Violence and Religion: Christian Perspectives*, 9–26, Cham, Switzerland: Palgrave Macmillan.

Collini, S. (2012), *What Are Universities For?* London: Penguin Books.

Comaroff, J. (2009), 'The Politics of Conviction: Faith on the Neo-liberal Frontier', *Social Analysis*, 53 (1): 17–38.

Connell, J. (2005), 'Hillsong: A Megachurch in the Sidney Suburbs', *Australian Geographer*, 36(3): 315–32.

Connolly, W. E. (2008), *Capitalism and Christianity, American Style*, Durham, NC and London: Duke University Press.

Coppock, V. and M. McGovern (2014), '"Dangerous Minds"? Deconstructing Counter-Terrorism Discourse, Radicalization and the 'Psychological Vulnerability' of Muslim Children and Young People in Britain', *Children & Society*, 28 (3): 242–56.

Corrigan, J. (2002), *Business of the Heart: Religion and Emotion in the Nineteenth Century*, Berkeley and Los Angeles: University of California Press.

Crenshaw, K. (1989), 'Demarginalizing the Intersection of Race and Sex: A Black Feminist Critique of Antidiscrimination Doctrine, Feminist Theory and Antiracist Politics', *University of Chicago Legal Forum*, 139–68.

Croft, S. (2012), *Securitising Islam*, Cambridge: Cambridge University Press.

Dahab, R. and M. Omori (2019), 'Homegrown Foreigners: How Christian Nationalism and Nativist Attitudes Impact Muslim Civil Liberties', *Ethnic and Racial Studies*, 42 (10): 1727–46.

D'Ancona, M. (2017), *Post-Truth: The New War on Truth and How to Fight Back*, London: Ebury Press.

Davie, G. (2002a), *Europe: The Exceptional Case – Parameters of Faith in the Modern World*, London: Darton, Longman and Todd.

Davie, G. (2002b), '"Praying Alone? Church-Going in Britain and Social Capital: A Reply to Steve Bruce', *Journal of Contemporary Religion*, 17 (3): 329–34.

Davie, G. (2015), *Religion in Britain: A Persistent Paradox*, 2nd edition, Chichester: Wiley Blackwell.

Davies, C. A. (1999), *Reflexive Ethnography: A Guide to Researching Selves and Others*, London: Routledge.

Davies, D. and D. Northam-Jones (2012), 'The Sea of Faith: Exemplifying Transformed Retention', in M. Guest and E. Arweck (eds), *Religion and Knowledge: Sociological Perspectives*, 227–43, Aldershot: Ashgate.

Davies, W. (2015), *The Happiness Industry: How the Government and Big Business Sold Us Well-Being*, London: Verso Books.

Davies, W. (2017), *The Limits of Neoliberalism: Authority, Sovereignty and the Logic of Competition*, London: Sage.

Day, A. (2013), *Believing in Belonging: Belief and Social Identity in the Modern World*, Oxford: Oxford University Press.

DeHanas, D. N. and M. Shterin (2018), 'Religion and the Rise of Populism', *Religion, State and Society*, 46 (3): 177–85.

Delanty, G. (2019), 'The Future of Capitalism: Trends, Scenarios and Prospects for the Future', *Journal of Classical Sociology*, 19 (1): 10–26.

Dinham, A. and M. Francis, eds (2015), *Religious Literacy in Policy and Practice*, Bristol: Policy Press.

Dinham, A., M. Francis and M. Shaw (2017), 'Towards a Theory and Practice of Religious Literacy: A Case Study of Religion and Belief Engagement in a UK University', *Religions*, 8 (12). doi:10.3390/rel8120276

Dolby, R. G. A. (1979), 'Reflections on Deviant Science', in R. Wallis (ed.), *On the Margins of Science: The Social Construction of Rejected Knowledge*, 27–8, Keele: University of Keele.

Duffy, B. and B. Page (2021), 'Culture Wars Uncovered: Most of UK Don't Know If "Woke" Is a Compliment or an Insult', *The Conversation*, 26 May. Available at: https://theconversation.com/culture-wars-uncovered-most-of-uk-public-dont-know-if-woke-is-a-compliment-or-an-insult-161529 (accessed 4 November 2021).

Du Mez, K. K. (2020), *Jesus and John Wayne: How White Evangelicals Corrupted a Faith and Fractured a Nation*, New York: Liveright.

References

Edgell, P. (2012), 'A Cultural Sociology of Religion: New Directions', *Annual Review of Sociology*, 38: 247–65.

Edgell, P., J. Gerteis and D. Hartmann (2006), 'Atheists as "Other": Moral Boundaries and Cultural Membership in American Society', *American Sociological Review*, 71 (2): 211–34.

Egorova, Y. (2018), *Jews and Muslims in South Asia: Reflections on Difference, Religion and Race*, New York: Oxford University Press.

Egorova, Y. and F. Ahmed (2017), 'The Impact of Antisemitism and Islamophobia on Jewish-Muslim Relations in the UK: Memory, Experience, Context', in B. Gidley and J. Renton (eds), *Antisemitism and Islamophobia in Europe: A Shared Story?*, 283–301, London: Palgrave Macmillan.

Einstein, M. (2008), *Brands of Faith: Marketing Religion in a Commercial Age*, London and New York: Routledge.

Ellingson, S. (2013), 'Packaging Religious Experience, Selling Modular Religion: Explaining the Emergence and Expansion of Megachurches', in F. Gauthier and T. Martikainen (eds), *Religion in Consumer Society: Brands, Consumers and Markets*, 59–74, Aldershot: Ashgate.

Emerson, M. and C. Smith (2000), *Divided by Faith: Evangelical Religion and the Problem of Race in America*, New York: Oxford University Press.

Engelke, M. (2014), 'Christianity and the Anthropology of Secular Humanism', *Current Anthropology*, 55 (10): 292–301.

Engelke, M. (2015), 'Secular Shadows: African, Immanent, Post-Colonial', *Critical Research on Religion*, 3 (1): 86–100.

Eroukhmanoff, C. (2015), 'The Remote Securitisation of Islam in the US Post-9/11: Euphemisation, Metaphors and the "Logic of Expected Consequences" in Counter-Radicalisation Discourse', *Critical Studies on Terrorism*, 8 (2): 246–65.

Fader, A. (2020), *Hidden Heretics: Jewish Doubt in the Digital Age*, Princeton, NJ: Princeton University Press.

Fea, J. (2018), *Believe Me: The Evangelical Road to Donald Trump*, Grand Rapids, MI: Eerdmans.

Fea, J. (2020), 'Evangelical Theologian Wayne Grudem Believes That Trump Does Not Tell Lies. Also, Anyone Who Believes Trump Is Trying to "Divide Us" Is "Bearing False Witness"', *Current*, 25 September. Available at: https://currentpub.com/2020/09/25/evangelical-theologian-wayne-grudem-believes-that-trump-does-not-tell-lies-also-anyone-who-believes-trump-is-trying-to-divide-us-is-bearing-false-witness/ (accessed 11 September 2021).

Feltmate, D. (2018), 'The Sacred Canopy as a Classic: Why Berger's Conceptual Apparatus Remains Foundational 50 Years Later', in T. Hjelm (ed.), *Peter L. Berger and the Sociology of Religion: 50 Years after* The Sacred Canopy, 67–84, London: Bloomsbury.

Fernandez, S. (2018), 'The Geographies of Prevent: The Transformation of the Muslim Home into a Pre-Crime Space', *Journal of Muslims in Europe*, 7 (2): 167–89.

Finke, R. and R. Stark (1992), *The Churching of America*, New Brunswick, NJ: Rutgers University Press.

Flanagan, K. (2001), 'Reflexivity, Ethics and the Teaching of the Sociology of Religion', *Sociology*, 35 (1): 1–19.

Flew, T. (2015), 'Foucault, Weber, Neoliberalism and the Politics of Governmentality', *Theory, Culture and Society*, 32 (7–8): 317–26.

Flory, R. and D. Miller (2008), *Finding Faith: The Spiritual Quest of the Post-Boomer Generation*. New Brunswick, NJ and London: Rutgers University Press.

Foucault, M. (1980), *Power/Knowledge: Selected Interviews*, Brighton: Harvester.

Freitas, D. (2017), *The Happiness Effect: How Social Media Is Driving a Generation to Appear Perfect at Any Cost*, New York: Oxford University Press.

Fuller, S. (2018), *Post-Truth: Knowledge as a Power Game*, London: Anthem Press.

Gaddini, K. (2020), 'Practising Purity: How Single Evangelical Women Negotiate Sexuality', in S.-J. Page and A. K. T. Yip (eds) *Intersecting Religion and Sexuality: Sociological Perspectives*, 103–21, Leiden: Brill.

Gallagher, S. (2003), *Evangelical Identity and Gendered Family Life*, New Brunswick, NJ: Rutgers University Press.

Gauthier, F. (2018), 'From Nation-State to Market: The Transformations of Religion in the Global Era, as Illustrated by Islam', *Religion*, 48 (3): 382–417.

Gauthier, F., T. Martikainen and L. Woodhead (2013), 'Acknowledging a Global Shift: A Primer for Thinking about Religion in Consumer Societies', *Implicit Religion*, 16 (3): 261–76.

Gauthier, F., L. Woodhead and T. Martikainen (2013), 'Introduction: Consumerism as the Ethos of Consumer Society', in F. Gauthier and T. Martikainen (eds), *Religion in Consumer Society: Brands, Consumers and Markets*, 1–24, Aldershot: Ashgate.

Gayle, D. (2019), 'UK's Prevent Guidance to Universities Unlawful, Court Rules', *The Guardian*, 8 March. Available at: https://www.theguardian.com/uk-news/2019/mar/08/uks-prevent -guidance-to-universities-unlawful-court-rules (accessed 21 May 2021).

Genz, S. (2006), 'Third Way/ve: The Politics of Postfeminism', *Feminist Theory*, 7 (3): 333–53.

George, C. V. R. (1993), *God's Salesman: Norman Vincent Peale and the Power of Positive Thinking*, Oxford: Oxford University Press.

Gerrard, J. (2014), 'All That Is Solid Melts into Work: Self-Work, the "Learning Ethic" and the Work Ethic', *The Sociological Review*, 62: 862–79.

Ghert-Zand, R. (2015), 'British Jews Say "No Thanks" to Nationalist Group's Support', *The Times of Israel*, 14 February. Available at: https://www.timesofisrael.com/british-jews-say-no-thanks -to-nationalist-groups-support/ (accessed 22 May 2021).

Giddens, A. (1991), *Modernity and Self Identity. Self and Society in the Late Modern Age*, Oxford: Polity.

Giddens, A. (1992), 'Introduction', in M. Weber (ed.), *The Protestant Ethic and the Spirit of Capitalism*, vii–xxvi, London and New York: Routledge.

Godelier, M. (1999), *The Enigma of the Gift*, Oxford: Blackwell.

Goffman, E. (1959), *The Presentation of Self in Everyday Life*, Reading: Penguin.

Goffman, E. (1963), *Stigma: Notes on the Management of Spoiled Identity*, New Jersey: Prentice-Hall.

Gökariksel, B. and K. Mitchell (2005), 'Veiling, Secularism and the Neoliberal Subject: National Narratives and Supranational Desires in Turkey and France', *Global Networks*, 5 (2): 147–65.

Gökariksel, B., and A. Secor (2010), 'Islamic-ness in the life of the commodity: Veiling fashion in Turkey', *Transactions of the Institute of British Geographers*, 35 (3): 313–33.

Goldstein, W. S., ed. (2006), *Marx, Critical Theory, and Religion: A Critique of Rational Choice*, Chicago, IL: Haymarket Books.

Gooptu, N. (2017), 'Religious Myths Retold: Masters and Servants in India's Corporate Culture', in D. Rudnyckyj and F. Osella (eds), *Religion and the Morality of the Market*, 72–93, Cambridge: Cambridge University Press.

Gorski, P. and A. Altinordu (2008), 'After Secularization?', *Annual Review of Sociology*, 34: 55–85.

Guest, M. (2010), 'Evangelicalism and Capitalism in Transatlantic Context', *Politics and Religion*, 4 (2): 257–80.

Guest, M. (2015), 'Religion and the Cultures of Higher Education: Student Christianity in the Contemporary UK', in L. Beaman and L. Aragon (eds), *Issues in Religion and Education: Whose Religion?*, 346–66, Leiden: Brill.

Guest, M. (2019), 'The Hidden Christians of the UK University Campus', in E. Arweck and H. Shipley (eds), *Young People and the Diversity of (Non)Religious Identities in International Perspective*, 51–67, Cham, Switzerland: Springer.

References

Guest, M. and K. Aune (2017), 'Students' Constructions of a Christian Future: Faith, Class and Aspiration in University Contexts', *Sociological Research Online*, 22 (1). Available at: http://www.socresonline.org.uk/22/1/12.html (accessed 28 February 2022).

Guest, M., E. Olson and J. Wolffe (2012), 'Christianity: Loss of Monopoly', in L. Woodhead and R. Catto (eds), *Religion and Change in Modern Britain*, 57–78, London: Routledge.

Guest, M., K. Aune, S. Sharma and R. Warner (2013), *Christianity and the University Experience: Understanding Student Faith*, London: Bloomsbury.

Guest, M., A. Scott-Baumann, S. Cheruvallil-Contractor, S. Naguib, A. Phoenix, Y. Lee and T. Al Baghal (2020), *Islam and Muslims on UK University Campuses: Perceptions and Challenges*, SOAS, Coventry University, Durham University and Lancaster University. Available at: https://www.soas.ac.uk/representingislamoncampus/publications/file148310.pdf (accessed 28 February 2022).

Hancock, A-M. (2016), *Intersectionality: An Intellectual History*, New York: Oxford University Press.

Harding, L., J. Elgot and A. Sparrow (2021), 'Accusations of Lying Pile Up against Boris Johnson. Does It Matter?', *The Guardian*, 30 April. Available at: https://www.theguardian.com/politics/2021/apr/30/accusations-of-lying-pile-up-against-boris-johnson-does-it-matter (accessed 4 November 2021).

Harsin, J. (2015), 'Regimes of Posttruth, Postpolitics, and Attention Economies', *Communication, Culture and Critique*, 8 (2): 327–33.

Harvey, D. (2007), *A Brief History of Neoliberalism*, Oxford: Oxford University Press.

Harvey, D. (2011), *The Enigma of Capital and the Crises of Capitalism*, New York: Oxford University Press.

Hayek, F. A. (1944), *The Road to Serfdom*, London: Routledge.

Heath-Kelly, C. (2016), 'Post-Structuralism and Constructivism', in R. Richard (ed.), *Routledge Handbook of Critical Terrorism Studies*, 60–9, London: Routledge.

Heath-Kelly, C. (2017), 'The Geography of Pre-Criminal Space: Epidemiological Imaginations of Radicalization Risk in the UK Prevent Strategy, 2007–2017', *Critical Studies on Terrorism*, 10: 297–310.

Heelas, P. (1996), *The New Age Movement: The Celebration of the Self and the Sacralisation of Modernity*, Oxford: Blackwell.

Heelas, P. and L. Woodhead (2005), *The Spiritual Revolution: Why Religion Is Giving Way to Spirituality*, Malden, MA, Oxford and Carlton: Blackwell.

Hefner, R. (2009), 'Religion and Modernity Worldwide', in P. Clarke (ed.), *The Oxford Handbook of the Sociology of Religion*, 152–71, Oxford: Oxford University Press.

Heinisch, R., A. Werner and F. Habersack (2020), 'Reclaiming National Sovereignty: The Case of the Conservatives and the Far Right in Austria', *European Politics and Society*, 21 (2): 163–81.

Herbert, D. and J. Bullock (2020), 'Reaching for a New Sense of Connection: Soft Atheism and "Patch and Make Do" Spirituality amongst Nonreligious European Millennials', *Culture and Religion*, 21 (2): 157–77.

Hirschle, J. (2010), 'From Religious to Consumption-Related Routine Activities? Analyzing Ireland's Economic Boom and the Decline in Church Attendance', *Journal for the Scientific Study of Religion*, 49 (4): 673–87.

Hjelm, T. (2014), 'Religion, Discourse and Power: A Contribution towards a Critical Sociology of Religion', *Current Sociology*, 4 (6): 855–72.

Hjelm, T. (2018), 'Assessing the Influence of *The Sacred Canopy*: A Missed Opportunity for Social Constructionism?', in T. Hjelm (ed.), *Peter L. Berger and the Sociology of Religion: 50 Years after* The Sacred Canopy, 157–74, London: Bloomsbury.

Hjelm, T. and P. Zuckerman, eds (2013), *Studying Religion and Society: Sociological Self-Portraits*, Oxford: Routledge.

HM Government (2011), *Prevent Strategy*, London: The Stationery Office Ltd. Available at: https://assets.publishing.service.gov.uk/government/uploads/system/uploads/attachment_data/file/97976/prevent-strategy-review.pdf (accessed 25 September 2021).

HM Government (2015), *The Counter-Terrorism and Security Act, 2015*. Available at: https://www.legislation.gov.uk/ukpga/2015/6/section/31/enacted (accessed 21 May 2021).

HM Government (2021), *Revised Prevent Duty Guidance for England and Wales (Updated 1 April 2021)*. Available at: https://www.gov.uk/government/publications/prevent-duty-guidance/revised-prevent-duty-guidance-for-england-and-wales (accessed 25 September 2021).

Hochschild, A. R. (1983), *The Managed Heart: Commercialization of Human Feeling*, Berkeley, CA: University of California Press.

Hochschild, A. R. (2016), *Strangers in Their Own Land: Anger and Mourning on the American Right*, New York: New Press.

Hofstadter, R. (1964), *Anti-Intellectualism in American Life*, London: Cape.

Holmwood, J. and T. O'Toole (2018), *Countering Extremism in British Schools?: The Truth about the Birmingham Trojan Horse Affair*, Bristol: Policy Press.

Hopkins, P., K. Botterill, S. Gurchathen and R. Arshad (2017), 'Encountering Misrecognition: Being Mistaken for Being Muslim', *Annals of the American Association of Geographers*, 107 (4): 934–48.

Houtman, D. (2020), 'Pillarization', in A. Possamai and A. J. Blasi (eds) *The Sage Encyclopedia of the Sociology of Religion*, 580–1, London: Sage.

Humphrey, M. (2009), 'Securitization and Domestication of Diaspora Muslims and Islam: Turkish Immigrants in Germany and Australia', *International Journal on Multicultural Societies*, 11 (2): 136–54.

Hunter, J. D. (1991), *Culture Wars*, New York: Basic Books.

Hutchings, T. (2017), *Creating Church Online: Ritual, Community and New Media*, London: Routledge.

Iannaccone, L. (1991), 'The Consequences of Religious Market Structure', *Rationality and Society*, 3 (April): 156–77.

Inge, A. (2016), *The Making of a Salafi Muslim Woman: Paths to Conversion*, Oxford: Oxford University Press.

Ivaldi, G., M. E. Lanzone and D. Woods (2017), 'Varieties of Populism across a Left-Right Spectrum: The Case of the Front National, the Northern League, Podemos and Five Star Movement', *Swiss Political Science Review*, 23 (4): 354–76.

Ivanescu, C. (2016), *Islam and Secular Citizenship in the Netherlands, United Kingdom and France*, London: Palgrave Macmillan.

Jackson, L. (2018), *Islamophobia in Britain: The Making of a Muslim Enemy*, London: Palgrave Macmillan.

Jaffrelot, C. (2009), 'Religion and Nationalism', in P. Clarke (ed.) *The Oxford Handbook of the Sociology of Religion*, 406–17, Oxford: Oxford University Press.

Jenkins, K. E. and G. Marti (2013), 'Warrior Chicks: Youthful Aging in a Postfeminist Prosperity Discourse', *Journal for the Scientific Study of Religion*, 51 (2): 241–56.

Johnson, J. (2010), 'The Citizen-Soldier: Masculinity, War, and Sacrifice at an Emerging Church in Seattle, Washington', *Polar-Political and Legal Anthropology Review*, 33 (2): 326–51.

Johnson, J. (2017), 'Megachurches, Celebrity Pastors, and the Evangelical Industrial Complex', in B. Forbes and J. Mahan (eds), *Religion and Popular Culture in America*, 3rd edition, 159–76, Oakland, CA: University of California Press.

Johnson, J. (2018), *Biblical Porn: Affect, Labor, and Pastor Mark Driscoll's Evangelical Empire*. Durham, NC: Duke University Press.

Jones, R. P. (2017), *The End of White Christian America*, New York: Simon and Schuster.

References

Jones, S. (2020), 'What is behind Austria's plan to outlaw "political Islam"?', *Financial Times*, 1 December. Available at: https://www.ft.com/content/3c8f761d-94cc-405f-904c-0785a11891a7 (accessed 28 February 2022).

Jones, S. H. (2020), *Islam and the Liberal State: National Identity and the Future of Muslim Britain*, London: I.B.Tauris.

Juergensmeyer, M. (2003), *Terror in the Mind of God: The Global Rise of Religious Violence*, 3rd edition, Berkeley, CA: University of California Press.

Kaplan, D. and R. Werczberger (2017), 'Jewish New Age and the Middle Class: Jewish Identity Politics in Israel under Neoliberalism', *Sociology*, 51 (3): 575–91.

Kapoor, N. (2013), 'The Advancement of Racial Neoliberalism in Britain', *Ethnic and Racial Studies*, 36 (6): 1028–46.

Karner, C. and D. Parker (2017), 'Words and Deeds against Exclusion: Deprivation, Activism and Religiosity in Inner-City Birmingham', in M. Guest and M. Middlemiss-Le Mon (eds), *Death, Life and Laughter: Essays on Religion in Honour of Douglas Davies*, 67–83, London: Routledge.

Kashyap, R. and V. A. Lewis (2013), 'British Muslim Youth and Religious Fundamentalism: A Quantitative Investigation', *Ethnic and Racial Studies*, 36 (12): 2117–40.

Katz, R., S. Ogilvie, J. Shaw and L. Woodhead (2021), *GenZ, Explained: The Art of Living in a Digital Age*, Chicago and London: University of Chicago Press.

Keeley, B. L. (2007), 'God as the Ultimate Conspiracy Theory', *Episteme: A Journal of Social Epistemology*, 4 (2): 135–49.

Kent, S. A. and T. A. Manca (2014), 'A War Over Mental Health Professionalism: Scientology verses Psychiatry', *Mental Health, Religion and Culture*, 17 (1): 1–23.

Ker-Lindsay, J. (2018), 'Turkey's EU Accession as a Factor in the 2016 Brexit Referendum', *Turkish Studies*, 19 (1): 1–22.

Kintz, L. (1997), *Between Jesus and the Market: The Emotions That Matter in Right-Wing America*, Durham, NC and London: Duke University Press.

Kiyagan, A. (2020), 'Austria drops "political Islam" from controversial bill', *Anadolu Agency*, 17 December. Available at: https://www.aa.com.tr/en/europe/austria-drops-political-islam-from-controversial-bill/2079476# (accessed 28 February 2022).

Klaver, M. (2015), 'Pentecostal Pastorpreneurs and the Global Circulation of Authoritative Aesthetic Styles', *Culture and Religion*, 16 (2): 146–59.

Klaver, M. (2016), 'Hillsong Megachurch Network: Christianity in Global Cities', in J. Kim, D. P. Baker et al. (eds), *Megachurch Accountability in Missions. Critical Assessment through Global Case Studies*, 150–60, Pasadena: William Carey Library.

Knox, Z. (2019), 'Jehovah's Witnesses as Extremists: The Russian State, Religious Pluralism, and Human Rights', *The Soviet and Post-Soviet Review*, 46 (2): 128–57.

Kruse, K. M. (2015), *One Nation under God: How Corporate America Invented Christian America*, New York: Basic Books.

Kühle, L. (2018), 'Policies of Radicalization as Anti- and Countercult Ideologies', *Journal of Muslims in Europe*, 7 (2): 211–36.

Kuloba, R. W. (2016), '"Homosexuality Is Unafrican and Unbiblical": Examining the Ideological Motivations to Homophobia in Sub-Saharan Africa – The Case Study of Uganda', *Journal of Theology in Southern Africa*, 154: 6–27.

Kundnani, A. (2012), 'Radicalization: The Journey of a Concept', *Race & Class*, 54 (2): 3–25.

Künkler, M., J. Madeley and S. Shankar, eds (2018), *A Secular Age beyond the West: Religion, Law and the State in Asia, the Middle East and North Africa*, Cambridge: Cambridge University Press.

Kvachev, V. (2019), 'From Weberian Bureaucracy to Networking Bureaucracy', *Russian Sociological Review*, 18 (2): 28–40.

Lawler, S. (2014), *Identity: Sociological Perspectives*, 2nd edition, Cambridge: Polity Press.

Lawrence, L. J. (2021), *Refiguring Universities in an Age of Neoliberalism: Creating Compassionate Campuses*, Cham: Palgrave Macmillan.

Lee, L. (2015), *Recognizing the Non-Religious: Reimagining the Secular*, Oxford: Oxford University Press.

Lewin, T. (2001), 'Sikh Owner of Gas Station Is Fatally Shot in Rampage', *New York Times*, 17 September. Available at: https://www.nytimes.com/2001/09/17/us/sikh-owner-of-gas-station-is-fatally-shot-in-rampage.html (accessed 11 May 2021).

Lindquist, G. and S. Coleman (2008), 'Introduction: Against Belief?', *Social Analysis*, 52 (1): 1–18.

Lindsay, D. M. (2007), *Faith in the Halls of Power: How Evangelicals Joined the American Elite*, Oxford: Oxford University Press.

Lofton, K. (2017), *Consuming Religion*, Chicago: University of Chicago Press.

Luckmann, T. (1967), *The Invisible Religion: The Problem of Religion in Modern Society*, New York: Macmillan.

Luhrmann, T. (2012), *When God Talks Back: Understanding the American Evangelical Relationship with God*, New York: Vintage.

Lury, C. (2011), *Consumer Culture*, 2nd edition, Cambridge: Polity Press.

Lynch, G. (2015), *Remembering Child Migration: Faith, Nation-building and the Wounds of Charity*, London: Bloomsbury.

Lyon, D. (2000), *Jesus in Disneyland. Religion in Postmodern Times*, Cambridge: Polity.

Lyon, D. (2018), *The Culture of Surveillance: Watching as a Way of Life*, Cambridge: Polity Press.

Maddox, M. (2012), '"In the Goofy Parking Lot": Growth Churches as a Novel Religious Form for Late Capitalism', *Social Compass*, 59 (2): 146–58.

Maddox, M. (2013), '"Rise Up Warrior Princess Daughters": Is Evangelical Women's Submission a Mere Fairytale?', *Journal of Feminist Studies in Religion*, 29 (1): 7–23.

Mahmood, S. (2005), *Politics of Piety: The Islamic Revival and the Feminist Subject*, Princeton, NJ: Princeton University Press.

Mahmood, S. (2010), 'Can Secularism Be Other-Wise?', in M. Warner, J. VanAntwerpen and C. Calhoun (eds), *Varieties of Secularism in a Secular Age*, 282–99, Cambridge, MA: Harvard University Press.

Mahmood, S. (2016), *Religious Difference in a Secular Age: A Minority Report*, Oxford and Princeton, NJ: Princeton University Press.

Malone, D. M. (2018), *From Single to Serious: Relationships, Gender, and Sexuality on American Evangelical Campuses*, New Brunswick, NJ: Rutgers University Press.

Marmor-Lavie, G., P. A. Stout and W. N. Lee (2009), 'Spirituality in Advertising: A New Theoretical Approach', *Journal of Media and Religion*, 8 (1): 1–23.

Marsden, G. (2006), *Fundamentalism and American Culture*, 2nd edition, New York: Oxford University Press.

Marti, G. (2008), *Hollywood Faith: Holiness, Prosperity, and Ambition in a Los Angeles Church*, New Brunswick, NJ: Rutgers University Press.

Marti, G. (2010), 'Ego-Affirming Evangelicalism: How a Hollywood Church Appropriates Religion for Workers in the Creative Class', *Sociology of Religion*, 71 (1): 52–75.

Marti, G. (2020), *American Blindspot: Race, Class, Religion, and the Trump Presidency*, Lanham: Rowman & Littlefield.

Martikainen, T. and F. Gauthier, eds (2013), *Religion in the Neoliberal Age: Political Economy and Modes of Governance*, Aldershot: Ashgate.

Martin, D. (1962), 'The Denomination', *British Journal of Sociology*, 13 (1): 1–14.

Martin, D. (1965), 'Toward Eliminating the Concept of Secularization', in J. Gould (ed.), *The Penguin Survey of the Social Sciences*, 169–82, London: Penguin.

Martin, D. (1978), *A General Theory of Secularization*, Oxford: Blackwell.

References

Marzouki, N. et al., eds (2016), *Saving the People: How Populists Hijack Religion*, London: Hurst & Co.

Mason, L., J. Wronski and J. V. Kane (2021), 'Activating Animus: The Uniquely Social Roots of Trump Support', *American Political Science Review*, 1–9. doi:10.1017/S0003055421000563

Mavelli, L. (2013), 'Between Normalisation and Exception: The Securitisation of Islam and the Construction of the Secular Subject', *Millennium: Journal of International Studies*, 41 (2): 159–81.

Mavelli, L. (2020), 'Neoliberalism as Religion: Sacralization of the Market and Post-Truth Politics', *International Political Sociology*, 14 (1): 57–76.

McGavran, D. (1970), *Understanding Church Growth*, Grand Rapids, MI: Eerdmans.

McGlynn, C. and S. McDaid (2019), 'Radicalization and Higher Education: Students' Understanding and Experiences', *Terrorism and Political Violence*, 31 (3): 559–76.

McGuire, M. (2008), *Lived Religion: Faith and Practice in Everyday Life*, New York: Oxford University Press.

McIvor, M. (2020), *Representing God: Christian Legal Activism in Contemporary England*, Princeton, NJ: Princeton University Press.

McKinney, J. (yet to be published), *American Evangelicalism and Hypermasculinity: Mark Driscoll and Mars Hill Church*.

Medeiros, J. D. (2018), *Conspiracy Theory in Turkey: Politics and Protest in the Age of 'Post-Truth'*, London: I.B. Tauris.

Meyer, B. (2007), 'Pentecostalism and Neo-Liberal Capitalism: Faith, Prosperity and Vision in African Pentecostal-Charismatic Churches', *Journal for the Study of Religion*, 20 (2): 5–28.

Meyer, B. and D. Houtman (2012), 'Material Religion: How Things Matter', in D. Houtman and B. Meyer (eds), *Things: Religion and the Question of Materiality*, 1–23, New York: Fordham.

Miera, F. and V. S. Pala (2009), 'The Construction of Islam as a Public Issue in Western European Countries through the Prism of the Muhammad Cartoons Controversy: A Comparison between France and Germany', *Ethnicities*, 9 (3): 383–408.

Moberg, M. (2017), *Church, Market, and Media: A Discursive Approach to Institutional Religious Change*, London: Bloomsbury.

Moberg, M. and T. Martikainen (2018), 'Religious Change in Market and Consumer Society: The Current State of the Field and New Ways Forward', *Religion*, 48 (3): 418–35.

Modood, T. (1990), 'Muslims, Race and Equality in Britain: Some Post-Rushdie Affair Reflections', *Third Text*, 4 (11): 127–34.

Modood, T. (2019), *Essays on Secularism and Multiculturalism*, London and New York: Rowman and Littlefield.

Moore, R. L. (1994), *Selling God: American Religion in the Marketplace of Culture*, New York and Oxford: Oxford University Press.

Moudouros, N. (2014), 'The "Harmonization" of Islam with the Neoliberal Transformation: The Case of Turkey', *Globalizations*, 11 (6): 843–57.

Mudde, C. (2016), 'Populist Radical Right Parties in Europe Today', in J. Abromeit et al. (eds), *Transformations of Populism in Europe and the Americas: History and Recent Tendencies*, 295–307, London: Bloomsbury.

Müller, J-W. (2017), *What Is Populism?* St Ives: Penguin.

Nichols, T. (2017), *The Death of Expertise: The Campaign against Established Knowledge and Why It Matters*, New York: Oxford University Press.

Niculescu, M. (2013), '"Find Your Inner God and Breathe": Buddhism, Pop Culture, and Contemporary Metamorphoses in American Judaism', in F. Gauthier and T. Martikainen (eds), *Religion in Consumer Society: Brands, Consumers and Markets*, 91–108, Aldershot: Ashgate.

Nielsen, J. S. (2010), 'Danish Cartoons and Christian-Muslim Relations in Denmark', *Exchange*, 39 (3): 217–35.

Norris, P. and R. Inglehart (2019), *Cultural Backlash: Trump, Brexit, and Authoritarian Populism*, Cambridge: Cambridge University Press.

Numbers, R. L. (2006), *The Creationists: From Scientific Creationism to Intelligent Design*, 2nd edition, Cambridge, MA and London: Harvard University Press.

Odone, C. (2013), 'Nigel Farage: we must defend Christian heritage'. *The Telegraph*. Available at: https://www.telegraph.co.uk/news/politics/ukip/10422169/Nigel-Farage-We-must-defend-Christian-heritage.html (accessed 28 February 2022).

Osella, F. and C. Osella (2003), 'Migration and the Commoditisation of Ritual: Sacrifice, Spectacle and Contestations in Kerala, India', *Contributions to Indian Sociology*, 37(1–2): 109–39.

Osella, F. and D. Rudnyckyj (2017), 'Introduction: Assembling Market and Religious Moralities', in D. Rudnyckyj and F. Osella (eds), *Religion and the Morality of the Market*, 1–28, Cambridge: Cambridge University Press.

O'Toole, T., N. Meer, D. N. Dehanas, S. H. Jones and T. Modood (2016), 'Governing through Prevent? Regulation and Contested Practice in State–Muslim Engagement', *Sociology*, 50 (1): 160–77.

Page, S.-J. and H. Shipley (2020), *Religion and Sexualities: Theories, Themes and Methodologies*, London: Routledge.

Page, S.-J. and A. Yip, eds (2020), *Intersecting Religion and Sexuality: Sociological Perspectives*, Leiden: Brill.

Pap, N. and V. Glied (2018), 'Hungary's Turn to the East: *Jobbik* and Islam', *Europe-Asia Studies*, 70 (7): 1036–54.

Parry, J. and M. Bloch, eds (1989), *Money and the Morality of Exchange*, Cambridge: Cambridge University Press.

Peck, J. (2010), *Constructions of Neoliberal Reason*, Oxford: Oxford University Press.

Perrin, R. H. (2020), *Changing Shape: The Faith Lives of Millennials*, London: SCM Press.

Perry, S. L., A. L. Whitehead and J. T. Davis (2019), 'God's Country in Black and Blue: How Christian Nationalism Shapes Americans' Views about Police (Mis)Treatment of Blacks', *Sociology of Race and Ethnicity*, 5 (1): 130–46.

Perry, S. L, A. L. Whitehead and J. B. Grubbs (2020), 'Culture Wars and Covid-19 Conduct: Christian Nationalism, Religiosity, and Americans' Behavior during the Coronavirus Pandemic', *Journal for the Scientific Study of Religion*, 59 (3): 405–16.

Pollack, D. and G. Rosta (2017), *Religion and Modernity: An International Comparison*, Oxford: Oxford University Press.

Possamai, A. (2018), *The I-zation of Society, Religion, and Neoliberal Post-Secularism*, Singapore: Palgrave Macmillan.

Possamai, A. and L. Murray (2011), 'Hyper-Real Religions: Fear, Anxiety and Late-modern Religious Innovation', *Journal of Sociology*, 47 (3): 227–42.

Quinn, B. (2016), 'French Police Make Woman Remove Clothing on Nice Beach Following Burkini Ban', *The Guardian*, 24 August. Available at: https://www.theguardian.com/world/2016/aug/24/french-police-make-woman-remove-burkini-on-nice-beach (accessed 4 November 2021).

Rashi, T. (2013), 'The Kosher Cell Phone in Ultra-Orthodox Society', in H. Campbell (ed.), *Digital Religion: Understanding Religious Practice in New Media Worlds*, 173–81, London: Routledge.

Research, Information and Communications Unit (RICU) (2007), *Counter Terrorism Communications Guidance*. Available at: https://assets.publishing.service.gov.uk/government/uploads/system/uploads/attachment_data/file/100382/11384_CT_communication_guidance.pdf (accessed 25 September 2021).

Rexhepi, P. (2018), 'Arab Others at European Borders: Racializing Religion and Refugees along the *Balkan Route*', *Ethnic and Racial Studies*, 41 (12): 2215–34.

References

Ringvee, R. (2013), 'Regulating Religion in a Neoliberal Context: The Transformation of Estonia', in T. Martikainen and F. Gauthier (eds), *Religion in the Neoliberal Age: Political Economy and Modes of Governance*, 143–60, Aldershot: Ashgate.

Ritzer, G. (2004), *The McDonaldization of Society*, revised New Century edition, Thousand Oaks: Pine Forge Press.

Roof, W. C. (1999), *Spiritual Marketplace. Baby Boomers and the Remaking of American Religion*, Princeton, NJ: Princeton University Press.

Rootham, E. (2015), 'Embodying Islam and laïcité: Young French Muslim Women at Work', *Gender, Place & Culture*, 22 (7): 971–86.

Roy, O. (2016), 'Beyond Populism: The Conservative Right, the Courts, the Churches and the Concept of a Christian Europe, in N. Marzouki, D. McDonnell and O. Roy (eds) *Saving the People: How Populists Hijack Religion*, 185–202, London: Hurst and Publishers.

Rudnyckyj, D. (2009), 'Spiritual Economies: Islam and Neoliberalism in Contemporary Indonesia', *Cultural Anthropology*, 24 (1): 104–41.

Runnymede Trust (1997), *Islamophobia: A Challenge for Us All*. Report available at: https://www.runnymedetrust.org/companies/17/74/Islamophobia-A-Challenge-for-Us-All.html

Sageman, M. (2008), 'A Strategy for Fighting International Islamist Terrorists', *The Annals of the American Academy of Political and Social Science*, 618 (1): 223–31.

Said, E. W. (1978), *Orientalism: Western Conceptions of the Orient*, London: Penguin.

Sandel, M. J. (2012), *What Money Can't Buy: The Moral Limits of Markets*, New York: Farrar, Straus and Giroux.

Sayer, A. (2009), 'Who's Afraid of Critical Social Science?', *Current Sociology*, 57 (6): 767–86.

Schlamelcher, J. (2013), 'The Decline of the Parishes and the Rise of City Churches: The German Evangelical Church in the Age of Neoliberalism', in T. Martikainen and F. Gauthier (eds), *Religion in the Neoliberal Age: Political Economy and Modes of Governance*, 53–67, Aldershot: Ashgate.

Schmid, A. P. (2013), 'Radicalization, De-Radicalization, Counter-Radicalization: A Conceptual Discussion and Literature Review', in *ICCT Research Paper 97*, The Hague: International Centre for Counter-Terrorism. Available at: https://icct.nl/app/uploads/2013/03/ICCT-Schmid-radicalization-De-radicalization-Counter-radicalization-March-2013_2.pdf (accessed 19 May 2021).

Scott-Baumann, A., M. Guest, S. Naguib, S. Cheruvallil-Contractor and A. Phoenix (2020), *Islam on Campus: Contested Identities and the Cultures of Higher Education in Britain*, Oxford: Oxford University Press.

Seubert, V. R. (1991), 'Sociology and Value Neutrality: Limiting Sociology to the Empirical Level', *The American Sociologist*, 22 (3/4): 210–20.

Shah, S. (2020), 'Ethnicity, Gender and Class in the Experiences of Gay Muslims', in S.-J. Page and A. K. T. Yip (eds), *Intersecting Religion and Sexuality: Sociological Perspectives*, 23–44, Leiden: Brill.

Sheldon, R. (2016), *Tragic Encounters and Ordinary Ethics: Palestine-Israel in British Universities*, Manchester: Manchester University Press.

Sherwood, H. (2020), 'UK Churches Urged to Wake Up to Spiritual Abuse of LGBT People', *The Guardian*, 17 October. Available at: https://www.theguardian.com/world/2020/oct/17/uk-churches-urged-to-wake-up-to-spiritual-abuse-of-lgbt-people (accessed 4 November 2021).

Singler, B. (2015), 'Big Bad Pharma: The Indigo Child Concept and Biomedical Conspiracy Theories', *Nova Religio: The Journal of Alternative and Emergent Religions*, 19 (2): 17–29.

Skeggs, B. (1997), *Formations of Class and Gender: Becoming Respectable*, London: Sage.

Smith, C. (1998), *American Evangelicalism: Embattled and Thriving*. Chicago and London: University of Chicago Press.

Smith, G. S. (2006), *Faith and the Presidency: From George Washington to George W. Bush*. New York: Oxford University Press.

Smith, G. S. and L. Woodhead (2018), 'Religion and Brexit: Populism and the Church of England', *Religion, State and Society*, 46 (3): 206–23.

Smith, L. T. (2012), *Decolonizing Methodologies: Research and Indigenous Peoples*, London: Zed Books.

Soares, B. (2017), '"Structural Adjustment Islam" and the Religious Economy in Neoliberal Mali', in D. Rudnyckyj and F. Osella (eds), *Religion and the Morality of the Market*, 138–59, Cambridge: Cambridge University Press.

Sødal, H. K. (2010), '"Victor, Not Victim": Joel Osteen's Rhetoric of Hope', *Journal of Contemporary Religion*, 25 (1): 37–50.

Spickard, J. V. (2017), *Alternative Sociologies of Religion: Through Non-Western Eyes*, New York: New York University Press.

Spring, M. (2020), 'The Causalities of This Year's Viral Conspiracy Theories', *BBC News*, 26 December. Available at: https://www.bbc.co.uk/news/blogs-trending-55355911 (accessed 4 November 2021).

Steger, M. B. and R. K. Roy (2010), *Neoliberalism: A Very Short Introduction*, Oxford: Oxford University Press.

Stern, J. and J. M. Berger (2016), *ISIS: The State of Terror*, London: HarperCollins.

Stievermann, J., P. Goff and D. Junker, eds (2015), *Religion and the Marketplace in the United States*, New York: Oxford University Press.

Stolz, J. (2006), 'Salvation Goods and Religious Markets: Integrating Rational Choice and Weberian Perspectives', *Social Compass*, 53 (1): 13–32.

Stolz, J. (2018), 'Economics of Religion on Trial: How Disestablishment Did Not Lead to Religious Revival in the Swiss Cantons of Geneva and Neuchâtel', *Journal of Contemporary Religion*, 33 (2): 229–46.

Stolz, J. and J.-C. Usunier (2018), 'Religions as Brands? Religion and Spirituality in Consumer Society', *Journal of Management, Spirituality & Religion*, doi:10.1080/14766086.2018.1445008

Stolz, J., J. Könemann, M. Schneuwly Purdie, T. Englberger and M. Krüggeler (2016), *(Un)Believing in Modern Society. Religion, Spirituality, and Religious-secular Competition*, London: Routledge.

Storm, I. (2013), '"Christianity Is Not Just about Religion": Religious and National Identities in a Northern English Town', *Secularism and Nonreligion*, 2: 21–38.

Strombeck, A. (2006), 'Invest in Jesus: Neoliberalism and the *Left Behind* Novels', *Cultural Critique*, 64: 161–95.

Sullivan, K. R. and H. Delaney (2017), 'A Femininity That "Giveth and Taketh Away": The Prosperity Gospel and Postfeminism in the Neoliberal Economy', *Human Relations*, 70 (7): 836–59.

Svitych, A. (2021), 'Voting for Jobbik and the Front National: Nostalgic, Deprived and Status-Frustrated', *European Review of International Studies*, 8: 49–76.

Swingewood, A. (2000), *A Short History of Sociological Thought*, 3rd edition, Basingstoke and London: Macmillan Press.

Taira, T. (2012), 'The New Atheism as Identity Politics', in M. Guest and E. Arweck (eds), *Religion and Knowledge: Sociological Perspectives*, 97–113, Aldershot: Ashgate.

Tarlo, E. (2010), *Visibly Muslim: Fashion, Politics, Faith*, New York: Berg.

Tasker, Y. and D. Negra, eds (2007), *Interrogating Postfeminism: Gender and the Politics of Popular Culture*, Durham, NC: Duke University Press.

Taylor, C. (2007), *A Secular Age*, Cambridge, MA and London: Belknap Press.

Taylor, D. (2021), 'Boy, 11, Referred to Prevent for Wanting to Give "Alms to the Oppressed"', *The Guardian*, 27 June. Available at: https://www.theguardian.com/uk-news/2021/jun/27/boy

References

-11-referred-to-prevent-for-wanting-to-give-alms-to-the-oppressed (accessed 26 September 2021).

Thiessen, J. and S. Wilkins-Laflamme (2020), *None of the Above: Non-Religious Identity in the US and Canada*, New York: New York University Press.

Thobani, S. (2014), 'European Education and Islam: Liberalism and Alterity', in K. H. Karim and M. Eid (eds), *Engaging the Other: Public Policy and Western-Muslim Intersections*, 67–87, New York: Palgrave Macmillan.

Thorleifsson, C. (2017), 'Disposable Strangers: Far-Right Securitization of Forced Migration in Hungary', *Social Anthropology*, 25 (3): 318–34.

Topgyal, T. (2012), 'The Securitization of Tibetan Buddhism in Communist China', *Politics and Religion*, 6 (2): 217–49.

Tranby, E. and D. Hartmann (2008), 'Critical Whiteness Theories and the Evangelical "Race Problem": Extending Emerson and Smith's *Divided by Faith*', *Journal for the Scientific Study of Religion*, 47 (3): 341–59.

Tremlett, P-F. (2007), 'The Ethics of Suspicion in the Study of Religions', *Diskus*, 8. Available at: http://www.basr.ac.uk/diskus/diskus8/tremlett.htm

Troeltsch, E. (1931), *The Social Teachings of the Christian Churches*, 2 volumes, London: Allen and Unwin.

Truong, F. (2018), *Radicalized Loyalties: Becoming Muslim in the West*, Cambridge: Polity Press.

Tuğal, C. (2012), 'Fight or Acquiesce? Religion and Political Process in Turkey's and Egypt's Neoliberalizations', *Development and Change*, 43 (1): 23–51.

Tylor, I. (2020), *Stigma: The Machinery of Inequality*, London: Zed Books.

Valenti, J. (2010), *The Purity Myth: How America's Obsession with Virginity Is Hurting Young Women*, Berkeley, CA: Seal Press.

Valentine, G., S. L. Holloway and M. Jayne (2010), 'Contemporary Cultures of Abstinence and the Nighttime Economy: Muslim Attitudes Towards Alcohol and the Implications for Social Cohesion', *Environment and Planning A*, 42 (1): 8–22.

Valeri, M. (2015), 'Weber and Eighteenth-Century Religious Developments in America', in J. Stievermann, P. Goff and D. Junker (eds) *Religion and the Marketplace in the United States*, 63–75, New York: Oxford University Press.

Virkama, A. (2017), 'Invisible Islam: Muslim Student Migrants' Everyday Practices in French Secular Universities', in K. Aune and J. Stevenson (eds), *Religion and Higher Education in Europe and North America*, 90–108, London: Routledge.

Voas, D. (2009), 'The Rise and Fall of Fuzzy Fidelity in Europe', *European Sociological Review*, 25 (2): 155–68.

Voas, D. and S. Bruce (2019), 'Religion: Identity, Behaviour and Belief over Two Decades', in J. Curtice, E. Clery, J. Perry, M. Phillips and N. Rahim (eds), *British Social Attitudes: The 36th Report*, 1–28, London: The National Centre for Social Research.

Voas, D. and A. Crockett (2005), 'Religion in Britain: Neither Believing Nor Belonging', *Sociology*, 39 (1): 11–28.

Wacker, G. (2015), 'Billy Graham, Christian Manliness, and the Shaping of the Evangelical Subculture', in J. Stievermann, P. Goff and D. Junker (eds), *Religion and the Marketplace in the United States*, 80–94, New York: Oxford University Press.

Wade, M. (2016), 'Seeker-Friendly: The Hillsong Megachurch as an Enchanting Total Institution', *Journal of Sociology* 52 (4): 661–76.

Wagner, R. (2013), 'You Are What You Install: Religious Authenticity and Identity in Mobile Apps', in H. Campbell (ed.), *Digital Religion: Understanding Religious Practice in New Media Worlds*, 199–206, London: Routledge.

Wallis, R. (1976), *The Road to Total Freedom: A Sociological Analysis of Scientology*, London: Heinemann.

Wallis, R. (1984), *The Elementary Forms of the New Religious Life*, London, Boston, Melbourne and Henley: Routledge and Kegan Paul.

Ward, P. (2020), *Celebrity Worship*, London: Routledge.

Warner, R. S. (1993), 'Work in Progress Toward a New Paradigm for the Sociological Study of Religion in the United States', *American Journal of Sociology*, 98 (5): 1044–93.

Watson, S. (2005), 'Symbolic Spaces of Difference: Contesting the Eruv in Barnet, London and Tenafly, New Jersey', *Environment and Planning D: Society and Space*, 23 (4): 597–613.

Webber, J. R. (2020), 'A Great Little Man: The Shadow of Jair Bolsonaro', *Historical Materialism*, 28 (1): 3–49.

Weber, M. (1947), *The Theory of Social and Economic Organization*, New York: The Free Press.

Weber, M. (1949), *The Methodology of the Social Sciences*, Glencoe, IL: The Free Press.

Weber, M. (1958), *The Protestant Ethic and the Spirit of Capitalism*, New York: Scribner's.

Weber, M. (2009), 'The Protestant Sects and the Spirit of Capitalism', in H. Gerth and C. W. Mills (eds), *From Max Weber. Essays in Sociology*, 302–22, London: Routledge.

Whitehead, A. L. and S. L. Perry (2020a), *Taking America Back for God: Christian Nationalism in the United States*, New York: Oxford University Press.

Whitehead, A. L. and S. L. Perry (2020b), 'How Culture Wars Delay Herd Immunity: Christian Nationalism and Anti-Vaccine Attitudes', *Socius*, 6: 1–12. doi:10.1177/2378023120977727

Whitehead, A. L., L. Schnabel and S. L. Perry (2018), 'Gun Control in the Crosshairs: Christian Nationalism and Opposition to Stricter Gun Laws', *Socius*, 4: 1-13. doi:10.1177/2378023118790189.

Whiton, Jacob (2021), 'Where Trumpism Lives', *Boston Review*, 19 January. Available at: http://bostonreview.net/politics/jacob-whiton-where-trumpism-lives

Wilkins, A. C. (2008a), *Wannabes, Goths and Christians: The Boundaries of Sex, Style and Status*, Chicago: Chicago University Press.

Wilkins, A. C. (2008b), '"Happier Than Non-Christians": Collective Emotions and Symbolic Boundaries among Evangelical Christians', *Social Psychology Quarterly*, 71 (3): 281–301.

Wilkinson, I. and A. Kleinman (2016), *A Passion for Society: How We Think about Human Suffering*, Oakland, CA: University of California Press.

Wilkinson, R. and K. Pickett (2009), *The Spirit Level: Why More Equal Societies Almost Always Do Better*, London: Allen Lane.

Williams, A. (2015), 'Postsecular Geographies: Theo-ethics, Rapprochement and Neoliberal Governance in a Faith-based Drug Programme', *Transactions of the Institute of British Geographers*, 40 (2): 192–208.

Williams, R. (1976), *Keywords. A Vocabulary of Culture and Society*, London: Fontana.

Williams, R. H. and G. Vashi (2007), 'Hijab and American Muslim Women: Creating the Space for Autonomous Selves', *Sociology of Religion*, 68 (3): 269–87.

Willis, P. (1977), *Learning to Labour: How Working Class Kids Get Working Class Jobs*, Farnborough: Saxon House.

Wilson, B. R. (1966), *Religion in Secular Society. A Sociological Comment*, Harmondsworth: Penguin.

Wilson, B. R. (1970), *Religious Sects: A Sociological Study*, London: Weidenfeld and Nicolson.

Woodhead, L. (2016), 'The Rise of "No-Religion" in Britain: The Emergence of a New Cultural Majority', *Journal of the British Academy*, 4: 245–61.

Wuthnow, R. (1988), *The Restructuring of American Religion*. Princeton: Princeton University Press.

Wuthnow, R. (2009), *Boundless Faith: The Global Outreach of American Churches*, Berkeley, CA: University of California Press.

Yabanci, B. and D. Taleski (2018), 'Co-opting Religion: How Ruling Populists in Turkey and Macedonia Sacralise the Majority', *Religion, State and Society*, 46 (3): 283–304.

INDEX

Index